Language Learning with Technology

Cambridge Handbooks for Language Teachers

This series, now with over 40 titles, offers practical ideas, techniques and activities for the teaching of English and other languages providing inspiration for both teachers and trainers.

Recent titles in this series:

Personalizing Language Learning
GRIFF GRIFFITHS and KATHRYN KEOHANE

Teaching Adult Second Language Learners
HEATHER MCKAY and ABIGAIL TOM

Teach Business English
SYLVIE DONNA

Teaching English Spelling
A practical guide
RUTH SHEMESH and SHEILA WALLER

Using Folktales
ERIC K. TAYLOR

Learner English (Second edition)
A teacher's guide to interference and other problems
EDITED BY MICHAEL SWAN and BERNARD SMITH

Planning Lessons and Courses
Designing sequences of work for the language classroom
TESSA WOODWARD

Teaching Large Multilevel Classes
NATALIE HESS

Using the Board in the Language Classroom
JEANNINE DOBBS

Writing Simple Poems
Pattern Poetry for Language Acquisition
VICKI L. HOLMES and MARGARET R. MOULTON

Laughing Matters
Humour in the language classroom
PÉTER MEDGYES

Stories
Narrative activities in the language classroom
RUTH WAJNRYB

Using Authentic Video in the Language Classroom
JANE SHERMAN

Extensive Reading Activities for Teaching Language
EDITED BY JULIAN BAMFORD and RICHARD R. DAY

Language Activities for Teenagers
EDITED BY SETH LINDSTROMBERG

Pronunciation Practice Activities
A resource book for teaching English pronunciation
MARTIN HEWINGS

Drama Techniques (Third edition)
A resource book of communication activities for language teachers
ALAN MALEY and ALAN DUFF

Five-Minute Activities for Business English
PAUL EMMERSON and NICK HAMILTON

Games for Language Learning (Third edition)
ANDREW WRIGHT, DAVID BETTERIDGE and MICHAEL BUCKBY

Dictionary Activities
CINDY LEANEY

Dialogue Activities
Exploring spoken interaction in the language class
NICK BILBROUGH

Five-Minute Activities for Young Learners
PENNY MCKAY and JENNI GUSE

The Internet and the Language Classroom (Second edition)
A practical guide for teachers
GAVIN DUDENEY

Working with Images
A resource book for the language classroom
BEN GOLDSTEIN

Grammar Practice Activities (Second edition)
A practical guide for teachers
PENNY UR

Intercultural Language Activities
JOHN CORBETT

Learning One-to-One
INGRID WISNIEWSKA

Communicative Activities for EAP
JENNI GUSE

Memory Activities for Language Learning
NICK BILBROUGH

Vocabulary Activities
PENNY UR

Classroom Management Techniques
JIM SCRIVENER

CLIL Activities
A resource for subject and language teachers
LIZ DALE and ROSIE TANNER

Language Learning with Technology

Ideas for integrating technology
in the language classroom

Graham Stanley

Consultant and editor: Scott Thornbury

CAMBRIDGE
UNIVERSITY PRESS

CAMBRIDGE UNIVERSITY PRESS
Cambridge, New York, Melbourne, Madrid, Cape Town,
Singapore, São Paulo, Delhi, Mexico City

Cambridge University Press
The Edinburgh Building, Cambridge CB2 8RU, UK

www.cambridge.org
Information on this title: www.cambridge.org/9781107628809

First published 2013

A catalogue record for this publication is available from the British Library

Library of Congress Cataloguing in Publication data
Stanley, Graham. Language learning with technology: ideas for integrating
technology in the language classroom /
Graham Stanley; Consultant and editor: Scott Thornbury.
  pages   cm. — (Cambridge Handbooks for Language Teachers)
  ISBN 978-1-107-62880-9 (pbk. : alk. paper)
  1. Language and languages—Computer-assisted instruction.   2. Language
and languages—Study and teaching—Technological innovations.
  3. Educational technology—Social aspects.   I. Thornbury, Scott,
1950- editor of compilation.   II. Title.

  P53.28.S73 2013 418.0078—dc23   2012048680

ISBN 9781107628809 paperback

Contents

Thanks ix

Acknowledgements x

Introduction 1

1 **Integrating technology** 9
1.1 Getting to know you 12
1.2 Technological survey 13
1.3 Visual class list 14
1.4 Favourite websites 15
1.5 Plan B 16
1.6 Our VLE 17
1.7 Dictionary race 18
1.8 Class audio recording 19
1.9 Unlocked achievements 21
1.10 Flip your classroom 23

2 **Building a learning community** 25
2.1 Learning together online 27
2.2 Who are my classmates? 29
2.3 Personal learning online 30
2.4 Class blog 32
2.5 Mystery guest 33
2.6 Blog exchange 34
2.7 Language wiki 35
2.8 What we need English for 36
2.9 Safety online 37

3 **Vocabulary** 39
3.1 In context 40
3.2 Digital camera scavenger hunt 41
3.3 Online word-game tournament 43
3.4 Word puzzles 44
3.5 Learner-generated quizzes 45
3.6 Memory posters 46
3.7 Alien vocabulary 48
3.8 Word associations 50
3.9 Making word games 52
3.10 Words and phrases 53

	3.11	Synonym swap	54
	3.12	Experimenting with antonyms	55
	3.13	Slang, register and style	56
	3.14	Multiple-meaning presentations	57
	3.15	Noticing collocations	58

4 **Grammar** **61**

	4.1	Audio gap-fills	63
	4.2	Grammar check	64
	4.3	Automatic cloze tests	65
	4.4	Questioning infographics	66
	4.5	Grammar fight	68
	4.6	Grammar-reference sites	70
	4.7	Common grammatical errors	71
	4.8	Real-world grammar	72
	4.9	Grammar safari	74
	4.10	Authentic word clouds	75
	4.11	If only …	77
	4.12	Grammar in context	79

5 **Listening** **81**

	5.1	Guess what I'm talking about	83
	5.2	Other people's interests	84
	5.3	Search the tube	86
	5.4	Reordered video story	87
	5.5	Talk-radio listening	88
	5.6	Guided tours	89
	5.7	Recorded poetry	90
	5.8	Online classroom guest	91
	5.9	Recorded stories	92
	5.10	Voice-recorder dictation	93
	5.11	Interview bingo	94
	5.12	Someone I know	95
	5.13	Altered interviews	96

6 **Reading** **99**

	6.1	Word-cloud warmer	101
	6.2	Video pre-reading warmer	102
	6.3	Quick-response reading race	103
	6.4	IWB skimming and scanning	104
	6.5	Pre-reading presentation	105
	6.6	Readathon	106
	6.7	Comparative texts	107
	6.8	Reviewer role play	109
	6.9	Coded message trail	110
	6.10	Ask the Internet	112

6.11 Identifying text-types 113
6.12 Big events 114
6.13 Kids' storytelling 116
6.14 Interactive fiction 117
6.15 Fan fiction 119

7 **Writing** **121**
7.1 Social-networking writing group 123
7.2 Writing on a class wiki 125
7.3 Using learner blogs 126
7.4 Blogging summary 127
7.5 Myths and legends 128
7.6 Five-sentence photo story 129
7.7 Speed writing 130
7.8 Interactive story 131
7.9 Developing a story 133
7.10 Crazy stories or poems 134
7.11 Art stories 136
7.12 Do you dream? 137
7.13 Message from the past 138
7.14 Report writing 139
7.15 Sensationalist reporting 140
7.16 Biographies 141
7.17 Translate to SMS 143
7.18 Pros and cons 144
7.19 Social network CVs 145
7.20 Academic writing 146

8 **Speaking** **147**
8.1 Spoken journals 149
8.2 Speaking pictures 151
8.3 Reading aloud 153
8.4 Unscripted and scripted dialogues 154
8.5 Mobile circle game 155
8.6 Guided tour 156
8.7 Virtual-world tourists 158
8.8 Talk-radio speaking 160
8.9 Current affairs 161
8.10 Train or coach? 163
8.11 Discussions of interest 165
8.12 Animated film 167
8.13 World issues 168

9 **Pronunciation** **171**
9.1 Class-vocabulary audio notebook 173
9.2 Phonemic dialogues 174

9.3	Howdjasayit?	175
9.4	Schwa what?	176
9.5	Phonetic games	177
9.6	Minimal-pair poems	178
9.7	Newsreader	179
9.8	Tongue twisters	181
9.9	Voice recognition	182
9.10	Smartphone app	183
9.11	What's the intonation?	184
9.12	Different accents	185
9.13	Guess the language	186
9.14	Re-recording speeches and scenes	187

10	**Project work**	**189**
10.1	Our e-book	191
10.2	Class magazine	192
10.3	Culture capsule	193
10.4	Class weekly learning podcast	194
10.5	TV magazine programme	195
10.6	Short film	196
10.7	Film festival	197
10.8	Our cookbook	198
10.9	Make your own webquest	199
10.10	IWB island	201

11	**Assessment and evaluation**	**203**
11.1	E-portfolio archive and showcase	205
11.2	Awarding badges	206
11.3	Comparing placement tests	207
11.4	Testing you	208
11.5	Testing me	209
11.6	Screen-capture video feedback	210
11.7	Self-assessing presentations	211
11.8	Evaluating classroom activities	212
11.9	Levelling up	213

Appendix A: Learning technologies guide	**217**
Appendix B: Technical notes and suggested software/websites by chapter	**221**
Index	**239**

Thanks

The author would like to thank Scott for initiating this journey, and for all his helpful advice and ideas. A big thank you to Karen and Debbie, and everyone else at Cambridge University Press for their hard work on this project. Thanks also to Farruca and Nano for keeping me company during those early morning writing sessions, and to Isabel de la Granja – I couldn't have written this without you by my side.

Special thanks to the committee and members of the IATEFL Learning Technologies Special Interest Group (http://ltsig.org.uk), my colleagues on the aPLaNet (http://aplanet-project.org) and iTILT (http://itilt.eu) EU projects, the terrific team of teachers I work with at the British Council in Barcelona. Last, but not least, thanks to all of you webheads out there who are part of my PLN – I couldn't have done this without your help.

This book is dedicated to my mother and father, for leading me nearer to the river's trembling edge.

Acknowledgements

Text

The authors and publishers acknowledge the following sources of copyright material and are grateful for the permissions granted. While every effort has been made, it has not always been possible to identify the sources of all the material used, or to trace all copyright holders. If any omissions are brought to our notice, we will be happy to include the appropriate acknowledgements on reprinting.

Screenshot on p. 40 by permission from Merriam-Webster's Learners Dictionary, copyright © 2012 (www.learnersdictionary.com) by Merriam-Webster, Inc. (www.merriam-webster.com);
Screenshot on p. 47 from Glogster EDU, www.glogster.com. Reproduced with permission;
Screenshot on p. 50 from Visuwords, www.visuwords.com. Reproduced with permission;
Education Games Network Ltd for the Game Builder screenshot on p. 52 from Wordia, www.wordia.com. Reproduced with permission;
Screenshot on p. 56 from Urban Dictionary, www.urbandictionary.com. Reproduced with permission;
Screenshot on p. 57 from Just the Word, www.just-the-word.com. Copyright © Sharp Laboratories of Europe Limited;
Screenshot on p. 58 from Compleat Lexical Tutor, www.lextutor.ca. Reproduced with permission;
Screenshot on p. 78 created using Popplet, http://popplet.com. Reproduced with permission;
Screenshot on p. 116 from LearnEnglish Kids. This story appears at www.britishcouncil.org/learnenglishkids and is reprinted with the permission of the British Council;
Adam Cadre for the IF game '9:05' on p. 117 from http://adamcadre.ac/if/905.html. Reproduced with permission;
Screenshot on p. 123 from Edmodo, www.edmodo.com. Copyright © 2012 Edmodo, Inc;
Screenshot on p. 132 from Carnegie Library of Pittsburgh. Image used with permission from Carnegie Library of Pittsburgh, www.carnegielibrary.org;
Screenshot on p. 133 from http://teacher.scholastic.com/activities/storystarters. Reprinted by permission of Scholastic Inc;
Screenshot on p. 134 from Mad Takes, www.madtakes.com. Reproduced with permission;
Screenshot on p. 141 from Timeglider, www.timeglider.com;
Screenshot on p. 151 from Blabberize, www.blabberize.com;
Screenshot on p. 152 from VoiceThread, www.voicethread.com. Reproduced with permission;
Screenshot on p. 157 from Woices, www.woices.com. Reproduced with permission;
Screenshot on p. 163 from National Express, www.nationalexpress.com. Reproduced with permission;
Screenshot on p. 165 from Voxopop, www.voxopop.com. Reproduced with permission;
Screenshot on p. 169 from Stop Disasters, www.stopdisastersgame.org. Copyright © Playerthree and UN/ISDR, www.playerthree.com.

Photos

The authors and publishers acknowledge the following sources of copyright material and are grateful for the permissions granted. While every effort has been made, it has not always been possible to identify the sources of all the material used, or to trace all copyright holders. If any omissions are brought to our notice, we will be happy to include the appropriate acknowledgements on reprinting.

p. 73 (TL): Kenneth Benjamin Reed/Shutterstock; p. 73 (TC): Jurgen & Christine Sohns/FLPA; p. 73 (TR): Vladimir Koletic/Shutterstock; p. 73 (BL): David Noton Photography/Alamy; p. 73 (BC): Comstock/Thinkstock; p. 73 (BR): Khoroshunova Olga Underwater/Alamy; p. 158: Carol and Mike Werner/Alamy; p. 123: Isabel de la Granja; Front cover photograph by © John Rensten/Corbis. T = Top, C = Centre, B = Below, L = Left, R = Right.

Introduction

Overview

Language Learning with Technology is a handbook for teachers interested in integrating technology into their classroom practice. The book makes a point of putting pedagogy at the forefront of the lesson, which is why content has been organised around specific learning content goals rather than specific technologies.

Each chapter deals with a different aspect of language learning, and use of technology is suggested only when it adds significant value to the learning. With over 130 activities to choose from, this book can be used by the teacher, as a classroom resource, to supplement an existing language course.

Who is this book for?

This book has been designed to be used by teachers who want to improve their own knowledge of how best to integrate a variety of learning technologies into their classroom practice.

It has been written to appeal to language teachers who are both new and experienced. Teachers may have had years of practice in using technology with their learners, or be looking to take their first steps in using it with a class.

A wide variety of activities has been provided for use with learners from beginner to advanced levels of proficiency. Although most activities have been written with the adult learner of general English in mind, many should be equally as effective when used with teenagers, or adapted for children, as well as for the teaching of any other foreign or second language.

Whatever your teaching context, we hope you will find this handbook an invaluable classroom guide to using learning technologies.

Why technology?

We now live in a world in which technology permeates every aspect of our lives. Apart from its time- and labour-saving function, technology can also inspire creativity and bring new opportunities to people, connecting them to new ideas and people they otherwise might not have met.

In language teaching and learning, technology can be used for:
- accessing information, including information about language
- exposure to the target language
- entertainment (i.e. reading/listening for pleasure)
- creating text
- publishing learner work
- communicating and interacting with other language users/learners
- creating community
- managing and organising learning (e.g. learning management systems, online vocabulary notebooks, etc.).

Benefits of learning technology

Many classroom teachers using technology have anecdotal evidence of their learners being motivated and engaged, and this is often a major reason for using learning technologies. There is also evidence that the use of technological tools empowers learners to transcend the traditional concept of the classroom (Drexler, 2010) and can lead to learners taking greater ownership of their learning (Terrell, 2011), especially through being actively involved together outside the classroom.

Technology can be a highly engaging and interactive tool, providing a source of real language, both written and spoken, in the classroom, and motivating learners to produce more language than they otherwise might have done.

Instant information

The Internet, in particular, has become a social phenomenon which 'pervades work, education, interpersonal communication' (Thorne & Black, 2008), and having internet access in the classroom opens up learning to the real world, beyond the confines of the classroom.

For instance, the Web can be an instant provider of information for the teacher, as it has fast become in the world outside the classroom. Rather than telling learners you will give them the answer to a question later, you can look it up there and then. You can also show the learners how to use reference tools, such as dictionaries, concordancers, a thesaurus and phonemic charts. By helping them help themselves, you are promoting their autonomy, as learners and users. A teacher also has more choice with the Web – more ways to answer vocabulary questions, for example. As well as explaining something or providing a definition or translation, you can look for example sentences, or show your learners a picture. I remember one class when a learner asked me the difference between the words *geek* and *nerd*. Rather than attempt a clumsy explanation, I turned to *Google Images*, and the learners were able to see the differences *and similarities* for themselves.

The Web is, of course, also a great source of listening. You can find video clips of people speaking countless varieties of English, as well as have access to songs, through sites such as *YouTube*. Apart from providing a large bank of authentic recordings, the Web allows you to personalise listening tasks and choose a video clip to complement something in the syllabus. You can also use the Web when your learners are particularly interested in a specific topic, or as a stimulus for speaking about a subject.

Real communication

There has also been a clear shift in the role of the Internet, away from it being a huge resource library towards what has been called *Web 2.0*, where communication takes the lead, which has led to an increase in internet use. A Web 2.0 site allows users to interact and collaborate with each other, as creators of user-generated content in a virtual community, in contrast to websites where users are limited to the passive viewing of content that was created for them. Examples of Web 2.0 include social-networking sites, blogs, wikis and video-sharing sites.

New studies show a growing interest in using these emerging web tools in language learning (Thomas, 2009), which shows promise for their role in the future, not only as learning tools, but also when used as authentic means of communication and relation building (Sykes et al., 2008).

Your learners can connect to other learners, or users of English, in real time (*synchronously*), or at different times (*asynchronously*), thereby providing opportunities for authentic language practice (i.e. real communication), rather than the practice for practice's sake that usually takes place in the classroom.

Publishing learners' work

Publication of learners' work online (e.g. via blogs, wikis, class webpages, etc.) is just one application that can have a positive effect on the quality and quantity of written work that learners produce. The fact that their work is being offered for reading to an audience beyond that of the teacher and the class can also be used to encourage process writing, and a focus on error correction, that would otherwise be difficult to achieve.

Even if you don't have internet access in your classroom, you can publish learners' work online and provide an audience that may include parents, other learners, etc.

A variety of different tools

Of course, it's not just about the Internet. The proliferation of hand-held devices, such as mobile phones, digital cameras, tablets, mp3 players and voice recorders, has led to what, for some teachers, is a sometimes bewildering choice of potential activities and resources. Even if mobile phones are banned in your classroom or institution, you can use your own (most mobile phones support this) to record learners (using the voice recorder or video recorder), and if it is a smartphone, there is a rapidly increasing number of applications to be made use of to help you in class.

As the potential of these devices is realised, and more and more learners have access to them, teachers are beginning to experiment with using these tools. The use of mobile devices is expected to lead to language learning becoming more informal and personal (Chinnery, 2006; Kukulska-Hulme & Shield, 2008), with many more learners studying or practising with manageable chunks of language wherever they are, and in their own time. This revolution in mobile learning is happening both inside and outside the classroom.

Pedagogy vs technology

This increase in the availability of technology has led to an explosion of interest in its use in the language classroom. Despite the potential for new ways of learning, the trap that teachers can fall into is one of being seduced by the 'wow factor' of new technology, with pedagogy being pushed to the sidelines.

Moreover, as language classrooms become more technologised, there is a real danger of teachers developing *Everest syndrome* (Maddux, cited in Gallo & Horton, 1994). Named after George Mallory's reason for wanting to climb Mount Everest, this refers to a situation where teachers can be tempted to use a specific technology just 'because it's there'. Care has to be taken, therefore, to make use of what we have available only when it serves the language aims of the lesson, and to avoid any use of 'technology for technology's sake'.

For this reason, the organisation of this book avoids prioritising technology over language learning. Many other handbooks for teachers, from the first guides to using the Internet

(Dudeney, 2000; Sperling, 1999; Teeler & Gray, 2000; Windeatt et al., 2000), through the second wave (Barrett & Sharma, 2003; Lewis, 2004), to the newer ones (Dudeney & Hockly, 2007; Hockly & Clandfield, 2010), are organised around different technologies, rather than the uses to which they can be put.

That is not to say, however, that an organisation around technology wasn't necessary when the first handbooks were written. Quite the opposite is true. Computer-assisted language learning (CALL) had just started to attract mainstream interest, marked by the emergence of the Internet, and there was a need to introduce language teachers to how it could be used, especially as CALL was still 'a peripheral interest in the language teaching community as a whole' (Levy, 1997).

Normalisation

At the turn of the century, the idea of there being a new generation gap of *digital immigrants* and *digital natives* (Prensky, 2001) struck a chord with many educators and seemed to describe a new technological landscape which educators needed to start exploring. However, this distinction no longer seems helpful as we move to a place where we are used to technology being in 'a state of perpetual beta' (Pegrum, 2009). In other words, technology is in a state of constant development, and it seems as if new tools and innovations emerge every day. It can be argued that learning technologies are now being used by many language teachers as a matter of course. This shows a move towards *normalisation*.

Normalisation (Bax, 2003) occurs in language education when technology is used without teachers being consciously aware of its role as technology. Few teachers consider dry-wipe board pens to be technology, for example, but the same cannot be said of the interactive whiteboard (IWB) and the electronic pens that go with it.

The concept was revisited by Bax (2011), and although the conclusion was that most technology, as other research indicates, is 'not yet normalised in language education' (Thomas, 2009), there are definite 'signs of a more fully integrated approach to CALL emerging because of Web 2.0' (Motteram & Stanley, 2011). With the danger of teachers using technology 'because it's there' forever lurking in the sidelines, it is clear that a new approach is required.

A principled approach

What is needed is an approach to using technology that has learning at its heart, where teachers question how and when to integrate technology into the classroom. A call for a more 'principled approach' has recently been made, with Hockly (2011) and Lyon-Jones (2011) both producing guidelines and checklists for teachers, which I have expanded upon here.

- *Why use the technology?* In other words, don't just use it because it is there. Are you trying to do something with the technology that can be better done without it? If learning is not enhanced by using the technology, then don't use it.
- *Who is the technology best for?* Is the technology appropriate for your learners? What age group is it suitable for, and what language level is required to use it? How much teaching / technical experience / training is required to use it effectively?

- *What is the technology best used for?* It is worth considering whether there is another technology that can be used instead that may better suit the learning objectives.
- *Where should it be used?* Is it more suitable for the classroom / connected classroom (i.e. with one computer and the Internet) / computer room / at home? Think also about classroom management issues here. Where in the classroom is the technology to be used and, if appropriate, what will the other learners be doing when one, or some, of them is using the technology (i.e. will they be engaged)?
- *When should the technology be used?* Not only when is the best moment during the class to use the technology (at the beginning/end, etc.), but also when in the term/syllabus? (It is best if used to enhance, and complement, what you are already doing with the learners, rather than as an added extra.)
- *How should the technology be used?* This shouldn't just be about what to do, but also how best to incorporate the technology into your class. Will using the technology be a more efficient use of a teacher's, or the learners', time?

This principled approach can do much to address the criticism of the use of technology in the language classroom, much of which tends to focus on time spent getting things to work – time which could have otherwise been spent practising language.

One example of this is the use of *clickers*, which are hand-held devices that work in combination with an IWB, and use infra-red signals to offer basic multiple-choice and polling options. Although they are popular with some subjects, and can be useful for concept testing in maths or physics, I am not yet convinced there is a place for them in the language classroom. First of all, I think the teacher would have to spend a large amount of time preparing an activity which might probably last only a few minutes in class, and which could be equally accomplished in most cases by asking the learners to raise their hands.

The IWB itself seems to have provoked a lot of criticism. One of the major reasons why this is so is misuse of the technology. Although the IWB looks like a standard whiteboard, this is deceptive, and teachers limiting themselves to using it to show *YouTube* videos, or simply picking up the electronic pen and writing on it, shows a misunderstanding of the affordances of this technology. In the hands of a teacher who knows how to use it well, the IWB can be a tool that encourages learner collaboration, is perfect for revision and helps with lesson organisation, as well as saving the teacher a lot of time.

Lack of training

Research suggests that the pedagogical exploitation of IWBs depends as much on the availability of teaching resources as it does on teachers' understanding of how best to use the technology (Cutrim Schmid & van Hazebrouck, 2010). This tends to indicate that training, therefore, is the key to effective use of the IWB or, indeed, of any technology.

The IWB is not the only example of a technology whose usefulness has been reduced by a lack of training. Training teachers how to use new technology is often a hidden cost that is not factored in when technology is introduced into an institution, which leads to a mismatch between what the institution expects teachers to know, in order to effectively use technology, and what their actual knowledge is. One of the aims of this book is to help teachers bridge this gap.

What technology?

This book draws upon a wide range of technologies for its activities, which many teachers have easy access to. The learning technologies used in the book are:

The Internet	Software	Hardware
automatic translators	apps	CD-ROMs
blogs	authoring software	computer room
comic-creator websites	concordancers	data projectors
image-creation software	ebooks	digital cameras
instant messaging	electronic dictionaries	DVDs
news websites	email	interactive whiteboards (IWBs)
online games	interactive fiction	laptops
podcasts	mind-mapping software	mobile phones
poster websites	music software	mp3 players
social networks	presentation software	netbooks
survey websites	quiz-making software	pen/flash drives
text and voice chat	screen-capture tools	tablets
text and voice forums	social bookmarking	video cameras
video-sharing websites	sound-editing software	voice recorders
wikis	word processors	webcams

Summary of aims

1. To provide a wide range of interesting and useful activities, where technology has been used only when there is clearly added value to language learning and practice.
2. To show how any teacher can use technology, alongside an existing language course, to enhance language learning.
3. To offer a reserve of activities which are suitable for all levels of proficiency, from beginner to advanced, and which include ideas for listening comprehension, grammar practice, oral production and fluency practice, amongst others.

How to use this book

The activities presented in this book have been divided according to learning focus, or language learning goals, rather than by tool. The outline of each activity begins with the following:

Main goals: the purpose of doing the activity.

Level: an indication of the proficiency level for which the activity is likely to be suitable.

Time: a rough guide to the time the activity is likely to take.

Learning focus: an indication of the specific language practised by doing the activity.

Preparation: what needs to be done before you do the activity with learners.

Technical requirements: the equipment and any special knowledge you, and your learners, need in order to do the activity.

In addition, many activities end with:

Variation: ideas on how to adapt the activity so that it practises another aspect of language, makes use of different technology, etc.

At the end of the book, Appendix A: *Learning technologies guide* is designed to help teachers by providing specific details about some of the software and hardware used in various activities. Appendix B: *Technical notes and suggested software/websites by chapter* will enable teachers to better understand what technology is required for each activity. Finally, look in the *Index* to see which activities focus on a specific language item or function. This book is also accompanied by a website (http://www.languagelearningtechnology.com) which is updated and maintained by the author. There are notes within the text which indicate for certain tasks that using this website would be helpful but it is not essential.

References

Barrett, B. and Sharma, P. (2003) *The Internet and Business English*, Andover: Summertown Publishing.

Bax, S. (2003) 'CALL past, present and future', *System*, 31 (1), 13–28.

Bax, S. (2011) 'Normalisation revisited: the effective use of technology in language education', *International Journal of Computer-Assisted Language Learning and Teaching (IJCALLT)*, 1 (2), 1–15. Available online at: http://www.igi-global.com/article/normalisation-revisited-effective-use-technology/53797.

Chinnery, G. (2006) 'Going to the MALL: mobile assisted language learning', *Language Learning & Technology*, 10 (1), 9–16.

Cutrim Schmid, E. and van Hazebrouck, S. (2010) 'Using the interactive whiteboard as a "digital hub"', *Praxis Fremdsprachenunterricht*, 4 (10), 12–15.

Drexler, W. (2010) 'The networked student model for construction of personal learning environments', *Australasian Journal of Educational Technology*, 26 (3), 369–85.

Dudeney, G. (2000) *The Internet and the Language Classroom*, Cambridge: Cambridge University Press.

Dudeney, G. and Hockly, N. (2007) *How to Teach English with Technology*, Harlow: Pearson Longman.

Gallo, M. A. and Horton, P. B. (1994) 'Assessing the effect on high school teachers of direct and unrestricted access to the Internet: a case study of an east central Florida high school', *Educational Technology Research and Development*, 42 (4), 17–39.

Hockly, N. (2011) 'The principled approach', *E-Moderation Station*. Available online at: http://www.emoderationskills.com/?p=551.

Hockly, N. and Clandfield, L. (2010) *Teaching Online: Tools and Techniques, Options and Opportunities*, Surrey: Delta Publishing.

Kukulska-Hulme, A. and Shield, L. (2008) 'An overview of mobile-assisted language learning: from content delivery to supported collaboration and interaction', *ReCALL*, 20 (3), 271–89.

Levy, M. (1997) *CALL: Context and Conceptualisation*, Oxford: Oxford University Press.

Lewis, G. (2004) *The Internet and Young Learners*, Oxford: Oxford University Press.

Lyon-Jones, S. (2011) 'Teaching with technology – a basic checklist', *The Edtech Hub*. Available online at: http://www.edtech-hub.com/resources/techteachchecklist.html.

Motteram, G. and Stanley, G. (2011) 'Preface: special issue on Web 2.0 and the normalisation of CALL', *International Journal of Computer-Assisted Language Learning and Teaching (IJCALLT)*, 1 (2), 1–15. Available online at: http://www.igi-global.com/Files/Ancillary/3b91f667-1863-46da-86c5-b262b319bafc_2155-7098_1_2_Preface.pdf.

Pegrum, M. (2009) *From Blogs to Bombs: The Future of Digital Technologies in Education*, Crawley, Australia: UWA Publishing.

Prensky, M. (2001) 'Digital natives, digital immigrants', *On the Horizon*, 9 (5), 1–6. Available online at: http://www.marcprensky.com/writing.

Sperling, D. (1999) *Dave Sperling's Internet Activity Workbook*, New York: Prentice Hall.

Sykes, J., Oskoz, A. and Thorme, S. L. (2008) 'Web 2.0, synthetic immersive environments, and mobile resources for language education', *CALICO Journal*, 25 (3), 528–46.

Teeler, D. with Gray, P. (2000) *How To Use the Internet in ELT*, Harlow: Longman.

Terrell, S. (2011) 'Integrating online tools to motivate young English language learners to practice English outside the classroom', *International Journal of Computer-Assisted Language Learning and Teaching (IJCALLT)*, 1 (2), 16–22. Available online at: http://www.igi-global.com/article/integrating-online-tools-motivate-young/53798.

Thomas, M. (ed.) (2009) *Handbook of Research on Web 2.0 and Second Language Learning*, Hershey, PA: IGI Global.

Thorne, S. L. and Black, R. W. (2008) 'Language and literacy development in computer-mediated contexts and communities', *Annual Review of Applied Linguistics*, 27, 133–60.

Windeatt, S., Hardisty, D. and Eastment, D. (2000) *The Internet*, Oxford: Oxford University Press.

1 Integrating technology

I am a firm believer that in order for learning technology to be successful, it should be integrated into the curriculum. According to a report published by the educational community Edutopia, this must happen 'in ways that research shows deepen and enhance the learning process', and 'in particular, it must support four key components of learning: active engagement, participation in groups, frequent interaction and feedback, and connection to real-world experts' (Edutopia, 2008).

Technology should always be part of what a teacher is currently doing with a class, and only be used to promote and extend learning. It shouldn't be something special, done as a break from regular classroom learning or as a reward for good behaviour. For this reason, whenever colleagues ask me for ideas on what to do in the computer room of our school, my first question to them is always, 'What are you doing with the class at the moment?' Once I have the answer to this question, then I can help them.

Of course, it's not always clear that incorporating technology into the pedagogical goal is the right way of doing things. I would hazard a guess that every teacher attracted to using technology in the classroom has been tempted to try using a new tool they have come across, even if the added value of using that tool was dubious. This urge to experiment is understandable, given we live in an age where technological change is happening at breakneck speed. Son (2011) calls for teachers to 'develop and implement CALL widely by exploring, selecting, using and evaluating the tools in a variety of contexts', and perhaps it is the *evaluating* aspect that teachers need to concentrate more on, in order to ensure that technology is not used for technology's sake.

So what comes first? Technology or learning objectives? The answer is, neither. The learners come first, and this is why one of the best ways of knowing if, and how much, technology should play a part in your class is by finding out from your learners their attitudes to using technology for language learning.

There are a couple of information-gathering activities in this chapter, but before you do these, you can simply ask your learners what they think of the idea of using more technology in class. If they are adults, perhaps the last thing they want to do after a long day sitting in front of screens at work is come to class and do the same! On the other hand, they may all have smartphones, and may appreciate their English teacher showing them how best to use them to practise English when they are commuting. Or you may teach teenagers who are bored with more traditional ways of learning English and who would be highly motivated by your spicing up your lesson with computers. What technology you use will also depend on what resources you, and your learners, have available. You may have an interactive whiteboard in the classroom, or a computer and a projector. If you are very lucky, you may have a class set of laptops, netbooks or tablets. In both of these cases, you will probably find yourself using technology in every class. You may have access to a computer room you need to book, or for which there is a sign-up sheet determining access. Your learners could all have smartphones, or other mobile devices, you can use. For this reason, determining what technology is at your disposal, and how you can make use of it (should you choose to do so), will be an important factor in deciding how to use technology in class.

Whatever your access to technology, one of the obvious choices of tools a teacher has is of electronic dictionaries, as well as other tools specifically designed to support language learning, such as the thesaurus. Introducing learners to these tools, and showing them when and how to use them, can help them help themselves at a later date. There is a suggestion in this chapter for how to introduce learners to electronic dictionaries.

One way of integrating technology into a course is to adopt a blended-learning approach.

Blended learning here 'refers to a language course which combines a face-to-face classroom component with an appropriate use of technology' (Sharma & Barrett, 2007: 7), and this definition implies the learners use technology at home. Although many teachers will believe that blended learning refers to when a face-to-face component has been added to an online course (i.e. 90% online; 10% face-to-face), the term can refer to the opposite: an online component is added to a face-to-face course.

One of the best ways teachers can adopt this type of blended-learning approach, and ensure technology is integrated into a course, is by using a *Virtual Learning Environment (VLE)*. VLEs come in various shapes and forms. Another term for a VLE is *Learning Management System (LMS)*. The most popular ones are currently *Moodle* and *Blackboard*, and larger institutions will often have available a VLE that teachers and learners can use. If this is the case in your situation, and you have been avoiding the VLE, now may be the time to start using it. If you don't have access to a VLE, then you can always set up your own for your learners to use, or (even better) talk to other teachers at your institution and set up one that can be used by a number of classes.

VLEs usually have tools that make it easy for teachers to see how often, and when, learners have accessed the system, and will let you set tests and record learner marks. Therefore, VLEs can be useful for assessment and evaluation.

VLEs, however, are very teacher-centric tools and don't encourage lifelong learning or learner autonomy. Usually, once a learner has stopped studying a course, or attending a particular institution, he/she will no longer have access to the VLE. For this reason, a popular alternative to the VLE is the *Personal Learning Environment (PLE)*. Rather than asking learners to join an institution-owned platform, they can be encouraged to set up a number of tools of their own. You can find out more about the PLE in Chapter 2 *Building a learning community*.

One activity in this chapter looks at the *flipped classroom*, which is an interesting approach to classroom practice that suggests teachers reverse the usual teaching model by delivering instruction at home (often by using teacher-created videos) – allowing them to spend more time in class for practice, with the idea of creating a more collaborative learning environment. Although perhaps best suited to content subjects, the flipped classroom can be used by language teachers as an alternative, for occasional use.

Finally, a common obstacle to integrating technology into a language course can be a teacher's fear of what to do if something goes wrong. A teacher using technology always needs to have a *Plan B* (i.e. a back-up plan). For this reason, an activity in this chapter looks at how best a teacher can prepare for the eventuality that the technology may not work as planned. Above all, this chapter is meant to be an introduction to integrating technology into the curriculum. Throughout the rest of the book, you will come across many more ideas for integrating technology, and for making teaching and learning English more meaningful and fun.

References

Edutopia (2008) 'Why integrate technology into the curriculum?: The reasons are many', *Edutopia*. Available online at: http://www.edutopia.org/technology-integration-introduction [accessed March 2012].

Sharma, P. and Barrett, B. (2007) *Blended Learning: Using Technology in and Beyond the Language Classroom*, Oxford: Macmillan Education.

Son, J. B. (2011) 'Online tools for language teaching', *TESL-EJ*, 15 (1). Available online at: http://www.tesl-ej.org/wordpress/issues/volume15/ej57/ej57int [accessed March 2012].

1.1 **Getting to know you**

Main goals	Ice-breaking
Level	All levels
Time	10 minutes
Learning focus	Review of question forms; basic structures
Preparation	Make sure all of the learners have mobile phones they can use in class. Write the names of everyone in the class on separate small pieces of paper.
Technical requirements	Mobile phones (one per learner) with voice recorders

Procedure

1 Hand out the pieces of paper with the learner names on them, one to each learner, and make sure nobody has their own name. Tell the learners that they are going to role play the part of a journalist and write a profile of the learner they have been assigned.

2 Ask the learners to take out their mobile phones and locate the voice recorder. Tell them that the first part of the profile is a description of the person, based on information they already have (this could be a physical description). Then ask the learners to record a description of their assigned learner, using the voice recorder.

3 Next, have the learners interview their assigned classmates. Tell them they can ask any questions they like, but they should find out as much as possible about the classmate, and record both the questions and answers on the voice recorder of their phone.

4 If learners find that the person they are going to interview is interviewing someone else, tell them they should wait their turn, listening to the interview.

5 When all of the interviews are finished, ask the learners to write the profiles of their classmates, starting with the description of the person, and then adding other information. They should aim to write about a paragraph.

6 Ask the learners not to transcribe the interview verbatim, but to use the answers to the questions to build a narrative (e.g. *Ruth lives in a small village, outside the city*, etc.).

7 When the profiles are finished, make a wall display in the classroom.

Variation

If the learners have applications for drawing on their phones, you can ask them to draw a quick sketch of their partner to go with the profile. Alternatively, you can ask the learners to take photographs with the mobile phones and print these out to go with the descriptions.

1.2 Technological survey

Main goals	Information gathering
Level	All levels
Time	10 minutes
Learning focus	Discovering experience with, and attitudes to, use of educational technology
Preparation	Choose a survey tool or questionnaire you can use to ask learners about the technology they use outside class, and their attitudes to using it. There are some suggestions of survey tools in Appendix B 1.2. Write down the questions you think are relevant to your class (see examples in Appendix B 1.2 – there are also some ready-made surveys you can use on the website accompanying this book, http://languagelearningtechnology.com).
Technical requirements	A computer room, or class set of laptops/netbooks/tablets. Alternatively, you can ask the learners to do the survey at home, or you can get an idea for how the class feels about using technology by using one computer and a projector (or IWB), and doing the survey as a whole-class activity. It is also possible, of course, to give the learners a photocopy of the questionnaire to fill in.

Procedure

1 Ask the learners how they feel about using technology in class, and get a feel for what they think it would be good to use it for and how often they think it should be used.

2 Ask the learners to complete the survey you have set up, or go through the questions and answer them in a whole-class setting. Here are some example questions:

Learning-technology survey

Part A – technology I use at home

1	I have a smartphone.	Yes / No
2	I use *Facebook* on a regular basis.	Yes / No

Part B – technology for language learning

1	I would like to use my mobile phone for language learning.	Yes / No
2	I would be happy to use *Facebook* for language learning.	Yes / No

---

3 Use the results of the survey to talk to your learners about how you plan to integrate technology into the syllabus.

4 Make sure to avoid using technology that some of your learners don't have access to (smartphones, for example), or to make this an optional part of whatever you do.

Variation

Learners work in pairs, or groups, and design their own survey, based on some example questions. They then change groups/pairs, interview each other and report the results to the whole class.

1.3 Visual class list

Main goals	Classroom management
Level	All levels
Time	10 minutes
Learning focus	Getting to know each other better
Preparation	Make sure you have the digital camera at hand, and that you can transfer the pictures you take to the computer (via cable, or other method, e.g. memory card). This activity is best done at the beginning of the year.
Technical requirements	An IWB, or computer with projector, and a digital camera, or mobile phone camera

Procedure

1   Tell the learners you would like to take a photograph of them to display on the board as a visual class list. Use the digital camera, or give it to the learners to take a class photograph of each other.

2   Let the learners take several class pictures, until they are happy with the results. If the learners prefer, they could send you individual digital photographs, or choose an icon to represent themselves. However, one of the reasons for taking class photographs is so you and the other learners can get to know each other better.

3   Transfer the photographs to the computer, and add them to the IWB, or (if you don't have an IWB) to a document.

4   You can use the photographs of the learners as a class list, at the beginning of each class, marking the time that learners arrive (if punctuality is an issue). You can also use the photographs to arrange groupings of learners, more easily displaying the seating arrangements for each class so the learners know where to sit when they arrive.

5   With an IWB, you can also use the learner photographs as a marker for board games, and to identify learners during quizzes and other activities.

1.4 Favourite websites

Main goals	Needs analysis / information gathering
Level	All levels
Time	10 minutes
Learning focus	Thinking about using English outside of class
Preparation	Make photocopies of the form below.
Technical requirements	None

Procedure

1   Ask the learners if they know of any websites in English, and if so, to fill in a form (similar to that below) about the websites they visit. To help them, provide a list of categories, such as sports, music, technology, news, etc.

Website	Category	Address	Why I like it

2   Apart from using the information you get from the learners in future classes, you can also make it the basis of a discussion with them about their interests.

1.5 Plan B

Main goals	Classroom management
Level	All levels
Time	Ongoing
Learning focus	Any
Preparation	Time to think about what you can do if the technology fails. See Appendix B 1.5 for help with specific contexts.
Technical requirements	None

Procedure

Before using a particular technology in class, think carefully what you will do if the technology doesn't work. Here are some ideas of what you can do:

- Ask your learners to help out if technology fails. Select a volunteer or two to help sort out the problem, while you conduct a discussion on 'Can we rely upon technology?' or 'What do you do when something goes wrong?'
- Have an alternative activity / lesson plan ready. Save what you had planned to do in this lesson for the next lesson.
- If using online video, play what you plan to play, all the way through, before class. This saves the file into a cache and means your learners won't need to wait for it to load.
- With online audio/video, try to download a copy to your computer so you don't have to rely on an internet connection. See Appendix B 1.5 for help with this.
- If you are using a video where there is a narrative storyline, another idea is to have photocopies of some screenshots of the video ready. You first describe what happens in the video, and then ask the learners to put the screenshots in order.

Note

Thanks to Sue Lyon-Jones of http://www.esolcourses.com for inspiring these ideas.

1.6 Our VLE

Main goals	Learner training; learner autonomy
Level	Elementary (A2) and above
Time	15 minutes
Learning focus	Encouraging homework and out-of-class communication
Preparation	If your institution has a *VLE* (*Virtual Learning Environment*, sometimes referred to as an *LMS* or *CMS*, i.e. *Language/Content Management System*), such as *Moodle*, *Blackboard*, etc., then use it for this activity. If not, choose a VLE from the list in Appendix B 1.6, and set up an account. Before doing so, make sure that using a VLE is acceptable with your institution. For obvious reasons, setting up the account is best done at the beginning of a course.
Technical requirements	A computer room, or class set of laptops/netbooks/tablets. Alternatively, you can use just one internet-enabled computer in the classroom, with a projector, to present the VLE, and the learners can access it outside of class.

Procedure

1 Tell the learners you are going to ask them to join a website and use it to submit homework for class. Tell them that they can also use the website as a way of communicating with you, and the other learners, between classes.

2 Introduce the learners to the features of the VLE you have chosen, and ask them to set up accounts (tell them to do this later if you are not using multiple computers in the classroom).

Features I recommend setting up on the VLE (they will obviously vary depending on the VLE you use) include:

Latest news: this is an area (usually a forum) where you can tell learners important news (inform them of homework, when exams are, etc.).
Learner blogs: learners can use these to write their written homework (unless you ask them to upload more formal documents).
Forums: you can have a number of these. One may be a Grammar Q & A, where learners can ask you questions.

Setting up these features depends on the VLE you choose, but you will be guided through the process on-screen, with drop-down menus you can choose.

3 Set the learners' first assignment. If this activity is done at the beginning of the course, then I suggest asking them to post an introduction in a forum, or on a blog. Ask the learners then to respond to these introductions, and you can also post messages responding to them, too.

4 Make sure you use the VLE regularly, refer to it in class and reward the learners who use it more frequently than others. Rewarding learners should encourage the others to use it more too.

1.7 Dictionary race

Main goals	Learner training; learner autonomy
Level	Elementary (A2) and above
Time	15 minutes
Learning focus	Using electronic/online dictionaries
Preparation	Choose an electronic, or online, dictionary you want to recommend to the learners (see Appendix B 1.7 for some examples), and prepare a list of words and phrases suitable for your class.
Technical requirements	A computer room, or class set of laptops/netbooks/tablets. You can also encourage the learners to use dictionaries they might have on their phones. Alternatively, you can use just one internet-enabled computer in the classroom, with a projector, to model the use of electronic dictionaries, and encourage the learners to use the dictionaries outside of class.

Procedure

1   Ask the learners if they use electronic/online dictionaries and if so, ask them to tell you what they use them for. Here are some of the responses they may give you:

> looking up words   checking spelling   checking grammar   checking pronunciation   finding synonyms

2   Tell the learners that they are going to try out a few electronic dictionaries (either ones they have on their mobile phone or others you recommend) and compare them to see which one(s) they prefer.

3   Ask the learners to work in pairs to look for the words/phrases you call out / write on the board and find definitions, pronunciation, etc. The first pair to define the word/phrase you call out wins a point. Alternatively, if you are using just one computer, ask for volunteers to take turns to use the dictionary. The other learners will follow along with the projected image.

4   After you have tried a few dictionaries, ask the learners which one(s) they preferred and why (easier to use, quicker, etc.).

Variation

With higher-level learners, you can challenge them to put the word/phrase into a sentence before they are awarded a point.

1.8 Class audio recording

Main goals	Giving language feedback
Level	Pre-intermediate (B1) and above
Time	Ongoing
Learning focus	Reflecting on language used; listening; pronunciation
Preparation	Don't try to second-guess when the learners are going to say something interesting. Record everything, but be selective about what you play back.
Technical requirements	A voice recorder (a mobile phone will suffice), with a built-in speaker (see Appendix B 1.8 for more information and suggestions).

Procedure

1 Before starting to record, ask the learners if it's OK to record what they say, and explain the reasons why you want to do so, i.e. to give immediate feedback on pronunciation, help the learners to better reflect on their errors, etc.

2 Activities that are good to record include any presentations the learners make, storytelling and role-playing dialogues, class discussions and debates, etc. When you start recording, be attentive for any language use you think it would be interesting for the learners to listen to / reflect upon, and note down the time in the recording where these language points occur, to make it easier to return to them.

3 When you hear someone say something you think it would be good to focus on, stop the recording, rewind and ask the learners about the language in question. Alternatively, wait until the activity comes to a natural end, and then return to the recording. You may use this approach for errors the learners make, particularly if they are frequent ones. It could be good to focus on times when the learners have difficulty expressing themselves, or when they manage to say something that could be improved upon. Be sure to praise the learners too, and to play back examples of language that are good.

4 Apart from using the voice recorder for correcting and developing language during a lesson, use the recordings on your own when planning/deciding what to do with the learners in class. They can help you become more aware of the learners' needs and what they should focus upon.

Variation 1

You can also use a voice recorder with a class, but the more learners you have, the less useful it will be to record the whole class. In these circumstances, choose carefully the activities you record: individual turns, presentations, group discussions, etc.

Variation 2

This activity works particularly well with small groups, or private (i.e. one-to-one) classes. In this situation, you can occasionally give the learners recordings of themselves to listen to, and ask them to focus upon specific features to improve (commonly recurring errors, etc.).

Variation 3

To help you evaluate learners' spoken language, do station work, and record the learners speaking (i.e. the learners work in small groups on different activities placed around the classroom, for 10 minutes at a time, with one of these stations being an oral exam with you). Station work allows you to concentrate on talking to the learners during the activity, and then later, you can assess the learners by listening to the recording.

1.9 Unlocked achievements

Main goals	Motivation; fun
Level	Pre-intermediate (B1) and above
Time	Ongoing
Learning focus	Motivating learners to work harder
Preparation	Use the IWB software (or a Word document if you don't have an IWB) to create a grid similar to the one below, with some achievements written in it.
Technical requirements	An IWB, or a computer in the classroom with a projector

Procedure

1 Write *unlocked achievements* on the board, and ask the learners if they know where they might see this term and what it means. If any of your learners play computer games in English, they will tell you that if someone *unlocks an achievement*, it means they have reached a particular target in a video game (e.g. they have found all of the hidden vehicles, completed all parts of a level, etc.). Tell the learners that *achievements* in video games are not essential to playing the game, but are extras, designed to increase motivation.

2 Tell the learners that you are going to add similar *achievements* to their English class. Show the learners the achievements grid you have started to create (below), and ask them to brainstorm other achievements to add to it.

Achievement	Who	Unlocked when	Level
Total class attendance	All the class	Everyone comes to class.	+1 (per lesson)
Total attendance	Individual learners	A student comes to class for one month without missing any classes.	+1 (per month)
Homework for all	All the class	Everyone completes all their homework.	+1 (each time)
Homework for you	Individual learners	A learner completes all the homework during one month.	+1 (per month)
Correct	Individual learners	A learner answers all the questions in an exercise correctly.	+1 (each time)
All correct	All the class	Everyone answers all of the questions in an exercise correctly.	+1 (each time)

3 Once you have decided on the achievements, you can start using the achievements grid in class, and refer to it from time to time. Make sure you keep a good record of the unlocked achievements – one way of doing this is having a list of them displayed at the beginning of class on your IWB (or use a Word document if you don't have an IWB).

Variation 1

You could add another column for *Reward* and reward the learners when they unlock an achievement, although in video games, unlocking the achievement is reward enough.

Variation 2

If you have the learners' email addresses, you can send them notification of the points (see Appendix B 1.9 for ideas on how best to do this).

Note

Adapted from a blog post originally published on http://www.digitalplay.info/blog

1.10 Flip your classroom

Main goals	Trying something new; learner autonomy
Level	Pre-intermediate (B1) and above
Time	Ongoing
Learning focus	Listening; understanding concepts
Preparation	Make a short video (three minutes or so) of yourself presenting a grammar point, or another language item. Upload the video to the class website, or to a video-sharing site (see Appendix B 1.10 for suggestions). Prepare a handout that supports the video with some practice activities on the language item presented in it (or the activities could be from a coursebook you are using).
Technical requirements	A video camera, for filming before the lesson. Learners should all have access to the Web from home.

Procedure

1 Towards the end of the lesson, when you would usually set homework, explain to the class the concept of a *flipped classroom*, i.e. a class where the learners do homework before a lesson, rather than afterwards, and that this homework involves a language presentation they will see on video. Tell them the advantage of doing homework this way is that they will then have more time in class to ask the teacher questions, and for practice. Finally, tell the learners that you are going to try out the concept of the flipped classroom with them, to see if they like this way of working.

2 Now tell the learners what their homework is. Tell them it is listening to you presenting a language item, followed by them practising the language presented. An example may be a grammar point you presented on video, followed by a worksheet. Another example could be a video of how best to structure a written report. See Appendix B 1.10 for links to examples.

3 Next class, ask the learners if they had any difficulties understanding the presentation, and go over the practice activity with the class. Follow up by further practice of the language in question.

4 Finally, ask the learners about their experience of the flipped classroom. Did they like it? Was it useful to do things in this way? Why? Why not? If the experience was positive, then think about continuing this way of working.

Variation 1

Flip the coursebook, which means you ask the learners to do parts of the book at home that you would normally do in class (reading, listening), leaving more time for speaking during lessons.

Variation 2

Instead of a video camera to record your presentation, use a virtual classroom (see Appendix B 6.6 for suggestions) which gives you access to a whiteboard, and means by which you can upload a presentation.

2 Building a learning community

It is difficult to understate the important role community has when it comes to learning, with community here meaning a group of people with shared values, a common purpose and similar goals. Were it not important, schools, colleges and universities would have little reason to exist. When it comes to language learning in particular, a community is arguably more important than with other subjects, especially as language is constructed in social contexts.

Perhaps the most notable contribution technology has made in creating communities is facilitating communication outside the classroom. Through online communities, built with the aid of tools such as email, threaded forum discussions, blogs and wikis, social learning can easily be extended, especially by making it easier for language users and learners to be in touch with one another. This can result in the building of a *community of practice* (Lave & Wenger, 1991: 98), a community that occurs when people with a common interest regularly interact to learn with each other over an extended period of time.

When talking to other language teachers about technology, I always encourage them to take advantage of the increase in popularity of social networking and of Web 2.0 tools, or user-centred tools, in daily life. Using these tools helps both teachers and learners to move away from regarding learning as an isolated activity, towards a more social model. In this chapter, I'll be looking at how social media and networking tools, such as blogs and wikis, can be used to connect learners and build community, inside and outside the classroom.

There are many opportunities for learning through the informational and personal connections that can be made through social media, and as a large majority of our learners already use many of these sites, they often can be persuaded to use them for language learning. Although many Web 2.0 tools were not originally designed for language learning, I hope the activities in this chapter show they can be adapted for this purpose.

One of the social-networking tools that can be used to connect learners with society is the blog. Blogging gives learners the opportunity to build a presence online, in an interactive space where they can display their different aptitudes, personality and talents. How you introduce blogs to learners will depend very much on the time you have available, and your choice between the three main types (Campbell, 2003) will depend very much on what your aims are; the options are a *tutor blog* (a blog owned by the teacher, with only learners able to post comments), a *class blog* (a blog where teacher and learners have equal posting rights) or a *learner blog* (a blog owned by a particular learner).

Another way of connecting learners is by using a social network, taking advantage of its possibilities for linking individuals together through common interests, and the production and sharing of text and other artefacts (photos, videos, etc.). Perhaps the most intriguing factor of social networking is its impact on our daily lives. Research has found that social networking can strengthen relationships, and there appear to be positive psychological benefits, including enhanced well-being and self-esteem.

Although some teachers may be wary about connecting with learners on popular social networks, such as *Facebook*, research has shown that it is advisable to use a learning environment that is already in use, or has been chosen by the learner (Brown & Duguid, 1996: 54). Privacy is an important issue, but setting up groups and negotiating guidelines can mean the social network can serve as a useful information point for learners, one that is effective for their learning outside the classroom.

Apart from *Facebook*, microblogging websites such as *Twitter* can also be used for learning and networking. Microblogging websites limit the number of words (140 characters in the case of *Twitter*) that can be written as a blog post; they, too, have the potential to extend learning beyond the boundaries of the classroom. Research (Antenos-Conforti, 2009: 59ff.) has shown that the use of *Twitter* leads to the development of community among learners, and that classroom dynamics are affected positively by its use.

One of the benefits of using *Twitter* is enhancement of social presence, because learners will have more exposure to each other's thoughts and opinions. *Twitter* can also support independent learning and help extend relationships beyond the time frame of a course. This benefit can help focus the learners on the idea of ongoing learning, and I have included activities in this chapter to promote this idea. These activities suggest ways a teacher can help learners build their own *Personal Learning Network (PLN)*, to help them continue learning long after a course has come to an end. A PLN is the group of people someone chooses to connect to (both online and offline) for help, support, advice, encouragement and knowledge.

If you are uneasy about using public social-networking tools such as *Twitter* and *Facebook*, but would like to try social networking to encourage learner and teacher conversations inside and outside the classroom in order to develop classroom community, there are other alternatives. These include private social-networking communities, such as http://www.edmodo.com (free) and http://www.ning.com (paid), which can work just as well and are ideal for connecting learners with others and for facilitating the sharing of information with peers.

Last, but not least, I have included an activity that looks at safety online, which I believe is something all teachers using technology should address with their learners, especially if you are encouraging them to connect with each other, and others, as part of your course.

References

Antenos-Conforti, E. (2009) 'Microblogging on Twitter: social networking in intermediate Italian classes', in L. Lomicka and G. Lord (eds.), *The Next Generation: Social Networking and Online Collaboration in Foreign Language Learning*, San Marcos, TX: The Computer Assisted Language Instruction Consortium (CALICO), 59–60.

Brown, J. S. and Duguid, P. (1996) 'Stolen knowledge', in H. McLellen (ed.), *Situated Learning*, Englewood Cliffs, NJ: Educational Technology Publications, 47–56.

Campbell, A. P. (2003) 'Weblogs for use with ESL classes', *The Internet TESL Journal*, 9 (2). Available online at: http://iteslj.org/Techniques/Campbell-Weblogs.html [accessed May 2012].

Lave, J. and Wenger, E. C. (1991) *Situated Learning: Legitimate Peripheral Participation*, New York: Cambridge University Press.

2.1 Learning together online

Main goals	Connecting with learners outside the classroom; homework platform
Level	All levels
Time	20 minutes
Learning focus	Socialising; supporting each other's learning
Preparation	Set up a private social network for your learners, using one of the websites recommended in Appendix B 2.1. This is best done at the beginning of a term or a year to get the most out of the social network and to promote good study habits.
Technical requirements	Your learners need to have internet-enabled computers to access the social network outside the classroom. A computer in the classroom with projector, or IWB, would be useful to present the social network to the class.

Procedure

1 Tell the learners they are going to be using a private social network outside class, and write some of the reasons for doing so on the board. Encourage them to suggest more uses.

We can get to know each other better.
If you can't come to class, you can see what you missed.
You can submit your homework online.
You can contact me, and the other learners, easily.
We can share online resources for learning together.

2 Once you have set it up, show learners the private social network and its features. Whichever social network you decide to use, it is likely to have the following features: user profile, status updates, blog and/or forum feature, folder and file sharing, and ways of setting assignments. Talk through each of the features, and negotiate how you are going to use them together:

User profile: information that learners choose to share about themselves
Status update: usually a short message about what a learner is currently doing
Blog: an online space for longer messages – can be used as a reflective learning journal
Forum: a place to ask/answer questions about language / the course, or for socialising online
Folder/file sharing: allows the teacher to submit assignments, and learners to submit work

3 Ask the learners to complete their *user profile* on the social-networking site, filling in basic personal information and adding a photograph, or a picture, representing themselves (if they prefer). You can also ask them to write their first *status update*, in which they introduce themselves.

4 Use the social network for setting pre-class activities, keeping track of homework and sharing extra ideas for websites that learners can access to improve their language (videos, etc.), and encourage the learners to share tips and links to resources they find.

Variation

Instead of a private social network, use a public one (*Facebook*, etc.) instead, which allows you to set up a private group. The advantage of a public network is that if learners are already members of this social network, they are more likely to make use of it. However, there is sometimes reluctance for learners (especially younger ones) to mix social life online with classwork, so check with them and their parents (if appropriate) beforehand, to gauge their feelings about this issue.

2.2 Who are my classmates?

Main goals	Building community in the classroom and outside
Level	Pre-intermediate (B1) and above
Time	20 minutes
Learning focus	Reading; speaking
Preparation	Learners need to accept each other as friends on a popular social network. If you don't want to use a public social network (*Facebook*, etc.), then you can use a private one, but learners must have set up a profile, and shared other information about themselves, for this activity to work.
Technical requirements	A computer room, or class set of laptops/netbooks/tablets. Alternatively, you can ask the learners to do this activity from home.

Procedure

1   This activity presents an example of a language lesson that uses public and private social networks. Start by asking the learners how well they know their classmates, and if they think they can get to know them better by using social networking.

2   Tell the learners to choose someone (or a couple of people) in the class they don't know very well, and ask the learners to find out more about these classmate(s) for the next class. Tell them they can do this in various ways: they can use the information they have already shared on the social-networking site, or they can contact the learner(s) directly on the site (in English!) and ask them questions they want answered.

3   Ask the learners to present what they learned in the next class and to focus, in particular, on what they found out and what (if anything) surprised them about the classmate(s) they chose.

2.3 Personal learning online

Main goals	Promoting autonomy; supporting learning online
Level	Pre-intermediate (B1) and above
Time	20 minutes
Learning focus	Socialising; supporting each other's learning
Preparation	If you don't already have one, build a *PLE* (*Personal Learning Environment*) and *PLN* (*Personal Learning Network*) by setting up accounts with a *microblogging* service, a social network and a blog (see Appendix B 2.3 for suggested websites) and connecting to people you think you can learn from (other teachers, etc.).
Technical requirements	One internet-enabled computer in the classroom, with a projector, or IWB. Learners should all have internet access at home, or outside the class.

Note: This is an alternative to that suggested in Activity 2.1, but it is not as easy for the teacher and learners to set up; therefore, it is recommended you use Activity 2.1 if you have not worked online with learners before.

Procedure

1 Write the words *Personal Learning Environment (PLE)* and *Personal Learning Network (PLN)* on the board, and briefly ask the learners if they know what they mean. If none of the learners can offer an explanation, tell them that a PLE is *a collection of online tools that learners can use to support their learning*, and a PLN is *a network of people that learners can connect to, to help them learn*.

2 Show the diagram below (or one that better represents your PLE), and then show the learners some of the tools that form the PLE.

3 Explain what each of the elements is, and show the learners each of the remaining tools that you have chosen to form the class PLE:

Wiki: a simple website that can be created and edited easily by a group of people
Social network: a space for socialising online and sharing information
Blog: an online writing space, which can be used as a reflective journal
Microblog: similar to a blog, but you are limited to very short messages

4 Tell the learners that most of the learning, when using a PLE/PLN, comes from being connected to other people, i.e. when you ask a question, someone answers; you share news, links and resources, to help others with their learning.

5 Ask the learners if they think setting up their own PLE/PLN would be useful, and if so, encourage them to start by setting up an account with a microblogging service, such as *Twitter*, and linking to each other.

6 Next, follow Steps 1–4 in Activity 2.1, and also help learners add other elements to their PLE (a blog, class wiki, etc.) over time.

7 Encourage learners to use the PLE/PLN between classes as a support system for their learning. You can do this in many ways:

- Share links to websites that are useful to the learners.
- Post questions, using the microblogging site, for learners to answer from home.
- Ask the learners to post plans for their writing assignments in their blog, and ask the other students to comment on them.
- Use the wiki to build a class grammar/vocabulary resource, with links to useful websites where the learners can find practice activities.
- Tell the learners to share what they do at the weekend by posting status updates on the social network, and/or microblogging platform, and ask the others to respond to their updates.

These are just some ways the PLE/PLN can be used – I'm sure you'll find others.

2.4 Class blog

Main goals	Getting to know each other
Level	Pre-intermediate (B1) and above
Time	20 minutes
Learning focus	Responding in writing to what other learners have written
Preparation	This activity is to encourage learners to use a blog and write comments on other learners' *class-blog* posts. Set up the class blog beforehand, and write an introductory post. The procedure below will explain how to set up a class blog (see Appendix B 2.4 for suggestions on blogging platforms).
Technical requirements	A computer room, or class set of laptops/netbooks/tablets. Alternatively, the learners can join the blog and write the comments for homework.

Procedure

1 If the learners don't already have a blog to use for class, ask them if they know what a blog is, and introduce them to the new class blog.

2 If using multiple computers, ask the learners to join the class blog and to write their first post, introducing themselves and saying three things they think most people in the class won't know about them.

3 As the learners finish, ask them to get to know more about their classmates by reading what they have written, and also to write a few comments on some of the learner entries. To help them, write some of the following on the board, and ask the learners to add to these possible ways of starting to write a comment.

This made me think about ...   *This is important because ...*
This makes me think of ...   *I don't understand ...*

4 Finish by setting another task for homework. Ask the learners to write a blog post on one of the following subjects:

What I find easy/hard about learning English   *What I like doing in class*
Where I am going on my next holiday   *My online life*

5 Continue the momentum by writing comments and referring to them in the next class. Use the blog as a way of communicating with learners outside of normal class times. If you use a class blog, you may want to set homework, as a blog entry, for the learners there. Finally, encourage the learners to write, but not only because you set homework; they can write about anything else that interests them.

Variation

Giving each learner their own blog can be more motivating, as learners have a greater sense of ownership and can individualise the look and feel of the blog. However, individual learner blogs also mean more work for you, the teacher, especially if you monitor what each learner writes and add comments to their posts, which is recommended. A compromise would be to divide learners into groups and set up a blog for each group of learners.

2.5 **Mystery guest**

Main goals	Encouraging participation
Level	Pre-intermediate (B1) and above
Time	Ongoing, over one to two weeks, for homework
Learning focus	Making predictions
Preparation	This activity is appropriate if you have a *class blog* (see Activity 2.4) with your learners and is good to use to keep interest from waning. Ask another teacher you know to be a mystery guest on your blog and to write a cryptic guest post, finishing with three questions about themselves for the learners to answer (e.g. *Where am I from? Where do I live now? What do I do?*).
Technical requirements	Learners should have internet access, outside of class, and should already have been introduced to the *tutor blog* or *class blog*.

Procedure

1　Tell the learners that you have invited a mystery guest to the blog, and that this person will be asking some questions for the learners to answer.

2　Ask the learners to respond, in the comments area, to the questions that the mystery guest posts, and to do their best to answer them. This activity can also be extended to other language-related games where learners guess information.

3　Be sure to talk in class about what the learners, and the guest, have written, making a clear link between what happens on the blog outside of class and what happens in class.

Note

Thanks to Barbara 'Bee' Dieu (http://barbaradieu.com) for introducing me to this activity in Brazil in 2003.

2.6 Blog exchange

Main goals	Connecting with other L2 speakers
Level	Pre-intermediate (B1) and above
Time	20 minutes
Learning focus	Sharing information
Preparation	Use a *class blog* (see Activity 2.4). Find another class (preferably in another country) to conduct an exchange with (see this book's accompanying website, http://www. languagelearningtechnology.com, for ideas on how to start a blog exchange, and Chapter 10 *Project work* for ideas for longer-term collaboration). Before this activity, both classes should have blogs, and learners should have, at least, written introductions on the class blog.
Technical requirements	A computer room, or class set of laptops/netbooks/tablets, with internet access. Alternatively, this activity is something learners can do at home.

Procedure

1   Tell the learners they are going to be connecting with another class in another country, and ask them to brainstorm all that they know about this country, using the following headings: *location*, *language* and *famous places*. Write the learners' ideas on the board. Follow this up by asking the learners what they would like to know about the other learners they are going to be connecting with (*daily activities, interests, school*, etc.).

2   Using what has been written on the board, ask the learners to come up with some questions they would like to ask a class in the other country. Tell the learners that these are the questions they are going to ask the other learners, and they are going to write them on their blogs.

3   Ask the learners to now predict what they think the learners in the other country will know about them and their culture. Tell the learners that they should write a post in which they introduce themselves and summarise their predictions. If using a class blog, then this step can be done as a class. If using learner blogs, then each learner can write a post individually.

4   Give the learners the address of the other class blog, and ask them to introduce themselves and write their questions, in the comments area, on this blog.

5   Continue the collaboration by asking the learners to respond, in their own blog, to the questions that the other class writes. These questions can be answered in another round of blog posts.

2.7 Language wiki

Main goals	Creating a class record of language/vocabulary
Level	Pre-intermediate (B1) and above
Time	20 minutes / ongoing
Learning focus	Revision
Preparation	Set up a *class wiki* (a simple website that can be easily edited), if you haven't already done so. See Appendix B 2.7 for recommended websites and help on how to set one up.
Technical requirements	A computer room, or class set of laptops/tablets/netbooks. Alternatively, you can use just one internet-enabled computer in the classroom. Learners can also be asked to do this activity from home if they have internet access.

Procedure

1   Tell the learners that you are going to create a class record of all of the language they choose to remember and focus on, recording it in a class wiki. Introduce them to the wiki and set up accounts / invite them to join via email, and ask the learners to look back on what they have done so far. Ask each of them (or each pair) to select an area of grammar or vocabulary, etc. they want to review.

2   Ask the learners to set up a new page on the wiki for the language review and to write, as a heading, the title they have chosen of the grammar item (e.g. *past perfect*, *irregular past verbs*, etc.) or vocabulary set (e.g. *phrasal verbs with 'out'*, *words related to transport*, etc.), adding some new example sentences. Alternatively, ask the learners to write some questions, using the language, at the end of their example sentences, to test the other learners on what they have written.

3   When the learners have finished, you should go through what they have written, either in class or at home, and make sure it is correct. Rather than correct what is wrong online, you can print out the relevant page, mark the errors on what the learners have written and give them the page, telling them to go back to the wiki to correct the errors.

4   If the learners write questions, on each page of the wiki where language is reviewed, to test the other learners, you could set the questions for homework over the coming weeks, and this way the learners will be encouraged to go back and revise what has already been done in class.

2.8 What we need English for

Main goals	Getting to know each other
Level	Pre-intermediate (B1) and above
Time	15 minutes
Learning focus	Reflecting on reasons for learning English
Preparation	Set up an account with an online noticeboard or digital poster site (see Appendix B 2.8 for suggestions).
Technical requirements	An IWB, or internet-enabled computer in the classroom. A digital camera is optional.

Procedure

1 Ask the learners to talk to each other and answer the following questions:

Why are you studying English?
Is English useful for you at the moment?
Will English be more important for you in the future? If so, how?
What do you need/want to do with your English?

2 When the learners have finished, ask each of them to write one sentence that summarises their reasons for learning English.

3 Use an online noticeboard, or digital poster site, which lets you post short notes in the form of sticky notes (see Appendix B 2.8 for suggested websites). Ask each learner to write their sentence on a digital sticky note. If you want to, take a picture of the learner, to place next to the sentence.

4 If you use a class website, blog or wiki, then link to the poster/noticeboard site, or (even better) embed the poster/noticeboard into the class website (you will find the code to do this on the noticeboard/poster site, under *sharing* options). Refer to the online noticeboard during the course, and ask the learners once every few months if they still feel the same about studying English, or if their reasons for learning English have changed.

2.9 Safety online

Main goals	Raising awareness about online safety
Level	Pre-intermediate (B1) and above (especially tweens/teenager learners)
Time	20 minutes
Learning focus	Being safe online
Preparation	Identify some resources you think will help your class with safety online (see Appendix B 2.9 for suggestions).
Technical requirements	One internet-enabled computer in the classroom, with projector, or IWB, would be useful for showing sites/information.

Procedure

1 Elicit what learners know about *safety online*, and ask your learners to discuss this topic in small groups. Here are some of the areas they may bring up:

personal information	*address and telephone number*	*real names*
bullying	*privacy*	*photographs*
email and chat	*videos*	*location*

2 Review imperatives beginning with *Don't*, *Never* and *Only*. Additionally, if you think it useful and the learners have a high enough level to understand, you can look at some existing website resources (see Appendix B 2.9) and check what advice is given there about various topics related to safety.

3 If your learners are tweens or teens, you could ask them to write a class guide for themselves and other learners. If you teach adults, they could work on producing a guide that gives advice to young people. Ask the learners to write a number of sentences using the imperatives you reviewed in Step 2.

3 Vocabulary

As every teacher knows, learning vocabulary can be very difficult. Not only must learners learn lots of words (upward of 5,000, according to some researchers), but they need to encounter vocabulary several times before they can retain it, and practise it in controlled situations before they can use it automatically. This means that reviewing and recycling vocabulary is very important. More than knowing just individual words, learners also needs a huge repertoire of word combinations – or 'chunks'. These aid fluency and also contribute to learners' 'idiomaticity', that is, the capacity to speak or write in a natural, idiomatic way. In most language courses, there is simply not enough time to learn all of the vocabulary that learners need, so much of it must be learned outside of class.

For these reasons, the teacher should focus on more than just teaching pre-selected words and phrases. Teachers need to introduce learners to strategies for learning vocabulary effectively and encouraging learner autonomy.

Some of the activities presented in this chapter, therefore, are designed to encourage learners to become more autonomous in their vocabulary learning. Introducing learners to online tools that they can easily use themselves outside of the classroom is one strategy, and here the teacher's role becomes one of selecting and introducing these tools and showing learners which vocabulary-learning strategies to use, and how they can use these tools to help themselves in the future.

There are activities aimed at helping learners notice meaning by looking at vocabulary in context. Encouraging learners to use online dictionaries, a thesaurus and concordance software can help them acquire new vocabulary.

The activities in this chapter are arranged by level: first the lower-level activities (word-game activities, etc.), followed by those that are more advanced (e.g. using concordance software, dealing with collocations, synonyms, etc.). Within this division, the activities are further arranged, with productive practice activities following on from receptive practice ones.

Apart from the tools mentioned above, technology can help learners learn vocabulary because it has been shown that vocabulary is more memorable if it is presented in an interesting way, and if the learners engage with words and phrases emotionally. So technology can help the teacher find different, and sometimes fun, ways to introduce vocabulary to the class.

Some of the activities in this chapter try to make the vocabulary that is reviewed relevant to learners, so emphasis is placed on the learners selecting the words they want to remember or revise. The learners can be encouraged to make their own vocabulary tests for their classmates, selecting the words and phrases, and writing their own definitions.

There are also activities that encourage learners to perform tasks with the vocabulary, because this can make the words more memorable, and activities that encourage them to look at different aspects of meaning that certain words and phrases can have.

3.1 In context

Main goals	Recognising and understanding words in context
Level	All
Time	5 minutes (ongoing)
Learning focus	Training learners to use context clues when they encounter new words
Preparation	Choose either an online dictionary for learners, with example sentences, or a concordancer (see Appendix B 3.1 for more information and suggested websites).
Technical requirements	One internet-enabled computer in the classroom, with a projector or IWB (optional)

Procedure

1   When looking at new vocabulary, select either an online dictionary (see example in Figure 3.1) or (with higher levels) a *concordancer* (see Appendix B 3.1) which displays example sentences so that learners can take note of the word in context.

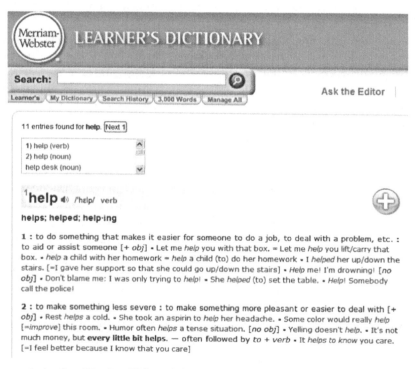

Figure 3.1: By permission from Merriam-Webster's Learners Dictionary © 2012 (www.LearnersDictionary.com) by Merriam-Webster, Inc. (www.Merriam-Webster.com)

2   Write the example sentences on the board. Then ask the learners to match them with the different definitions and, if relevant, parts of speech, and encourage the learners to write example sentences in their vocabulary notebooks.

3.2 Digital camera scavenger hunt

Main goals	Identifying words; recycling vocabulary; describing location
Level	All levels
Time	30 minutes
Learning focus	Classroom and school vocabulary; prepositions
Preparation	Write a list of vocabulary that can be found in or near the classroom, suitable to your learners' level. Make sure the items are easily accessible, and if items are located outside the classroom, then (important) check with the school management that you can let the learners out of class.
Technical requirements	Learners should have enough digital cameras (one per group of three learners), or they should use the cameras on their mobile phones.

Procedure

1 Tell the learners that they are going to work in teams of three and take part in a scavenger hunt: their goal is to find a number of vocabulary items and take pictures of them. Set a time limit, and tell them that each team will gain a point for each vocabulary item they take a photograph of. Also tell them that extra points will be awarded for the best photographs.

2 Give the learners the vocabulary lists or, alternatively, ask them to make a list of words that they think they can find in, or near, the classroom. Examples (this will depend on the learners' level and your situation) may include:

board	*blinds*	*board eraser*	*library*	*broom*	*smoke alarm*
corridor	*hinge*	*window frame*	*houseplant*	*receptionist*	*switchboard*

3 At this stage, don't explain the meaning of words learners don't understand (it's more fun to let them guess, or if they are more advanced, some of them can ask the meaning of words from anyone they happen to meet when they are doing the activity).

4 Start the activity and monitor the learners, making sure they are safe and don't cause too much disruption (especially if they are young learners).

5 When time is up (10 minutes is a good amount of time), ask them to come back to the classroom and either display the photos (if this is possible without too much fuss) or take turns in looking at the photos on the camera, or on each other's mobile phone screens.

6 Give points for each photograph that a team has taken of a correct object, and deduct a point if they have taken an incorrect photo. Award an extra point to the team with the best photograph of each item.

7 Encourage the learners to describe their photographs, saying where they found the items (i.e. *it was near the stairs*, *it was next to the door*, etc.).

8 Make copies of some of the photographs and then, in a later class, return to them and see how many words the learners can remember.

Variation 1

Instead of giving the vocabulary out first, ask the learners to take photographs of things in, or near, the classroom that they don't know the words for in English (or, if they do this for homework, at home or in the town/city where they live), and then to bring the photographs back to class. In class, check to see if any of the other learners know the meanings of the words, or tell learners the meaning. You can also print the photographs and build a classroom wall display of vocabulary that is new to the learners.

Variation 2

If it isn't possible for you to do this activity during class time, or if it goes well and you want a follow-on activity, then give the learners a list of words that they can find at home, or in the town or city where they live, and ask them to take the photos for homework. Check the images in the next class, and award points as above.

3.3 Online word-game tournament

Main goals	Using word games
Level	All
Time	Ongoing
Learning focus	Increasing awareness and knowledge of vocabulary
Preparation	Choose an online word game (e.g. Scrabble) that you think your learners will like and have access to (e.g. one on a social network you know they use). See Appendix B 3.3 for more information and suggested websites.
Technical requirements	One internet-enabled computer in the classroom, with a projector or IWB (optional)

Procedure

1 Tell the learners that you would like them to play a word game for homework, and that you want to see who is the class champion. Introduce them to the game and show them how to play it (in case they don't know).

2 Set a time limit (e.g. one month), telling them that this is to be a tournament, and the winner will be declared in class. Participate yourself, and encourage the learners to challenge you, and others, to a game.

3 Be sure to keep track of the learners' progress, and mention the word game every class, asking them how they are doing. At the end of the month, look at the scores and declare the winner.

4 If the learners take to this activity, introduce them to a different word game and hold another competition.

3.4 Word puzzles

Main goals	Encouraging vocabulary learning; having fun
Level	All
Time	20 minutes
Learning focus	Word definitions and extending knowledge of words
Preparation	Choose a word-puzzle site (see Appendix B 3.4 for more information and suggested websites).
Technical requirements	A computer room, or class set of computers, with internet access. A printer is required to make paper copies of the word puzzles.

Procedure

1   Introduce the class to the word-puzzle site you have chosen (a website that enables them to create a word puzzle for someone else to complete), and choose a type of puzzle (crossword, word search, etc.) suitable for their level.

2   Ask learners to choose a number of words that they have recently come across in class and to create a word puzzle for their classmates. Your choice of puzzle will depend on the level of your class. The puzzle site will generate puzzles with only a group of words, but you should encourage the learners to write clues which are definitions, gapped sentences or mother-tongue translations.

3   Monitor the learners as they do the activity, and provide help as needed.

4   When learners have finished making the word puzzle, ask them to print a copy, and collect the puzzles. You can then either use them as warmers/fillers in future classes or give them out from time to time for learners to do for homework.

3.5 Learner-generated quizzes

Main goals	Vocabulary revision
Level	All levels
Time	20 minutes
Learning focus	Recycling vocabulary
Preparation	Create a class account with a test-/quiz-generator website (see Appendix B 3.5 for more information and suggested websites).
Technical requirements	A computer room, or class set of laptops/netbooks/tablets

Procedure

1 Ask the learners to work in pairs and to select a number of vocabulary items that they would like to revise from work that has already been done. You can give different pairs of learners different topic areas, or let them choose which types of words to focus on (phrasal verbs, adjectives, etc.).

2 Ask the learners to make a list of 10 words or phrases and to write definitions of them (they can use dictionaries to make it easier).

3 Once they have their lists, they create their tests using the quiz-generator website, entering the words/phrases and definitions. The software will automatically generate a vocabulary test from these. While learners are doing the task, monitor them and check the words/phrases are spelled correctly and the definitions make sense.

4 When learners have finished, invite them to try some of the tests created by their classmates.

5 You can set some of the tests for the learners to do at home, too.

Note

For more ideas on how to use technology for learner-generated testing, see Chapter 11 *Assessment and evaluation*.

3.6 Memory posters

Main goals	Vocabulary revision
Level	All levels
Time	10 minutes
Learning focus	Recycling vocabulary topics
Preparation	Create a class account at a digital poster-creation website (see Appendix B 3.6 for more information and suggested websites), and prepare an example digital poster.
Technical requirements	A computer room, or class set of laptops/netbooks/tablets, for the creation of the posters. For the follow-up activity, a connected classroom (i.e. an internet-enabled computer and data projector in the classroom) is ideal.

Procedure

1   Ask the learners to work in pairs / small groups and for each group/pair to select a different topic from the syllabus – one that you have already looked at (see Step 2 for examples). Tell them they are going to make posters to revise vocabulary.

2   Each of the groups/pairs chooses a number of words or phrases (e.g. 10) from a vocabulary topic that they think is important to remember, and they take note of the words and expressions and their meaning. Typical examples of topics could be:

Holidays	*House and home*	*Family and friends*	*Education*
Shopping	*Eating and drinking*	*Leisure activities*	*Music*

3   Once groups have their 10 words/phrases, introduce the learners to the poster-creation website, and tell them they are to create a poster illustrating the vocabulary they have chosen with images from the software image library. Show them the example you created and ask them to guess the words that are missing (see image of example poster in Figure 3.2 below).

4   The learners start to make their posters, adding text and using the tools of the website to illustrate the words and phrases with images and videos. Because learners can spend a lot of time creating their posters if they are allowed to do so, be sure to set a time limit (20–30 minutes, for example) for this activity. If they don't finish, then ask them to complete the poster for homework.

5   When the posters are ready (the next class if necessary), display them one by one, and ask the other pairs/groups to take turns guessing the vocabulary.

6   Award points to the pairs/groups for correct answers. The posters can be added to a class wiki or blog (see Chapter 2 *Building a learning community*).

7   In later lessons, perhaps just before the beginning or the end of a class, you can display one of the posters and call on learners to guess the words.

Figure 3.2: Poster created with Glogster: http://www.glogster.com, a free poster-creation site

Variation 1

If time is short, or access to computers restricted, the poster-creation activity can be done by the learners entirely at home.

Variation 2

Instead of testing vocabulary, learners can create posters using vocabulary related to the topic and then give a short presentation in class of the vocabulary on their posters.

Note

Adapted from Lindstromberg, S. (2004) 'Memory poster circles', *Language Activities for Teenagers*, Cambridge: Cambridge University Press: 156.

3.7 Alien vocabulary

Main goals	Talking about unfamiliar vocabulary words
Level	All levels
Time	30 minutes
Learning focus	Describing unfamiliar vocabulary
Preparation	Make sure you have permission to use some spaces with interesting objects outside the classroom (a garden is a good space, for example). Prepare an example video to give the learners an idea of what is required of them, or use one of the examples on the website accompanying this book (http://languagelearningtechnology.com).
Technical requirements	Learners should have enough digital video cameras (one per group of three learners) or should use the video cameras on their mobile phones. The learners need to be able to leave the classroom (or ask them to do this part outside of class, in which case they can describe anything they find).

Procedure

1   Tell the learners they are going to work in pairs and take on the role of visiting aliens on an *ethnographic* mission to Earth. Tell them their mission involves filming and providing a recorded description of interesting objects made by people. This information will be sent back to their home planet in order to build a database of the Earth and the capabilities of humans.

2   Play one or two example videos. If you feel it helpful, play only the sound of the video, and ask the learners to guess what is being described. Here is a transcript of someone talking about a streetlight:

Here we have an interesting object used by the humans when there is no natural light in their world. For several hours a day, these objects become bright, which helps the humans find their way home.

3   Ask the learners to leave the classroom and to film and record themselves talking about any objects they think their alien planet would find it interesting to know about. Alternatively, the filming is something each of the learners can do outside of class.

4   Watch and listen to the recordings together. After you have watched the videos together and commented upon them, ask each of the learners to transcribe their recordings, and then ask them if they could be improved upon. Monitor while this is happening and offer suggestions on how to improve the descriptions.

5   Ask the learners to record another video with the improved texts (although persuade them to read from notes rather than from the texts, as reading the texts will sound artificial), or to record a voiceover to the original videos.

6   If there is enough interest, collect the videos together on the class website or set up a wiki to share them (see Chapter 2 *Building a learning community* for help with this).

Variation

Instead of asking the learners to find their own objects, you can ask them to find, and video, specific objects in the vicinity (show them photographs of the things you want them to talk about), or give them coordinates (via an online map) to specific objects you want them to visit and film. If you do the latter, then the activity could be turned into a race.

Note

Based on Driver, P. (2012) 'Invader', an idea presented at the *IATEFL* conference in Glasgow, Scotland, http://www.digitaldebris.eu

3.8 Word associations

Main goals	Awareness of semantics; word associations
Level	Pre-intermediate (B1) and above
Time	5 minutes (ongoing)
Learning focus	Making associations between words
Preparation	Choose a *visual dictionary* (an online dictionary that allows learners to visualise the relationships between words) to use in class (see Appendix B 3.8 for more information and suggested websites).
Technical requirements	One internet-enabled computer in the classroom, with a projector or IWB (optional)

Procedure

1 Make use of tools such as visual dictionaries to strengthen learner knowledge of the associations between different words. When learners come across a word that would benefit from looking at word maps, use a visual dictionary (see example in Figure 3.3) to show how this word links to other words.

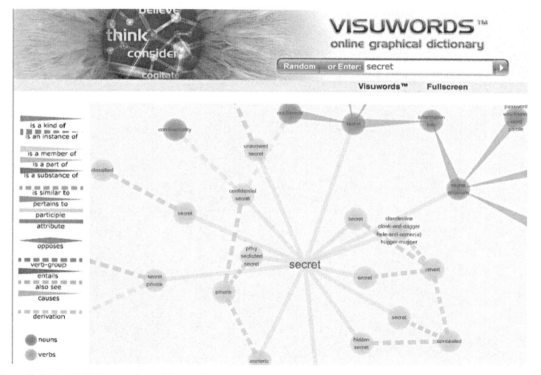

Figure 3.3: Visual dictionary: http://www.visuwords.com

2 After accessing a word map that the visual dictionary will bring up when you search on a particular word, you can play a memory game with the learners. Give them two minutes to study the words; then minimise the browser or turn the projector off.

3   Working in pairs or small groups, the learners try to remember as many words as they can. Award a point for each word, and extra points if they can say what part of speech (noun, verb, adjective, etc.) the words are.

4   After looking at the visual dictionary for the first time, ask the learners when they think this kind of tool would be useful to use (e.g. to complement or use instead of a more standard dictionary, to help with writing, etc.).

Variation

With higher levels, instead of asking learners just to remember the words (Step 3), ask them to re-create the word map, to see if they can link the words in the same way.

3.9 Making word games

Main goals	Fun with vocabulary; revision
Level	Pre-intermediate (B1)
Time	30 minutes
Learning focus	Learning vocabulary form; spelling
Preparation	Choose a word-game site, such as the one in Figure 3.4, that allows you to create your own games by uploading your own bank of words (see Appendix B 3.9 for more information and suggested websites).
Technical requirements	A computer room, or class set of laptops/netbooks/tablets. Alternatively, the games can be played in a whole-class setting (using an IWB, or computer and projector), with the learners creating the games for homework.

Procedure

1   Ask the learners to use a dictionary and select a list of words and definitions, and to write example sentences if the definitions do not provide them.

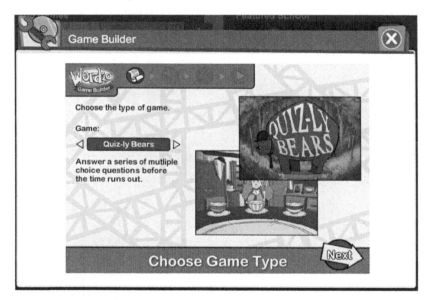

Figure 3.4: Word-game builder: http://www.wordia.com

2   Either in class or at home, the learners next upload the word list to the word-game site and select a game from those available. The game may test the form or spelling, etc., depending on what the learners choose.

3   Once the games have been made, you can play them together in class as revision, or ask the learners to do so (if you have access to multiple computers).

3.10 Words and phrases

Main goals	Introduction to a concordancer; learner autonomy
Level	Intermediate (B1+) (EAP)
Time	15 minutes
Learning focus	Checking frequency and collocation of words
Preparation	Choose a concordancer tool suitable to use with your class (see Appendix B 3.10 for more information and suggested websites).
Technical requirements	A computer room, or class set of laptops/netbooks/tablets. Alternatively, the concordancer can be presented in class with one computer and a projector.

Procedure

1 Introduce the learners to the concordancer (an index of texts produced by a computer that helps you look at meaning in context), and tell them that it can be used to enhance their knowledge of vocabulary, particularly collocations. Explain that a collocation is a grouping of words (sometimes set phrases) that are commonly found together (e.g. *change your mind*, *a business deal*).

2 Demonstrate how to conduct a concordance search (see Appendix B 3.10 if you need help), and how to demonstrate the results of such a search by using a word which has multiple meanings or which is used as different parts of speech, e.g. *sort* (noun and verb), or *fast* (adverb and adjective). Show the learners how they can see which of the meanings are most frequent and how collocations are displayed in the concordancer.

3 Continue the demonstration by focusing on a specific aspect of collocation, such as verbs + dependent prepositions (e.g. *rely on*, *agree with*, etc.), or commonly confused words (*borrow/lend*, *affect/effect*, etc.). Ask the learners to use the concordancer to find the rule.

4 Ask the learners to work in pairs and to make a list of other words that they have doubts about, or that they would like to check using the concordancer. Alternatively, give them a list of words that have caused problems in class recently. If the learners are using multiple computers, let them do the activity on their own. Otherwise, take examples from each of the pairs and conduct a concordance search.

5 Finish by asking the learners if they think that using a tool such as this will help them, and how they think it could best be used for independent study.

3.11 Synonym swap

Main goals	Expanding learners' vocabulary; using a thesaurus; rewriting texts
Level	Intermediate (B1+) and above
Time	30 minutes
Learning focus	Synonyms
Preparation	This activity is especially appropriate for single- or integrated-skills classes that have writing as a component, or for writing classes. Do this activity after learners have their written texts in hand. The overall organisation of the learner texts (e.g. paragraphing, etc.) should be acceptable. If this is not the case, then work should be done on the texts before the synonym-swap activity. To help the learners, you can mark (use a highlighter) parts of the text that would benefit from the use of synonyms for the words they have used.
Technical requirements	A computer room, or class set of laptops/netbooks/tablets; access to an online thesaurus (see Appendix B 3.11 for more information and suggested websites)

Procedure

1 Establish what a synonym is – either by asking the class, telling them or giving examples, i.e. *it's a word that has the same meaning.*

2 Tell learners they are going to use a thesaurus / synonym finder to change some of the words in the texts they wrote before, and to see if changing the words improves their writing. Explain some of the reasons for finding synonyms (e.g. to avoid repetition, to express the same thing more formally, etc.).

3 Ask them to read the text and to think about synonyms for the words and phrases that have been highlighted. Tell the learners to think carefully about whether their chosen synonyms improve the text.

4 Now using the computers, ask the learners to go to the thesaurus website and to look for synonyms of the highlighted words.

5 Encourage learners to check the definitions of the synonyms they choose in a dictionary if they have any doubts whether the new words are suitable or not.

6 As the learners work on their texts, monitor and check their work, and give help and advice as needed.

Variation 1
This activity works well when combined with other process-writing tasks (see Chapter 7 *Writing*).

Variation 2
Rather than improving texts (to make them clearer, etc.), change the focus to register, and stress that you want the learners to change their informal texts to formal ones (or vice versa), using the thesaurus website to help them. If you do this, then be sure to give the learners advice on the difference between formal and informal language beforehand.

Variation 3
If some of the learners have access to smartphones, then they could use a thesaurus app., instead of a website, when they are looking for synonyms.

3.12 Experimenting with antonyms

Main goals	Expanding learners' vocabulary; using a thesaurus; rewriting texts
Level	Intermediate (B1+) and above
Time	30 minutes
Learning focus	Antonyms
Preparation	Choose a number of suitable texts for your learners' level (from a coursebook, a magazine or a news website). Texts that work particularly well with this activity include reviews and celebrity interviews.
Technical requirements	A computer room, or class set of laptops/netbooks/tablets; access to online thesaurus or antonym finder (see Appendix B 3.12 for more information and suggested websites)

Procedure

1 Tell the learners they are going to work in pairs (or small groups) to change the meaning of a text by replacing some of the words with antonyms. If using reviews, then the opinion of the reviewer should be the opposite of what it is in the original text. If doctoring celebrity interviews, encourage the learners to make them humorous.

2 Ask the learners to look at the text(s) that you have pre-selected and to choose, and highlight/underline, the words they think they need to change in order to substantially change the meaning of the review, interview, etc.

3 Introduce the learners to the thesaurus/antonym website, and encourage them to use it to find words that mean the opposite to those in their text. Monitor the pairs/groups while they are doing the activity, and help them with the language.

4 When the groups have finished, look at some of the texts together, comparing them with the originals. You can ask volunteers to read out the new texts while the remaining learners are reading the old ones, noticing the changes.

5 Ask the learners to finish by making a list of the synonym/antonym pairs. If you have a class wiki (see Activity 2.7), then learners can add these pairs to the vocabulary section of this site.

Variation

Turn the activity into a game by asking the learners to compare the two text variants and decide which ones are the originals and which the doctored texts.

3.13 Slang, register and style

Main goals	Focus on register and style of words
Level	Upper-intermediate (B2) and above
Time	30 minutes
Learning focus	Register of slang words
Preparation	Make a list of typical slang words suitable for your class, and choose an online dictionary (see Appendix B 3.13 for more information and suggested websites). You may choose to focus on particular slang expressions (e.g. those used to express emotions, etc.).
Technical requirements	One internet-enabled computer in the classroom with a projector, or IWB

Procedure

1 Ask the learners to tell you any English slang words or expressions they know, and write the ones you think are most interesting up on the board. If they struggle to think of any, use words from the list you created earlier, or look at the lyrics of a couple of pop songs and see if the learners can identify any slang words. Be certain to choose songs that would not be offensive in any way.

2 Ask the learners to work in groups and to choose some of the words. Then ask them to a) decide on a definition of them and b) think of an alternative way of expressing the slang more formally.

3 When the learners have finished, ask them to share what they think with the rest of the class. Make use of a dictionary of slang to check meaning (see example in Figure 3.5).

Figure 3.5: From a dictionary of slang: http://www.urbandictionary.com

3.14 Multiple-meaning presentations

Main goals	Learning the meaning of new words; using concordancer software
Level	Upper-intermediate (B2) and above
Time	20 minutes
Learning focus	Understanding words with multiple meanings
Preparation	Prepare a list of vocabulary you think your class may have difficulty with, choosing words that have several meanings, and make a copy for each learner. Choose a concordancer tool that you think the learners will find easy to use (see Appendix B 3.14 for more information and suggested websites). An example of a concordancer appropriate for this activity is shown below.
Technical requirements	A computer room, or class set of laptops/netbooks/tablets. Alternatively, the learners can do the activity at home and present their findings in the next class. For the presentation, there should be a computer with a projector in the classroom.

Procedure

1 Present the list of words, and ask each learner to choose one. Tell the learners that they are all words with more than one meaning, and that each learner is going to find out the various meanings and then present them to the class.

2 Introduce the learners to a concordancer tool such as the one in Figure 3.6 (see Appendix B 3.14 for more information), and show them an example (e.g. *effect*) and how there are various meanings.

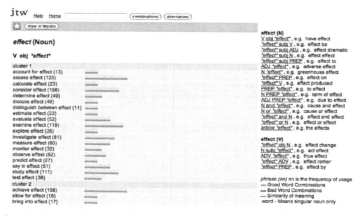

Figure 3.6: Concordancer that can be used with Activity 3.14: http://www.just-the-word.com

3 Tell the learners that the software will show which meanings are most frequent and that they should try to spot this frequency. They should then choose three of the most frequently found meanings of the word and select example sentences to present to the rest of the class.

4 Help the learners as they choose the best word combinations, as displayed by the software, or (alternatively) the word combinations they think are best, and put together a presentation of the meanings, with examples.

5 When learners are finished, they should each give their short presentation to the rest of the class.

3.15 Noticing collocations

Main goals	Noticing collocations; promoting learner autonomy
Level	Upper-intermediate (B2) and above (EAP)
Time	15 minutes
Learning focus	Vocabulary collocation; error correction
Preparation	Collect samples of learners' written errors to correct, especially any errors of meaning.
Technical requirements	A computer room, or class set of laptops/netbooks/tablets; access to online concordance software (see Appendix B 3.15 for more information and suggested websites).

Procedure

1 Present some examples of the learners' written errors, and explain how learners can use the Internet to check the correct meaning. Tell them that they can use a search engine such as *Google*, which will give them interesting examples, but using a *concordancer* such as the one in Figure 3.7 (an index of texts produced by a computer that helps you look at meaning in context) will often be more accurate and produce more relevant returns (see Appendix B 3.15 for further information).

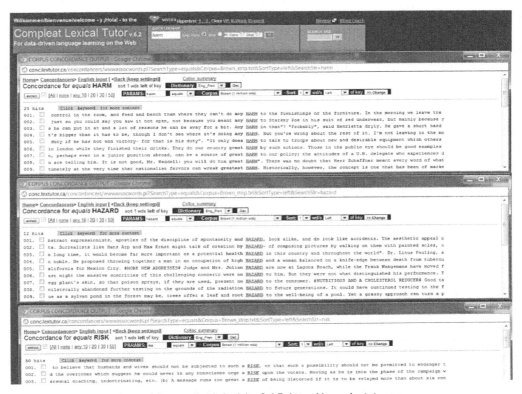

Figure 3.7: Concordancer that can be used with Activity 3.15: http://www.lextutor.ca

2   Ask learners to work in groups. Armed with their lists of errors, learners start entering them into the concordancer to see if they can find examples that help them understand the correct meaning of the words, and also if they can find sentences that show *collocations* (i.e. words that commonly co-occur).

3   Once the learners have the correct examples, ask them to change groups and share their examples to check if they have the same ones.

4   Ask learners to check the meaning, in a dictionary, of the different uses of the word represented in the concordances. Finally, choose learner volunteers to report to the whole class. Ask the learners what helped them best understand the meaning – the example sentences, the dictionary definitions or both together.

Variation 1

Prepare a few sets of commonly confused words (for example, *harm*, *risk* and *hazard*) that your learners have difficulty with, or ask your learners to find concordances as homework, before the lesson begins.

Ask the learners to choose two or three example phrases for each of the commonly confused words (tell them they don't have to be complete sentences) and to copy and paste them into another document. With the example words above, they might be:

> *I meant him no harm.*
> *… can't do any harm to …*
> *… may do more harm than good*
>
> *… take the risk of …*
> *… should not be subjected to such a risk*
> *… at their own risk*
>
> *… were no hazard to him*
> *… a potential health hazard*
> *… to hazard comments*

Variation 2

The activity in Variation 1 can also be used to compare the difference in usage of other words and phrases. Some examples are: *used to* and *am used to*, *however* and *although*, conditional sentences, phrasal verbs, etc.

Variation 3

Rather than asking the learners to use the computers, search for the examples before class and remove the key words (the highlighted words that are the focus of the search), giving the learners photocopies of the examples and asking them to guess what the key words are. Then continue as above, using the dictionaries to look for definitions, etc.

Variation 4
For Business English learners, use a different concordancer which uses a corpus of business letters (see Appendix B 3.10 for suggestions of concordancers).

Variation 5
Ask the learners, in pairs or small groups, to prepare worksheets to test each other on examples. Ask the learners to write additional sentences with the same meaning of the words that the concordancer provided, or create multiple-choice questions, with similar words in the distractors.

4 Grammar

What is *grammar*? It can refer to either the structure of a language as it is used by its speakers and writers (*descriptive* grammar), or the structure of a language as certain people (most often teachers) believe it is or should be used (*prescriptive* grammar). It is perhaps best described as 'the structural foundation of our ability to express ourselves. The more we are aware of how it works, the more we can monitor the meaning and effectiveness of the way we and others use language ... all teaching is ultimately a matter of getting to grips with meaning' (Crystal, 2004: 24).

The focus of this chapter is on grammar, and the activities included here aim to show teachers how technology can support the attempt by teachers and learners to *get to grips with meaning*. What can a technology-supported approach to grammar teaching and practice offer learners and teachers? Specifically, it can offer support for both *descriptive* and *prescriptive* grammar through:

- *Engagement and motivation*. Grammar does not have to be dull, and technology can help the teacher vary the way grammar is both presented and practised.
- *Access to data*. The Web has an enormous collection of texts of different types, which means teachers and learners have access to a wealth of real-world examples of grammar.
- *Description*. Declarative knowledge of grammar is readily available online in the form of rules, often illustrated by examples.
- *Noticing / awareness raising*. Learners can discover rules from examples of features found in texts on the Web, helping input become intake as they notice patterns and organisation of real language use.
- *Feedback*. There are some tools (especially spellcheckers and grammar-checkers) included in word-processing software, or available online, which give feedback on errors.
- *Opportunities for practice*. Technology can be used in different ways by learners to help them practise grammar. Some examples can be found in the activities in this chapter.

It is worthwhile for teachers to spend some time becoming familiar with, and introducing learners to, the various ways that grammar can be supported by technology, as mentioned above. The tools are not just useful classroom tools. Many of those presented in this chapter are used by people every day to check their own grammar knowledge and support their writing. These include those found in browsers (e.g. the 'find' feature), online tools, such as automatic-translation websites, and tools embedded in word processors (spellcheck and grammar-check tools), which learners may or may not be familiar with, but which can be very useful to them, both when they are learning a language and in their daily life.

Apart from day-to-day needs, grammar is also important to learners who want to pass exams, and exam practice is looked at here, with Activity 4.3 asking learners to produce their own cloze tests. This is a way of helping learners become more familiar with the kinds of features found on language exams.

The activities in this chapter are organised according to level. The chapter starts by giving teachers some alternative ways of practising grammar with learners. Some of these ways suggest using learners' own writing (4.1–4.3) or error correction (4.7) as the basis of the activity. Using real-world texts for noticing grammar, and raising awareness, is the focus of activities 4.8–4.10 and 4.12.

Teachers often follow the same format when presenting grammar, writing structures on the board and then asking learners to look at examples, more often than not contained in a text they have to read. There are activities in this chapter that suggest looking at authentic examples of grammar found in texts on the Web (4.4, 4.5, 4.11) – a more descriptive approach – and activities which focus on a number of different prescriptive grammar sites (such as 4.6) and require the learners to take a critical approach to what they find there.

References

Crystal, D. (2004) 'A 21st century grammar bridge', *The Secondary English Magazine*, Birmingham, UK: National Association for the Teaching of English. Available at: http://www.davidcrystal.com/ DC_articles/Education3.pdf [accessed June 2012].

4.1 Audio gap-fills

Main goals	Guessing grammar from context
Level	All levels
Time	20 minutes
Learning focus	Specific grammar items (e.g. verb tenses, adverbs, articles, etc.)
Preparation	Either give the learners short texts (mini-sagas – texts containing exactly 50 words – or urban myths work well), or use ones the learners have produced in a previous lesson.
Technical requirements	One audio-recording device for at least every three learners in your class (learners could also use their mobile phones)

Procedure

1 Choose a grammar item in an area learners have been studying (e.g. present-tense verbs), hand out the texts and ask the learners to work in pairs or groups of three. Get the voice recorders ready.

2 Ask the learners to read the texts and record themselves. Tell them that when they come to the chosen grammar item, they should say 'blank' instead of the actual word(s). When recording, learners in each group should take turns saying each of the sentences. When the recording stage has finished, collect the texts from the learners.

3 Next, ask the learners to swap the recording devices with another pair/group and listen to the recording, without pausing it.

4 Now ask the learners to listen again and to make a note of the missing words. This time, they can pause the recording and listen as many times as they want.

5 Exchange recorders again and ask the learners to listen to a different story, repeating Steps 3 and 4 above. Do this again, as long as there is interest from the learners.

6 Pin the original texts on the walls of the classroom, and ask the learners to find the texts they listened to and to check their answers.

Variation 1

Instead of just having learners fill in the missing words, you could ask them to rewrite the whole of the recorded texts (as they would with a dictation). If you choose this variation, you probably wouldn't want them to do it with more than one text.

Variation 2

To make the activity more difficult, instead of selecting a specific item of grammar, you can ask the learners to 'blank out' a combination of grammar features (prepositions, articles, etc.), and then ask the learners to guess what kinds of words are missing.

4.2 Grammar check

Main goals	Noticing and correcting mistakes in grammar and spelling; raising awareness of useful tools for writing
Level	All levels
Time	20 minutes
Learning focus	Grammar and spelling in general
Preparation	This activity assumes the learners have completed a piece of writing. The learners can use the grammar-checking tools built into their word processor, and also external ones (see Appendix B 4.2 for more information).
Technical requirements	One internet-enabled computer in the classroom and/or multiple computers (computer room, class set of laptops/netbooks/tablets); word processor with grammar and spellchecker and/or grammar-checking website (see Appendix B 4.2)

Procedure

1 Ask the learners if they ever use the spelling and grammar-checking software on their word processors, or other grammar-checking programs on the Web. If they do, ask them if they find it useful / easy to use / etc.

2 Show the learners how to change the language in the word processor and how to check the grammar/spelling, using the in-built word-processor tools and a grammar-/spellcheck website.

3 Now ask the learners either to check the written work they have previously produced (if using multiple computers), or to go through some of their writing and check it with the grammar-checking software. Ask them to try both the in-built grammar-checker and one on the Web to compare their effectiveness.

4 Using the word-processor grammar-/spellchecker will probably show both grammar and spelling errors. If this happens, tell the learners to correct the grammar errors first and then to correct the spelling mistakes.

5 After 10 minutes or so, ask the learners for feedback. Do they think the grammar-/spellchecker was useful? Is it perfect (i.e. did the grammar-checker catch everything? Did it say something was a mistake when it wasn't? etc.)?

4.3 Automatic cloze tests

Main goals	Raising awareness of grammar; revision of tenses; encouraging learners to correct writing
Level	All levels
Time	10 minutes
Learning focus	General grammar
Preparation	Ideally, this should be done after the learners have produced some writing which has been *code corrected* (with indications to the learners about what needs to be changed: e.g. *wo.* = *word order*, *t = tense*, *sp. = spelling*, etc.). Select a cloze-test generator (see Appendix B 4.3 for suggested websites) to use, and try it out beforehand.
Technical requirements	A computer room, or class set of laptops/netbooks/tablets

Procedure

1 Give the learners back their writing that has been code corrected. Ask the learners to work in pairs, helping each other to correct their texts. While they are doing this, monitor them and help with the corrections.

2 Once the learners have corrected their texts, they create the cloze tests. Each of the pairs then should decide which feature to base their cloze test on. Alternatively, you can tell the learners to focus on a particular language item (articles, prepositions, linking words, etc.) – preferably one they have recently studied – and to remove some examples of this item in the text. (Some websites allow you to choose and automatically remove the selected words.)

3 When the learners have finished, share the links to the tests, or print the tests out for the learners to do in class.

Variation

Instead of learner writing, you can ask the learners to use another text they are interested in that has examples of grammar you are practising in class. The learners remove the verbs (or other grammar items) and prepare their texts for other learners to correct.

4.4 Questioning infographics

Main goals	Opportunities for practice
Level	All levels
Time	25 minutes
Learning focus	Wh- and yes / no question formation, and language of comparisons
Preparation	Find an infographic (graphic representation of information, data or knowledge) that you think will interest your learners, and which has information represented as answers to questions. To find an infographic, either search using *Google*, use a special infographic search engine or look for an infographic repository. (See Appendix B 4.4 for more information and suggested websites.)
Technical requirements	One internet-enabled computer in the classroom, with projector (or IWB)

Procedure

1   Before class, choose an infographic of interest to your learners. The subject may be to do with social sciences, science, the arts, something related to current events, etc. You should base your choice on the level and interests of the learners.

2   Write the title of the infographic that you have chosen on the board, and ask learners to brainstorm the kinds of specific information they think the image will show. Depending on the infographic, write these ideas on the board in the form of a mind map or graph, like the example infographic in Figure 4.1. Alternatively use mind-mapping software (for specific software, please refer to Appendix B 4.4).

3   Next, ask the learners to work in pairs, and turn the ideas in the mind map into questions (i.e. *What is the most popular type of webpage? How many people like cinema websites?* etc.).

4   Ask the learners to stand up and mingle, to ask their classmates the questions and to record the answers.

5   Finally, show the learners the original infographic, and ask them to compare their predictions (either spoken or written) with the information displayed in the image. Ask them if they were surprised by any of the differences.

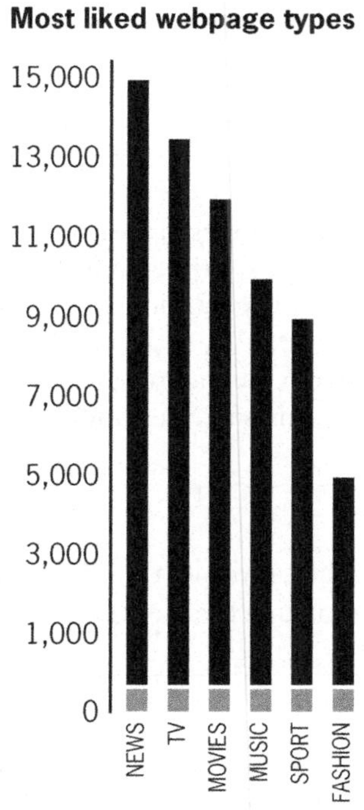

Most liked webpage types

Figure 4.1: Monthly average of websites liked (2012)

4.5 Grammar fight

Main goals	Using the Web to check grammar usage
Level	All levels
Time	20 minutes
Learning focus	Specific grammar structures (e.g. adverbs of frequency)
Preparation	Prepare a list of statements with mistakes in the grammatical structure that you want learners to practise (e.g. adverbs of frequency in the example below), adjusting the number of adverbs and accompanying structures to match the level of your class
Technical requirements	One internet-enabled computer in the classroom with a projector, or computer room or class set of laptops/netbooks/tablets, and search engine (see Appendix B 4.5 for more information and suggestions)

Procedure

1　Show the statements you prepared earlier to the learners (similar to the examples below), and ask them to decide if they are true or false, asking them to ignore the grammar for the moment.

European customs: true or false?

1　French people shake hands generally when meeting people for the first time.
2　The Spanish don't eat lunch usually before 3 p.m.
3　Shops in Portugal close at lunchtime often.
4　In Britain, young people leave typically home when they are 18.
5　Children never are allowed to stay up very late in Greece.
6　Italians always have eaten at least one plate of pasta per day.
7　Norwegians wear sometimes national dress at weddings and festivals.

From *Language Learning with Technology* © Cambridge University Press 2013　　　　　PHOTOCOPIABLE

2　Now ask the learners to focus on the grammar in each of the statements and to correct it if they think it's wrong.

3　Once the learners have made their corrections, ask them if they think there's a way of checking on the Web to see if what they decided seems to be true.

4　After the learners have had a chance to respond, and if nobody mentions it, tell them that one way they can check their sentences is by using *Google* to see how many results are returned when they search for a particular grammar item. Stress that although this does not always work as a way to check grammatical accuracy, if there are more examples of a structure used in a particular way, then it's likely to be more frequently used by people.

5　Tell the learners that one fun way of comparing results on *Google* is by using a website called *Googlefight*, and ask them to check the number of uses of a particular structure. For example, the learners can put in variations of the verb/auxiliary/adverb, using quotation marks.

6 Finish with the learners writing their own similar statements and checking the variations of grammar in *Googlefight*. When they are done, ask them to share the sentences with the rest of the class.

Variation

This activity can be used with a variety of different grammatical structures, especially non-standard forms that are used by people. Some examples are: *If I'd known* vs *If I'd have known*; *different from* vs *different to*, etc.

Note

Adapted from Thornbury, S. (2004) 'Grammar – rule discovery (grammar of structure)', *English Teaching Professional*, 32, 40–1. Available online at: http://thornburyscott.com/assets/grammar%20 ETP.pdf [accessed 3 July 2012].

4.6 Grammar-reference sites

Main goals	Introducing learners to grammar-reference websites; learner autonomy
Level	Pre-intermediate (B1) and above
Time	20 minutes
Learning focus	Examining grammar explanations on different websites
Preparation	Choose a selection of grammar-reference websites (see Appendix B 4.6 for more information and suggested websites).
Technical requirements	Ideally, a computer room or class set of laptops/netbooks/tablets, with internet access, although the activity could be done with the class as a whole if you have one internet-enabled computer in the classroom and projector (or IWB).

Procedure

1　Ask the learners if they ever consult online grammar-reference sites and, if they do, ask them which ones they prefer (if any). Write these on the board, and add the ones that you have pre-selected.

2　Tell the learners that they are going to work in pairs and review a selection of grammar-reference websites to decide which ones are the best. Give the learners copies of the form below, and ask them to start looking at the sites on the board. If you don't have multiple computers, you can go through these one by one and ask learners to make notes.

Name of website	Address (URL)	What we liked	What we didn't like

From *Language Learning with Technology* © Cambridge University Press 2013　　　　PHOTOCOPIABLE

3　When the learners have finished, ask them to rate the websites from 1 to 10 (with 10 points being the maximum), and then collect the points for each of the websites to see which one(s) the learners prefer. Some sites have more detail than others; a few have games or exercises for practice. When the results are in, ask the learners to say what they particularly liked about the winning website(s).

4　Act on the learners' choices by using the favourite grammar-reference website in future lessons.

4.7 Common grammatical errors

Main goals	Checking for mistakes
Level	Pre-intermediate (B1) and above
Time	15 minutes+
Learning focus	Common grammatical errors / non-standard grammar
Preparation	Choose a grammar-checking site (see Appendix B 4.7 for more information and suggested websites), and collect a list of common mistakes that your learners make, or examples of non-standard grammar according to level.
Technical requirements	One internet-enabled computer in the classroom with a projector, or a computer room / class set of laptops/netbooks/tablets with internet access

Procedure

1   Present the learners with some of the common mistakes that they make or that are made by other learners (*I'm looking forward to go, I have twelve years old*, etc.), or a list of non-standard grammar (e.g. popular expressions or catchphrases, such as *I'm loving it, What's up, doc?* etc.), and ask the learners if they think these are correct.

2   If using multiple computers, ask the learners to use the grammar-check websites to see if the examples are correct, or if you have only one computer in the classroom, take each example, in turn, and vote on it before checking the website.

3   With the non-standard expressions, ask the learners to check for examples, using a search engine, and see if they can discover the origin of some of these phrases (advertising, TV and film, etc.), and if there are other similar examples that fit the pattern.

4.8 Real-world grammar

Main goals	Looking at real-world examples of grammar
Level	Pre-intermediate (B1) and above
Time	20 minutes
Learning focus	Revision of grammar
Preparation	Make photocopies of the example on p. 73, or create another example more suitable to your class.
Technical requirements	A computer room or class set of laptops/netbooks/tablets; access to a shopping site for books/films (see Appendix B 4.8)

Procedure

1 Tell the learners that they are going to look for real-world examples of grammar, looking for titles of books/films and then writing a continuation of the title.

2 Working in pairs, the learners choose different grammar items and search on a phrase in the shopping site to see what they can find. Here are some examples you can give them:

If I were ...	*They went ...*	*All I needed ...*	*Whatever you ...*
... since I ...	*I wish ...*	*Always ...*	*Things I have ...*
Living with ...	*... even if ...*	*... used to ...*	*Whose ...?*

3 Ask the learners to choose the most interesting six film/book titles, resulting from the search, and to copy and paste the book/film images into a Word document.

4 Once the learners have the examples, ask them to extend the title if they need to and add their own ideas (as in the example, using conditionals, below). Their ideas could include another sentence that explains what the book is about. Monitor the learners while they do this step, making sure the language they write is correct. Give them help as needed.

5 The learners then create a poster from the images. Tell them to write their sentences out of order below the images (as in the example below), because their classmates will later be looking at the poster and guessing which sentences go with which images.

6 Print out the posters and display them on the classroom walls or project them next class (if you have a computer/projector in the classroom), and ask the other learners to try to match the images with the sentences on each poster.

Variation 1

Instead of just completing the titles, as the learners choose one or two images, ask them to try to imagine what the film/book is about. They then write a paragraph or two in the present tense about the plot. With higher-level classes, ask learners to use a range of different adjectives. You can follow this up next class by holding a 'press conference' where the learners take on the roles of writer/publisher or director/producer and 'launch' their film or book. The other learners ask them questions.

Variation 2
Instead of books or films, song or album titles and online music software can be used.

Note
Adapted from Keddle, J. (2011) 'Book puzzle'. Available online at: http://lessonstream.org/ [accessed May 2012].

Match the titles to the phrases below.

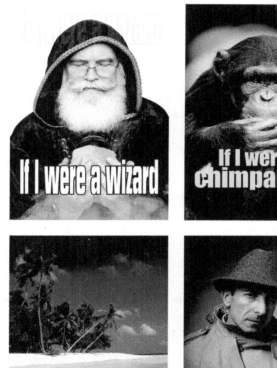
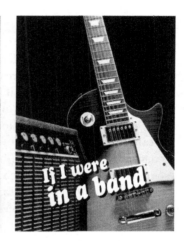

From *Language Learning with Technology* © Cambridge University Press 2013   PHOTOCOPIABLE

1   ... *I wouldn't like to live in a zoo.*
2   ... *I would have an exciting but dangerous life.*
3   ... *I would explore the oceans.*
4   ... *I would be very happy.*
5   ... *I would make people happy playing music.*
6   ... *I would use magic to change the world.*

4.9 Grammar safari

Main goals	Noticing usage of grammar; using browser tools to find example language
Level	Intermediate (B1+) and above
Time	15 minutes
Learning focus	Grammar usage (e.g. present perfect)
Preparation	Best done after a lesson on the grammatical structure to be practised
Technical requirements	One internet-enabled computer in the classroom with a projector, or a computer room / class set of laptops/netbooks/tablets

Procedure

1 If using multiple computers, ask the learners to choose a news article they are interested in, or decide on one together if you are using one computer in the classroom. Once an article has been found, ask the learners to skim it for a few minutes to get a sense of what it's about.

2 Tell the learners they are not going to read the article but, instead, are going to find examples of how the writer has used the grammar in question (e.g. the present perfect).

3 You or the learners select the 'Find' function (in the Edit menu of the browser) and type in what the learners want to search for (in this case, they can search on *have* and *has* and ignore any non-present perfect instances). Ask them to record examples of the grammatical structure they find (or you do this on the board), along with any time phrases that accompany tenses.

4 Once finished, share the examples on the board, and ask the learners if they were surprised (in the example, by *how the present perfect was used*).

5 Finally, ask the learners to write sentences using the verbs they found in the article, remembering the original ones, if possible, or making new sentences up.

Variation

Instead of using just one news article, ask the learners to use a search engine and check for examples on the Web, in general. Instead of just one grammatical structure, ask them to look for a variety of structures (phrasal verbs, conditionals, modals, etc.). This may be a good moment to help learners with search engines, using wildcards (such as * *and ?*), etc. For help with wildcards, see Appendix A, *Search engines*.

4.10 Authentic word clouds

Main goals	To increase learner awareness of authentic written communication
Level	Intermediate (B1+) to Advanced (C1)
Time	40 minutes
Learning focus	Authentic written communication, such as relative clauses
Preparation	Find an authentic news text, with interesting examples of complex sentences, from a newspaper website, and paste the entire text into a word-cloud creator (see recommended websites in Appendix B 4.10). Make enough copies for your class to share.
Technical requirements	Word-cloud creator (see Appendix B 4.10)

Procedure

1   Hand out the photocopies of the word-cloud text (see example in Figure 4.2), give the learners a little background to the original text (i.e. it's from a news website) and ask them to work in pairs to make guesses as to what the text is about.

Figure 4.2: Word cloud made from a news text: *Why do people climb Mount Everest?*

2   Now ask the class to tell you what they think the text is about, and write their ideas on the board. After a few minutes, write the headline on the board, and check to see if any of the learners know more about this news story. If they do, encourage them to tell the class what they know. If nobody knows about the news story, tell the learners briefly what it concerns.

3   Choose an example sentence from the original text, and write it on the board, e.g. *Before his attempt to climb the mountain, which was fatal, Mallory said people who climb Everest do so 'because it's there'.*

4   Ask the learners to look at the word cloud again and to see if they can make similar sentences from the other words (i.e. in the example, ones containing relative clauses). Tell them they can add as many words as necessary in order to make their sentences grammatically correct.

5 Write their examples on the board. Then ask the class to review them and decide a) if they are likely to be sentences from the text and b) if they are grammatically correct.

6 Read the original text together, and talk about anything that is interesting or surprising in the news.

7 Finally, look at the learners' examples and the original text, and point out any examples of structures you particularly wish to focus on.

Variation

Rather than using a news article, try inputting lyrics from songs into the word-cloud software, and then ask the learners to re-create the lyrics, as best they can. This works best if the learners are not familiar with the song lyrics. Afterwards, hand out copies of the original lyrics, ask the learners to compare them with what they wrote themselves, and point out examples of structures they have studied. Finish by playing excerpts of the songs.

4.11 If only …

Main goals	Practising contrary-to-fact conditionals
Level	Intermediate (B1+) to Advanced (C1)
Time	10 minutes
Learning focus	Conditionals
Preparation	Prepare a story beforehand.
Technical requirements	A computer and projector in the classroom; a class account with mind-map software (see Appendix B 4.11 for more information and suggested websites)

Procedure

1 Write *The date that never was* on the board, and ask the learners to imagine what the story is about.

2 You can either make up a story together with the learners or use the example below, or another one you have previously prepared.

The date that never was

Lesley and Nick met at a party and got on well.

They arranged to meet at a restaurant the next day.

Lesley took Nick's mobile number.
Nick didn't get Lesley's mobile number.
Lesley lost Nick's mobile number.
Nick thought they had arranged to meet at 11.30 am.

Lesley remembered they had agreed to have lunch at 1.00 pm.

Nick waited at the restaurant for an hour.

Lesley arrived half an hour after Nick had left.

Nick went home thinking he had been stood up.

Lesley was upset thinking Nick had forgotten about the date.

From *Language Learning with Technology* © Cambridge University Press 2013   PHOTOCOPIABLE

3 Write the stages of the story in the mind-mapping software, or paste the story you have brought to class. When the story has been entered in the mind-mapping software, check that certain learners understand the original story. If the mind map doesn't provide sufficient clues, hand out a copy of the full story.

4 Ask the learners to brainstorm, in pairs or small groups, the things that might have been different. Do this for each stage of the story.

5 Ask the learners to present the ideas they've brainstormed, and encourage them to express themselves using the conditional (i.e. *If they hadn't gone to the party, they wouldn't have arranged to meet later*).

6 Create a branching story (see screenshot in Figure 4.3) by asking the learners hypothetical questions (e.g. *What would have happened if ...* etc.).

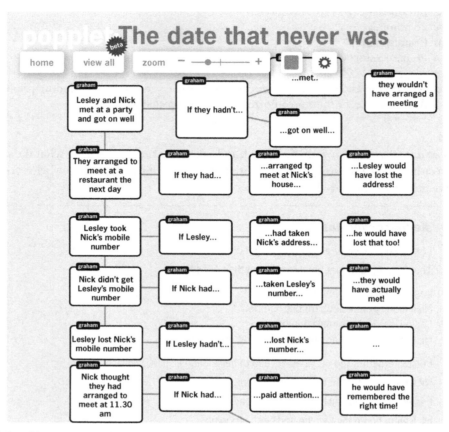

Figure 4.3: Conditional story produced using http://popplet.com

4.12 Grammar in context

Main goals	Raising awareness of how grammar is used in a real-world communicative context
Level	Intermediate (B1+) to Advanced (C1)
Time	15–20 minutes
Learning focus	Revision of grammar (e.g. phrasal verbs, past perfect, etc.)
Preparation	Learners should have recently been looking at the grammar in question. Be prepared to revise this if necessary.
Technical requirements	A computer room, or class set of laptops/netbooks/tablets, and access to a microblogging site (see Appendix B 4.12 for information and suggested websites)

Procedure

1 The learners brainstorm, in pairs or groups, examples of the grammar in question (e.g. phrasal verbs). Write the examples on the board, and check the meaning by asking the learners to help you write example sentences using the same phrasal verbs.

2 Introduce the class to the microblogging site (a blog that allows users to write brief text updates), and make certain learners understand what one is. Tell the learners that they are going to find out how people on this site are using the grammar the class looked at.

3 Ask the class to go to the microblogging site and search for some of the examples they brainstormed in Step 1. Tell the learners to use quotation marks when searching for the examples.

4 Ask the learners to take note of sentences that are different in meaning from the ones on the board, or which they find funny, interesting or confusing.

5 Now, with the computers turned off, ask the learners to share what they found with the rest of the class. Deal with any doubts about meaning, and ask the learners what they have learned about the grammar and what they think of the microblogging site as a way of displaying real language.

Variation 1

Rather than looking at one grammatical structure, learners can search for a variety of grammar items they have previously brainstormed. Ones that work well with this activity include future forms, past perfect, de-lexical verbs (*have a rest*, *take a look*, etc.) and conditional sentences.

Variation 2

Instead of using a microblogging site, you can use concordance software or search a specific corpus (see Appendix B 3.10 for help), to bring up examples of a particular structure. This is especially recommended if doing this with a class of young learners or teenagers, as language on microblogging sites can be particularly adult-orientated.

Variation 3

With lower-level learners, use example sentences from texts they have already read or written themselves. Alternatively, especially if the learners are young learners or teenagers, lines from popular songs or fairy tales can be used instead.

5   Listening

Technology has a long history of supporting language learning, starting from the wax cylinders produced by Linguaphone in 1901 and the phonograph records of the 1925. The revolutionary magnetic tape of the 1950s led to the establishment of language laboratories, with sound booths and the recording and playback of learners' voices. Later came digital audio on CDs in the 1980s, but it could be said that things started to get interesting only with the rising influence of the Internet, through podcasting and other online audio. The aim of this chapter is to show you that technology, when used well and applied to listening, can help teachers help learners with the challenge of understanding spoken language in the real world.

The listening process is an active process in which listeners select and interpret information that comes from auditory and visual clues, in order to define what is going on and what the speakers are trying to express (Thompson & Rubin, 1996: 331). Comprehension, which can be defined as 'the process of relating language to concepts in one's memory and to the references in the real world' (Rost, 2002: 59), is key to forming an accurate understanding of a situation. Given communicative language learning and teaching's emphasis on speaking, it follows then that listening is an equally important skill.

However, listening is a skill which is difficult to teach successfully, and results are not easily demonstrable. Its intangible, transient nature, and a general belief that listening can be 'picked up' by passive exposure to language, means teachers often adopt a 'practice makes perfect' comprehension approach. Listening is usually neglected or undervalued in the classroom (Field, 2008: 3), and it is often the skill which teachers cut when there is pressure on contact hours, because it is viewed as the least manageable of the four skills. This can lead to listening being *tested* rather than *taught* in the classroom.

How can using technology help? There is an argument that a focus on sustaining motivation, promoting practice and listening outside the classroom should be the goals. Teachers can use technology, especially the Internet, to prepare learners to take advantage of the sources of information in the real world, by getting them to engage with language and tasks which have personal relevance to them.

This chapter contains activities that help learners with listening for gist (5.1, 5.4), listening for inference (5.1), listening for detail (5.4, 5.6, 5.12, 5.13) and listening for information (5.5, 5.6, 5.8, 5.9, 5.11), or understanding a range of different people speaking about different things (5.2). Some activities make use of the wealth of authentic listening material on *YouTube* (5.3, 5.4), are aimed at improving listening skills (5.10), include listening to rhymes (5.7) and listening just for fun (5.5).

Apart from the Internet, many of the activities in this chapter make use of voice recorders (mobile phones or mp3 players can also be used) for recording people known to the teacher and learners, or use the IWB, telephony tools (such as *Skype*) or audio-editing software.

Technology can also provide variety outside of the usual 'listening and comprehension-question' approach. Using *YouTube* and other video-sharing websites, as well as Web 2.0 tools, such as the voice forums (5.2) or audio-guide websites (5.6), increases the opportunity for learners to get input, interaction and feedback, and are powerful in that they can connect people from different parts of the world instantly, without the restrictions of time and place.

Encouraging learners to listen to *podcasts* outside the classroom can also give learners exposure to comprehensible input while they are engaged in authentic listening. Podcasts are audio and video files made available on the Internet, designed to be downloaded and listened to on a portable mp3 player of any type, or on a personal computer. Podcasts can be used to increase the time a learner allocates to language learning and 'provide a meaningful experience that is motivating, stimulating and useful for a language learner' (McMinn, 2008).

Listening to podcasts can help learners to become more effective autonomous learners in the future. Most podcasts have not been produced primarily with language learners in mind, so learners have easy access to a repository of authentic oral texts and can choose subjects they are interested in. Listening can be repeated at will, and the audio on podcasts can also be slowed down, using tools such as *Audacity* (see Appendix A, *Audio recording and editing*).

Although not covered by the activities in this chapter, teachers should certainly encourage learners to listen to podcasts and can introduce them to ones that are relevant to the learners' level and interests (see suggestions on the book's accompanying website: http://www.languagelearningtechnology.com).

I hope that the activities presented here can be fitted into whatever you are doing in the classroom. If these tools are used judiciously by the teacher, and integrated into the syllabus, it's possible to move beyond the idea of technology as a novelty.

References

Field, J. C. (2008) *Listening in the Language Classroom*, Cambridge: Cambridge University Press.

McMinn, S. W. J. (2008) 'Podcasting possibilities: increasing time and motivation in the language learning classroom', *iLearning Forum, European Institute for E-learning*. Available online at: http://www.eife-l.org/publications/proceedings/ilf08/ [accessed May 2012].

Rost, M. (2002) *Teaching and Researching Listening*, Harlow: Pearson Education.

Thompson, I. and Rubin, J. (1996) 'Can strategy instruction improve listening comprehension?', *Foreign Language Annals*, 29 (3), 331–42.

5.1 Guess what I'm talking about

Main goals	Listening to different people talking about a subject
Level	All levels
Time	15 minutes
Learning focus	Listening for gist and inference (listening for information not directly stated)
Preparation	Ask a number of colleagues or friends / family members (three to five) to talk briefly about a subject, without mentioning what they are talking about. Some example subjects could be: *something I enjoy doing, a birthday present I really liked, my favourite food/film/book*, etc. Record them using a voice recorder (see Appendix B 5.1 for help with recording).
Technical requirements	Voice recorder (mobile phone or mp3 player with microphone), and speakers to play back the audio in the classroom

Procedure

1 Tell the learners that they are going to listen to a number of people talking about something, and that their task is to guess the general topic that they are talking about.

2 After playing each recording, stop and ask the learners to guess what the person is talking about. At this point, don't tell them the answer or verify if their answers are right or wrong. Write their guesses on the board, leaving spaces to write other words next to each guess.

3 Ask the learners to tell you what words they heard that made them think they knew the answer, and write these down next to the learners' guesses.

4 Play the recordings again, and this time ask the learners to listen out for any key words that capture the gist of what the person is talking about and to make a note of them.

5 This time, tell the learners if they have guessed correctly, and ask them to tell you which words helped them.

6 Ask the learners to listen again, but now instead of listening for information, ask them to make inferences (i.e. to guess from clues about things that are not directly stated). Tell the learners to listen to how the person speaks and to guess why the speaker says certain things, and how he/she feels about the subject.

7 Finally, use the recordings as the basis of a discussion. Talk to the learners about which of the recordings were the most difficult for them to understand, and ask them why (a person talking fast, the accent, the subject, etc.).

5.2 Other people's interests

Main goals	Authentic listening; understanding people from different countries talking about their interests
Level	All levels
Time	20 minutes
Learning focus	Expressing likes; vocabulary related to hobbies, sports, free time
Preparation	Use a site which has recordings of speakers talking about things that interest them (sports, hobbies, etc.) – a voice forum, for example (see Appendix B 5.2 for suggestions) – and choose one or two recordings where a range of people speak about things they are interested in. Listen to the recordings, and make a note of the names of the people speaking and some other details (e.g. where they come from, what they say they like, etc.).
Technical requirements	One internet-enabled computer in the classroom, with speakers

Procedure

1 Ask the learners to talk in small groups about what people usually do in their free time in the place where they live. After a few minutes, stop the learners and ask a spokesperson from each group to summarise what they talked about.

2 Direct the learners to several discussions from a voice forum where people talk about things they are interested in. Tell the learners what a forum is (an online space where people ask and answer questions and give their opinions), and tell them the discussions are organised into threads (i.e. a number of different people's recordings about the same topic).

3 Tell the learners they are going to listen to some recordings of people speaking about their interests. Write the names of the people in the first recording on the board, and ask the learners to predict where each one comes from. Then ask the learners to predict what each person will say.

4 Start to play the first recording, and ask learners to listen and fill in information in a grid similar to the one below. Make a note on the board of any interesting language.

Speaker	Hobby	How long?	Who with?

5 After each recording, look more closely at any language you have made a note of, and ask the learners if they remember who said it and if they know what it means.

6 If there's enough learner interest, continue and repeat the activity with the other recordings you have chosen.

Variation 1

If you have access to a computer room or a class set of laptops/netbooks/tablets, you can ask the learners to record their own responses to the discussions they have listened to on the site.

Variation 2

If using multiple computers, follow up with a task where the learners access the listening texts in pairs, listen for detail in the recordings and then write questions for their classmates. After they have finished, they can ask another pair to listen to the same recordings and answer the questions.

5.3 Search the tube

Main goals	Awareness of how videos can be used for learning English
Level	All levels
Time	20 minutes
Learning focus	Various
Preparation	None required
Technical requirements	Multiple computers (computer room or class set of laptops, etc.). Alternatively, an IWB, or one internet-enabled computer in the classroom with a projector

Procedure

1   Ask the learners to talk in small groups about what they watch on video-sharing sites such as *YouTube*, and after two to three minutes, stop them and ask if any of them mentioned any of the following:

'How to' videos	*Interviews with famous people*	*Short films*
Funny videos	*Recordings with different accents*	*Advertisements*

2   Explain any of the terms the learners don't understand, and then tell the learners that they are going to work in groups to look for a video to recommend to the class, with each group choosing one of the categories above. If you have access to only one computer in the classroom, the learners can do this step for homework, and then you can watch the videos together in class.

3   Ask each group to present the video they have found, describing it before the class views it and mentioning why they chose it.

Variation 1

Ask the learners to share their favourite internet *meme* (a phenomenon that becomes popular through the Internet, e.g. viral videos passed from user to user, songs, web celebrities, catchphrases, etc.). Before watching the chosen video, ask the learners to talk to the rest of the class about the *meme* and why they like it (see Appendix B 5.3 for some example *memes*).

Variation 2

Instead of using a video-sharing site, ask the learners to search for and select a podcast to recommend to the class (a downloadable audio file that can be subscribed to), using Apple's *iTunes*, or searching directly on the Web.

5.4 Reordered video story

Main goals	Listening for gist and for detail
Level	All levels
Time	20 minutes
Learning focus	Re-creating a story
Preparation	Choose a short video with a story to it that has interesting language suitable to the level of your class (short films* work well for this activity – see the book's accompanying website, http://languagelearningtechnology.com, for suggestions), and make 6–10 screenshots (i.e. images of your screen) of key moments of the story. You can use software to do this (see Appendix B 5.4 for suggestions), or simply press the 'Print-screen' button. Paste the images into a Word document, mix up the order of the images and make copies of the document for your learners.
Technical requirements	One internet-enabled computer in the classroom with speakers, and access to a video site

Note: Please ensure the short films you choose are in the public domain and that you have appropriate legal permission.

Procedure

1 Tell your learners they are going to listen to a video with the screen turned off, and they should try and guess the plot of the film. Play the video with the screen blanked, and then ask the learners to talk in pairs or small groups about what they heard and what they think the story of the film is.

2 After the pairs/groups have had time for discussion, ask them to tell you what they think happens in the story, and write their ideas on the board.

3 Next, give them the handout of the images in the wrong order, and ask them to try to put the images in the correct order, according to what they thought the story was about.

4 Ask the learners to listen again, and this time tell them to try and focus on listening for details about what is happening in the images. When the learners have finished listening, ask them to talk together about what is happening in each of the images.

5 Ask the learners to compare their answers and then, finally, play the video (this time with the screen turned on) so they can check that what they thought was happening in the story, and each of the images, was correct.

5.5 Talk-radio listening

Main goals	Listening to peers
Level	All levels, particularly young learners and teenagers
Time	10 minutes
Learning focus	Listening for information; listening for fun
Preparation	Requires you to have made a 'talk-radio programme' with another class (see Chapter 8 *Speaking*). The other class should have scripted, and then recorded, a radio programme with different sections, including some of those mentioned below.
Technical requirements	One internet-enabled computer in the classroom, with a set of speakers

Procedure

1 Record a talk-radio show with a different class (see Activity 8.8), or alternatively, split this class into two groups and record two radio shows, one with each group.

2 Tell the learners that another class you teach has recorded a talk-radio show, and ask them if they know what that is (i.e. a radio show based on information, rather than music).

3 Ask them to predict what sections the radio programme includes. Some suggested answers include:

   news   gossip   interviews   weather   sports   horoscope

   Confirm with the learners which sections are included in the programme (there could be three to four different ones), and tell them the order in which they appear, to help them.

4 Tell the learners they are going to work in pairs and play bingo, predicting some of the words and phrases the learners said during the radio show, by adding words to a grid similar to the one below. Ask them to write the name of the sections in the first column.

Section	What I think they'll say	What they actually said

5 To help the learners, tell them something about what was talked about in some of the sections (e.g. *in the news section, the learners talked about their favourite school subjects*).

6 Play the recording, and ask the learners to listen and cross off any word they hear someone say. Stop the recording every so often (after each section, or earlier, if necessary), check comprehension and find out how many words the students have heard. Play the recording several times until learners have accurately filled in all of the words used.

7 Next, ask the learners to use the words in the column 'What they actually said' to reconstruct the gist of what was said in each section, comparing their ideas with a partner and then reporting to the class.

8 You can finish by asking the class if they would like to plan, write and record a similar radio show. If they want to, this is something you can start preparing for next class.

5.6 Guided tours

Main goals	Asking learners to listen critically to audio produced by others; describing places
Level	All levels
Time	20 minutes
Learning focus	Listening for information and detail
Preparation	Choose an audio-guide site with guided tours in English (see Appendix B 5.6 for suggestions), or make your own recording with another class (see Chapter 8 *Speaking*).
Technical requirements	One internet-enabled computer in the classroom with speakers

Procedure

1 Ask the learners to think about what a typical tourist to the capital city of their country (or the place where they live if it is large enough and a well-known tourist attraction) would need to know and see. Get them to talk in groups about this topic and to come up with a list of five to six essential sites to visit.

2 When the learners have finished, tell them that you are going to introduce them to a website where people have recorded commentaries about places in the city, and ask them to predict, for each of the sites they have chosen, three to four features that would have been mentioned about the places (e.g. *The Tour Eiffel is the tallest building in Paris*; *It was built for the 1889 World's Fair*, etc.).

3 Once the learners have their predictions, find out which places each group has chosen, and write the five most popular places and comments on the board, in order from the most to the least popular.

4 Starting with the most popular place commented on, search the audio-guide site and find the place in the city. If there is a recording for it, play it and ask the learners to tick each of the features they predicted would be mentioned.

5 Continue with the list of predictions, playing the recordings and asking the learners to check whether their guesses were accurate.

6 Finally, ask the learners what they thought of the audio guides, if anything that was said surprised them and if they thought any of the information was false or could have been presented in a better way.

Note

Thanks to Ian James (http://teflteacher.wordpress.com) for inspiring this activity.

5.7 Recorded poetry

Main goals	Listening and identifying vowel sounds and rhymes
Level	All levels (especially young learners)
Time	30 minutes
Learning focus	Vowel sounds; rhyming words
Preparation	Choose a video of a poem you think the learners will like, and which they would be able to understand, or ask the learners to find a number of videos for homework and then vote on their favourite. See Appendix B 5.7 for specific poems that rhyme and also have videos that work well with this activity. Make photocopies of the poem to give to the learners.
Technical requirements	One computer in the classroom

Procedure

1   Play the video of the poem to the learners and ask them if they like it.
2   Hand out the photocopies of the poem to the learners, and play the poem again, this time asking them to mark the words that rhyme (i.e. have the same vowel sounds).
3   Check the answers with the learners, and then ask them to look at the rhyming pairs and write alternative rhymes, changing the words but making sure the poem still rhymes.
4   Finish by asking the learners to read out their versions of the poems. If you like, record these – this way you can justify asking the learners to spend more time rehearsing how the poems sound before recording them.

Variation

Use special software which 'auto-tunes' the poems and turns them into songs (see the book's accompanying website, http://languagelearningtechnology.com, for details), to surprise the learners when you play them back next lesson.

5.8 Online classroom guest

Main goals	Motivating learners to listen
Level	All levels
Time	20 minutes
Learning focus	Listening for information
Preparation	Find a relative, a friend or a colleague who lives in another country and is willing and able to speak to your class using *Skype* or other internet telephony software (see Appendix B 5.8 for suggestions).
Technical requirements	One computer in the classroom with microphone and internet telephony software (e.g. *Skype*) installed. Although not necessary, it's better if both you and your guest have a webcam.

Procedure

1 In the class before, tell your learners that you have invited a special guest to join you in the next class, and ask them to guess who it is. You can play the game '20 Questions' with them, letting them find out information by answering their yes / no questions (e.g. *Is it a man? Is he from the UK?* etc.).

2 After the class has a general idea of who you have invited to speak to them, show them a photograph of the person and talk a little about him/her. Tell the learners where the person lives, what he/she does and how you know the person, etc.

3 Now ask the learners to work in pairs or groups and to think of questions they want to ask the guest. These questions could be related to a project you are doing with the class (see Chapter 10 *Project work*) or could be general questions related to the culture/background of your guest, etc. For lower-level classes, you may need to prompt learners by giving them key words or partial questions.

4 During your next class, arrange a date and time for your guest to join you on Skype in the classroom, and ask the learners to be ready to ask some of their questions.

5 While your guest is speaking, ask the learners to take notes on the answers to their questions. You can also take note of any interesting language that the guest uses, especially language that may not be familiar to your learners.

6 After the interview, review what the guest said with your learners, and ask them to write a thank-you note to your guest which you can share with him/her.

Variation 1

Instead of revealing the identity of your guest, you can ask him/her to be mysterious. Give some clues as to the person's home (e.g. *She lives in a country without mountains*) and profession (e.g. *She works indoors, but is visited by many people*), etc., and ask the learners to write questions that will help them guess the person's identity.

Variation 2

Provided you obtain permission from the learners and your guest, you can make a recording of the occasion with a voice recorder or internet-recording software (see the book's accompanying website, http://languagelearningtechnology.com, for suggestions) and revisit it later, looking at particular features of the language that was used.

5.9 Recorded stories

Main goals	To practise speaking using narrative tenses; to encourage learners to listen to themselves and self-correct
Level	All levels
Time	10 minutes
Learning focus	Listening for information
Preparation	This is a good activity to do after you have done work on narrative tenses.
Technical requirements	One voice recorder / mobile phone with recorder per table of learners

Procedure

1 Tell the learners they are going to work in groups and record a story together, but before they do so, each group has to decide what kind of story it's going to be (i.e. the genre). Help the learners by brainstorming different genres of stories and writing these on the board. Suggestions may include:

horror science fi tion romance comedy historical fairy tale mystery

2 Once groups have decided the genre, they should then decide the names of the main characters in their story and some detail about their lives (how old they are, where they come from, what they do, etc.). After this, tell the learners that they are ready to begin, and hand out the voice recorders.

3 Tell them that they are now ready to make up a story about the characters. Learners take turns recording the sentences. When someone in the group thinks of a sentence, that learner takes the voice recorder and says that sentence, recording themselves. Tell the learners that if they want to write down the sentence first, they can do so.

4 Also tell the learners that everybody in the group should take a turn (i.e. once somebody has spoken, that learner cannot say another sentence until the last member of the group has said something).

5 Ask the learners to continue until they think they have reached the end of the story.

6 Once everyone has finished, they can listen to the entire story from the beginning, and then swap the voice recorders with the other groups and listen to each of the stories. Alternatively, you can listen as a class to each of the stories.

Variation

Instead of asking learners to record a story, get them to sit in a large circle, and tell them they are going to have an unscripted conversation about anything they want to talk about. When any of the learners wants to say something, ask them to put their hand up, and their line of dialogue is recorded. Just as in Community Language Learning (CLL), if learners don't know how to say something in English, they can ask the teacher beforehand, trying it out and asking the teacher to correct it before it is recorded. Once the activity is finished, play back the conversation, and ask the learners to work in pairs to transcribe it. Show the transcription on a projector to focus on features of vocabulary or grammar.

5.10 Voice-recorder dictation

Main goals	To encourage learners to listen to themselves; to understand and reflect on their own use of English
Level	Elementary (A2) to Intermediate (B1+)
Time	20 minutes
Learning focus	Improving listening skills, and general speaking and writing
Preparation	Make sure there are enough voice recorders to go round. Choose a number of relevant written texts (four) that your learners will read, not too long and at a suitable level for your class. Make sufficient copies for each pair of learners in your class.
Technical requirements	A voice recorder or other recording device for each pair of learners. Nowadays, most mp3 players and mobile phones have voice recorders built into them.

Procedure

1   Give each pair of learners a copy of Text A, B, C or D, and ask them to skim their text in order to have a general understanding of what it's about.

2   Tell them to take turns reading aloud the paragraphs of the texts and to ask you when they have any doubts how to pronounce a particular word. Monitor the learners while they are doing this, and help them if they have difficulties with any particular part of a text.

3   Hand out the voice recorders, or ask learners to use their mobile phones to make a recording of them reading the text.

4   Take the texts back and swap the voice recorders so each of the pairs of learners listens to a different text. Ask the learners to listen to the recording and to transcribe the text exactly. If the learners don't understand something, they can rewind and listen again. Tell the learners you want them to write the text as accurately as possible.

5   Give out the original texts so the learners can check their version, and ask them to count and correct the mistakes.

6   Finish by asking the learners to tell the others about the texts they have read.

Variation

You can choose texts that have been written by the learners and ask the groups to correct and improve upon these, once the dictation activity has finished.

Note

Although when making the recordings, the classroom could end up being noisy, the noise simulates a real-life task, as learners need to learn how to focus on a specific conversation while other people are talking.

5.11 Interview bingo

Main goals	Predicting before listening
Level	Intermediate (B1) and above
Time	15 minutes
Learning focus	Listening for information; listening to natural connected speech
Preparation	none required
Technical requirements	One internet-enabled computer in the classroom, with speakers

Procedure

1　Ask the learners to tell you the name of a singer/actor/celebrity they like, or use someone in the news. Take a vote on the most popular one.

2　Search for an interview, on a video site such as *YouTube*, with the person the class voted for. This activity works best if the interview is with a celebrity who is using natural, connected speech.

3　Ask the learners to draw a four-column by two-row table.

4　Establish what the person is talking about (from the title, or by playing the introduction or from the first question the interviewer asks). Then ask the learners to brainstorm eight words that might appear in the interview and to write their eight predictions in the table, one word per space. The words they use must be verbs or nouns; adjectives or adverbs; and they cannot choose people or places or brand names, or any words that already appear in the title.

5　Play the interview, and ask the learners to cross out any of the words on their tables that they hear the person mention.

6　After the first listening, check to see which learner predicted the most words. If none of the learners heard all of their words mentioned, ask the learners to change the words they haven't heard for other ones, based on what they thought the person said.

7　Tell the learners that the first person to hear all of their words should shout out, 'Bingo!' Play the video again, stopping it when someone has crossed out all of their words.

5.12 Someone I know

Main goals	Listening practice; providing role models for learners
Level	Intermediate (B1+) and above
Time	20 minutes
Learning focus	Listening for detail
Preparation	Interview a relative/friend about learning a language, and make a recording of the interview to play in class (optional).
Technical requirements	Learners should have mobile phones with a voice-recording or video-recording feature (most mobile phones do nowadays). Alternatively, they can record at home, using an mp3 player or a computer with a microphone. You will need a set of speakers you can plug into a mobile phone to allow you to play the recordings in class.

Procedure

1   Tell the learners that you want them to interview a relative or friend and then give/send you the recording or bring the recorder into class so everyone can listen to it. Tell them they can interview the person about anything they want (i.e. their experience of learning English, their job, a holiday, etc.). At this stage, you may want to give them help with the questions they can ask.

2   Talk to the learners about the practicalities of recording the interview. Ask them to take out their mobile phones and find the voice-recording option. Alternatively, they can video record their chosen person using another method (mp3 player or computer with microphone).

3   Once the learners have made the recording, ask them to give or send you an mp3 file you can play back in class, or they can simply bring the phones into class, and you can plug them into a set of speakers to play back the recordings.

4   Before the next class, listen to the interviews and write down, in a Word document, the interview questions each learner asked, turning each interview into a worksheet by leaving spaces for the answers. Make enough copies of the worksheets for learners to listen to three to four of the interviews, and ask the learners to listen and record the answers.

5   After the learners listen to three to four interviews and check the answers, ask them to work in groups and compare answers.

6   Finish by asking the learners to compile a list of some of the things that the interviewees said in the interviews, and turn this into a class poster.

5.13 Altered interviews

Main goals	Listening for fun
Level	Intermediate (B1+) and above
Time	50 minutes
Learning focus	Listening for detail
Preparation	This activity requires the teacher to have some knowledge of how to edit audio (principally, cutting and pasting) by using audio-editing software (see Appendix B 5.13 for help). Interview one of the learners before the lesson, and edit the audio as an example to play in class. Change the order of the answers, and remove words so that the resulting audio is funny (see example transcript below).
Technical requirements	A computer room, or class set of laptops/netbooks/tablets, with audio-editing software installed (see Appendix B 5.13)

Procedure

1 Interview and record a learner, and then edit the audio (as described above) before the next class.
2 Play the edited audio to the whole class, and then ask the learners to guess what you did to the interview. If you have time, give them a transcript of the original audio, play it again and ask them to highlight, or underline, the parts that have been changed. See the example below.

Original interview with learner

Teacher Hello, could you tell everyone your name and what you do?
Learner Yes. My name is Pablo, and I am an engineering student.
Teacher Where do you live, Pablo?
Learner I live in Barcelona.
Teacher What do you like doing in your free time?
Learner I like playing football and meeting my friends.
Teacher Where do you think is the worst place to live?
Learner Under a bridge, I think.
Teacher What things don't you like doing?
Learner Hmm … homework and washing dishes.
Teacher What job would you not like to do?
Learner A cleaner. I don't think I would like it.
Teacher What's your favourite animal?
Learner I think it's a dog.
Etc.

Edited interview

Teacher Hello, could you tell everyone your name and what you do?
Learner Yes. My name is Barcelona, and I am a cleaner.
Teacher Where do you live, Pablo?
Learner Under a bridge, I think.
Teacher What do you like doing in your free time?
Learner I like homework and washing dishes.
Teacher Where do you think is the worst place to live?
Learner Barcelona.
Teacher What things don't you like doing?
Learner Playing football and meeting my friends.
Teacher What job would you not like to do?
Learner An engineering student, I don't think I would like it.
Teacher What's your favourite animal?
Etc.

3 Show the learners the audio-editing software and how you cut and pasted what the learner said into different places. Tell them that they are going to record each other and create similar 'distorted gossip' about a person.
4 Ask the learners to brainstorm questions to ask each other, and then to interview each other and make voice recordings using the audio software.
5 The learners then work on the audio they recorded to produce funny distorted recordings.
6 When the learners have finished, play some of the recordings aloud for all of the class to hear.

Note
Sometimes it is better to ask the learners to record interviews before they know what you want them to do with the resulting audio. Other times, you will see they are more creative with their questions if they know they are going to create distorted audio recordings.

6 Reading

Reading is a complex and multifaceted skill, and notions of how best to teach reading have been in constant revision, especially with the rise of the Internet. The International Reading Association (2009) has said that 'to be fully literate in today's world necessitates proficiency in the new literacies of information and communication'. You can, therefore, argue that teachers need to help learners develop reading skills required for reading new media. Different reading strategies are often needed when it comes to electronic texts (how to deal with hyperlinked texts, for example), and the nature of a text itself has changed, with new genres of text emerging (email, chat, microblogging, etc.), as well as new combinations of text and image. All of these new texts require a new set of skills, usually clustered under the umbrella term of *digital literacy*.

Digital literacy refers to 'a person's ability to perform tasks effectively in a digital environment' and 'includes the ability to read and interpret media, to reproduce data and images through digital manipulation, and to evaluate and apply new knowledge gained from digital environments' (Jones-Kavalier & Flannigan, 2006). It is connected to *critical literacy*, which has become more important because of the increasing ease of publication online, and which means learners need to be more critical about sources of information they refer to.

In this chapter, we will look at some activities designed to help the teacher use technology to facilitate reading-skills development. These activities are intended as examples of how a teacher can use technology to enhance the different types of more traditional reading that occur in the language classroom (those usually connected with print texts). Different reading sub-skills are examined here, which include skimming (6.4), scanning (6.4, 6.9), reading for gist (6.3), activating schema (6.5) and inferencing (6.15). The activities try to use technology in ways that make it easier or more motivating to practise these sub-skills.

The activities also deal with different areas of reading, such as extensive reading (6.6, 6.15), reading aloud (6.6, 6.13), comparing reading texts (6.7), reading for information (6.8, 6.12), integrating reading and writing (6.10, 6.14), identifying different text-types (6.11), reading and summarising (6.12) and reading for pleasure (6.6, 6.13, 6.14, 6.15).

The last of these seems to be particularly important, as anecdotal evidence indicates that many teachers complain nowadays that their learners (especially teenagers) don't read and don't like reading. The global *Harry Potter* and *Twilight* phenomena show that this is not always the case, though, and reading for enjoyment can often be one of the most motivating reading tools at a teacher's disposal. It should be emphasised that there is 'no magic bullet; no single explanation for what teachers can do to ensure that their learners learn to read a second or foreign language' (Hudson, 2007: 297).

References

Hudson, T. (2007) *Teaching Second Language Reading*, Oxford: Oxford University Press.
International Reading Association, Board of Directors (2009) 'New literacies and 21st-century technologies position statement', *International Reading Association* [online]. Available

at: http://www.reading.org/General/AboutIRA/PositionStatements/21stCenturyLiteracies.aspx [accessed June 2012].

Jones-Kavalier, B. R. and Flannigan, S. L. (2006) 'Connecting the digital dots: literacy of the 21st century', *EDUCAUSE Quarterly*, 2, 8–10. Available online at: http://net.educause.edu/ir/library/pdf/EQM0621.pdf [accessed June 2012].

6.1 Word-cloud warmer

Main goals	Activating learners' existing knowledge and interest in a reading text
Level	All levels
Time	15 minutes
Learning focus	Various
Preparation	Select a reading text and a website for creating word clouds (see Appendix B 6.1 for suggestions), and follow the steps below before using the reading text in class.
Technical requirements	One internet-enabled computer to use before class

Procedure

1 Using word-cloud software can be a quick and easy way of creating a pre-reading task with any text on a website. First, find the text you wish to use on a news or other website.

2 Copy and paste the first paragraph from the text into the word-cloud software, and create the word cloud. Frequent words will be larger in the picture the word cloud creates (see example in Figure 6.1), which makes it really easy for learners to focus on key words.

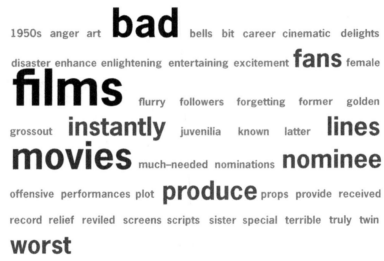

Figure 6.1: Word cloud of the first paragraph of an article about bad films

3 Give out the word cloud as a pre-reading task, and ask the learners to work in pairs and guess what the text is about. Ask them to write notes.

4 Next, give the learners the reading text, and ask them to check their notes with the first paragraph of the text in order to confirm their guesses.

5 Optionally, take away the text, and ask the learners to use their notes to reconstruct the text, telling each other about it. If necessary, before taking the text away, ask learners to first expand their notes to cover all paragraphs, as needed.

6.2 Video pre-reading warmer

Main goals	Creating an interesting pre-reading task
Level	All levels
Time	15 minutes
Learning focus	Pre-reading
Preparation	Create a pre-reading video task for a text that you have decided to read in class (from the coursebook or other source), following the procedure suggested below. Use one of the video-warmer websites (see Appendix B 6.2 for information and suggested websites).
Technical requirements	One internet-enabled computer in the classroom, with a projector or IWB

Procedure

1 Using one of the suggested video websites, create a short video as a warm-up to the reading text. Start by entering the title of the text and perhaps a photograph related to it (either take a photo from the article, or choose an image related to the subject of the text). Next, feed in some of the key content words that appear in the reading text, and create a video of the themes presented there. The video can be short – some five screens or so should be enough.

2 Show the learners the video as a pre-reading task. Once the learners have watched the video, write two to three questions you'd like them to guess the answer to before starting to read the text.

Variation

Instead of a pre-reading video, create a post-reading video with some statements from the reading. The learners then have to decide if they are true or false. Using one of the video sites, input some of the statements that came out of the text (either as true/false questions, as mentioned, or alternatively as questions/opinions), and ask the learners to discuss them.

6.3 Quick-response reading race

Main goals	Comparing images to descriptions
Level	All
Time	20 minutes
Learning focus	Reading for gist
Preparation	Use a QR (quick-response) code generator (see Appendix B 6.3 for help with this and suggested websites). QR codes are types of bar codes which contain information that can be scanned and revealed by a bar-code reader (now available for many mobile phones). Choose a series of short texts (150–200 words) with 8–10 images. Alternatively, choose a series of images, and write descriptions to go with them. This activity works well with images and descriptions of people, famous paintings, rooms of a house, holiday photographs, etc. Print out the images on separate pieces of paper, and add each written description to a separate webpage or online document (see Appendix B 6.3). Create a QR code for each webpage, and print these out, too.
Technical requirements	This activity requires learners working in groups of three, with each group having access to a mobile phone (smartphones are better) with a camera and bar-code reading software (this is a free app which can be downloaded if not already on the phone). Make sure your learners are happy about using their own phones for this activity before you suggest it. You will also need Wi-Fi access for the learners to access the webpages.

Procedure

1 Place the images around the classroom, and put a QR code next to them (the QR codes should not match the images).

2 Tell the learners that they are going to have a reading race, and they have to work in groups of three to go to each of the images, scan the QR code and read what the text says. They should then decide quickly if the text relates to that particular image or another one.

3 Ask the learners to continue scanning the QR codes and reading the texts. As they do so, they should try to match the images with the texts.

4 When the learners have finished, check the answers and declare the winning team. Then look at specific features of the texts you want to draw their attention to.

Note

Adapted from Singh, J. (2011), an original idea presented at the 2011 AsiaCALL conference, Gujarat, India.

6.4 IWB skimming and scanning

Main goals	Skimming and scanning of reading texts
Level	Elementary (A2) and above
Time	20 minutes
Learning focus	Skimming and scanning practice
Preparation	Choose a number of online texts (five to six) suitable for the level of your class (see Appendix B 6.4 for information and suggested websites), and using the IWB software, block out the titles/headlines in the text. Think of some alternative titles and subheadings to give the learners, and produce a handout for the learners with these new titles.
Technical requirements	One internet-enabled computer in the classroom, with a projector, as well as an online newspaper (or other suitable) website

Procedure

1   Give the learners the handouts, and tell them they are going to practise skimming a number of different texts (i.e. reading to get a general impression about what the text is about). Emphasise the need for speed during these tasks, but don't make the activity feel like a competition.

2   Tell the learners that they are to start by skimming the first text to decide which of the titles is the most appropriate. Tell them to mark the answer on the handout and then put their hands up when they have finished. Take note of the time it takes for the learners to find the answers, and after all of the learners have finished, check their answers.

3   Continue with the other texts and repeat Step 2. Ask the learners when they have finished reading the last text if they thought they were getting better at skimming.

4   Go back to the first text, and tell the learners that you now want them to practise scanning (i.e. looking for specific information in a text). Tell them that, this time, you are going to ask them to read each text quickly to find the answer to a question you ask. The types of questions you ask will depend on the text, but they may be similar to these:

What was the name/age of the person?
In which paragraph is the proposed solution suggested?
How many times does the word 'this' occur?

5   Finish by asking the learners which of the texts they found most interesting.

Variation

Instead of asking for specific information, ask the learners to read for the main ideas of the texts, and set a time limit (e.g. one minute) using the timer tool on the IWB (or blank the projector after the allotted time).

6.5 Pre-reading presentation

Main goals	Activating interest in reading
Level	Intermediate (B1+) and above
Time	10 minutes
Learning focus	Activating schema and interest before reading
Preparation	Use the presentation software on your computer (or software suggested in Appendix B 6.5), and create a pre-reading task for a text you are going to use in class (follow the suggested procedure below), adding related pictures and videos found on the Web.
Technical requirements	An internet-enabled computer in the classroom with a data projector, or IWB

Procedure

1 Activate the learners' schema (i.e. what they already know about the subject) by showing a picture related to the reading text and asking them to predict what they are going to be reading about.

2 Now display the title of the article, using the presentation software, and find out what the learners know about the subject by asking them for any words they think may occur in the article. Ask them to write these down.

3 If you find a related video, you could play it, or part of it, after the initial presentation or save it to use after the learners have read about the subject.

4 Give the learners the reading text (or ask them to look for it in their coursebooks), and ask them to read quickly to see how many of the words they predicted earlier occur in the text. The learners then continue reading and can answer comprehension questions about details related to the text.

6.6 Readathon

Main goals	Extensive reading; reading aloud
Level	Pre-intermediate (B1) and above
Time	20 minutes
Learning focus	Reading for pleasure
Preparation	The learners should be reading a book in class. This activity could also be organised with other classes collaborating, or even a whole school.
Technical requirements	One internet-enabled computer in the classroom, with a microphone and a virtual classroom (see Appendix B 6.6 for information and suggested websites). Alternatively, the activity can be set as homework.

Procedure

1   Make sure learners understand that a *readathon* is a long reading activity (a variation of a *telethon* – a long TV programme, usually to raise funds for charity), and tell the learners they are going to participate in one.

2   Tell the learners that, together, they are going to read aloud extracts from a number of books and broadcast these extracts live online in a virtual classroom, and they can invite their friends and family, other classmates, etc. to attend. At this point, you can show the virtual classroom and show how it works (see Appendix B 6.6), explaining how to communicate by using the microphone and how to respond to the people who are attending virtually. (The virtual classroom allows people to come together for webinars or classes in real time. It is a live event.)

3   Ask the learners to choose a book from the class or school library, or use one they are already reading. Tell them that they need to choose a chapter they want to read aloud during the readathon, and they should write a short introduction to the book, mentioning the main theme, the author and any other relevant details.

4   Arrange a day/time for the live readathon (this could be during class time, or it could be done at home if all of the learners can connect). Ask a volunteer learner to create a poster/flyer that you can put up around the school to advertise the readathon, and get the learners to promote the event so that you have an online audience on the day it takes place.

5   Before the actual day, ask the learners to practise reading the chapter aloud for homework, and tell them to ask you if they have any doubts about pronunciation, etc.

6   On the day of the readathon, make sure you have an audience, as this will make it more meaningful for the learners. You can also record the video and audio of the readathon taking place in the virtual classroom, and the learners can watch themselves reading passages from a book at a later point.

6.7 Comparative texts

Main goals	Reading short texts and comparing them
Level	Pre-intermediate (B1) and above
Time	20 minutes
Learning focus	Variable (in the example below: predicting and comparing)
Preparation	Find three to four different websites that publish similar types of texts (e.g. horoscopes), and check that they are appropriate for your class. Create a handout based on the text-type (see example for horoscopes), and make copies for each pair of learners.
Technical requirements	A computer room, or class set of laptops/netbooks/tablets. Alternatively, you can use just one internet-enabled computer in the classroom, with a projector.

Procedure

1 Ask the learners to discuss questions about the text-type you have chosen (the example below is about horoscopes) in pairs / small groups:

Do you believe people can predict the future?
What do you think of horoscopes?
What star sign are you?
Do you ever read your horoscope?
Has anything in your horoscope ever come true?

2 Once the learners have finished discussing the questions, ask them to give you feedback to get an idea of what the class think of the text-type in question. For example, do they read their horoscopes for advice or just for fun?

3 If you are using one computer in the classroom, then open up the first website that includes the text-type you have chosen. Prepare a handout prior to class where learners will rate aspects of the website, and give the learners the handout (see example below).

4 After the learners have made notes, ask them to rate features and content of the first website on a scale of 1–10. Once they have had time to look at one site, display another one, and ask them to compare the features and content on the new site to the previous one. If your learners are using multiple computers, they can go to the websites, in turn, and read individually or in pairs, comparing the features and rating each site. Continue for three to four different sites.

5 After the learners have finished, ask them to compare their results in small groups. Did they all prefer the same website(s)? Why? What were the main differences between the sites? Things that may be mentioned are: the length of the texts, the tone (e.g. was it more or less serious?), whether the information was better on one website, etc.

6 Finish by asking the learners if any of them have now changed their minds about the text-type in question, or whether they still hold the same opinions as when they started the activity. Reasons (e.g. with horoscopes) why they might change their minds include that they read something they think was true, or they hadn't compared different horoscopes before.

Variation

Other text-types that would work well include recipes (learners compare different versions of the same well-known dish), biographies of famous people, medical information, etc.

Horoscopes

Online horoscope websites: do they offer similar advice?

Compare what different horoscope websites say about your specific star sign.

	Horoscope 1	Horoscope 2	Horoscope 3	Horoscope 4
Friends				
Family				
Romance				
Work/study				
Money				
Home				
Travel				

Tick (√) if the horoscope mentions one of the topics listed in the chart, and give each horoscope site a mark out of 10 (1–10). Make some notes about what they say. After reading three to four horoscope sites, decide which was the best one.

From *Language Learning with Technology* © Cambridge University Press 2013   PHOTOCOPIABLE

6.8 Reviewer role play

Main goals	Reading for information
Level	Pre-intermediate (B1) and above
Time	20 minutes
Learning focus	Language used in reviews
Preparation	Pre-select a website where customers post reviews and comments (i.e. a travel-review site, in the example below).
Technical requirements	A computer room, or class set of laptops/netbooks/tablets, with internet access

Procedure

1   Tell the learners they are going to play the role of reviewers (or travel agents, in the example below) and make recommendations for various groups of people. Hand out the card below (profiles of travellers) or brainstorm different profiles.

Group 1

A family of four on holiday for a week. The couple have two children: a boy aged 10 and a girl aged 16. The couple are fond of history and architecture.

Group 2

A young couple on their first trip abroad together. They want to go somewhere exotic and are both keen on gastronomy. A week's holiday.

Group 3

Three friends on a limited budget. They want to spend a fortnight in Europe somewhere and have fun, without spending too much money. Interested in photography.

From *Language Learning with Technology* © Cambridge University Press 2013   PHOTOCOPIABLE

2   Tell the learners to work in pairs and think of a recommendation for each group (e.g. a holiday they would like, in the example above) and then go to the website that has the reviews.
3   On the website, the learners should search for what they have chosen (e.g. the place they would go on holiday) and then select a few examples (e.g. hotel, a couple of restaurants and some places to visit), based on the criteria in the card (above) and what the website recommends.
4   Ask the learners to write down a few of the comments from the website, marking down whether the reviews by the customers are favourable, unfavourable or neutral, so they can justify their choices when they make their suggestions.
5   After the learners have finished, look at each group, in turn, and hear what each pair of learners have suggested for a holiday (e.g. the places chosen by each pair).

6.9 Coded message trail

Main goals	Making reading fun
Level	Pre-intermediate (B1) and above
Time	20 minutes
Learning focus	Scanning; reading for specific information
Preparation	For this game to work, you'll need to be able to allow the learners to move outside the classroom to other spaces in your institution. Create a series of clues (see example below), leading from the classroom to other places in your building (and outside if you have a garden, etc.). Use a QR code generator (see Appendix B 6.9 for information and suggested websites), create one QR code per clue and place them in order near the places you have chosen for the trail.
Technical requirements	One internet-enabled computer to create the QR codes. Learners working in groups of three should have one mobile phone with a camera and bar-code scanner per group (check these work in the class before).

Procedure

1   Display the first clue on the board, and ask the learners to scan the QR code and read the clue. If you want to make the game more interesting, then create four different trails that converge into one later on. For the game to work well, each group should have about five QR codes to scan. Here are some example QR codes:

Group 1    *Group 2*

Group 3   *Group 4*

The clues that learners see when they scan the bar codes are:

Group 1

> Leave the classroom and turn left. Walk along the corridor until you reach the fire extinguisher. Look next to this.

Group 2

> Walk out of class and turn right. Walk along the corridor and take the second left. Look next to the landscape painting.

Group 3

> Leave the room and go to the main entrance. Look under one of the chairs for the next code.

Group 4

> Go into the garden and walk to the tree near the wall on the left. To the right of this near the ground is the next clue.

2 Tell the learners the game is a race to reach the end. If you like, leave a prize at the last location. While each group may follow the clues in a different order, all groups should have the same clue in the final location.

3 Let the learners go off in their groups and follow the trail. Monitor them and help, if necessary, with language they do not understand.

4 Back in class, once the trail is over, ask the learners to reconstruct the clues as best they can, writing the directions down as a post-reading task.

5 Ask the learners to check what they have written by giving them the text of the clues.

Variation

If you want to add an extra layer of difficulty, you can code the messages so the learners have to decipher them before they can understand where the next clue is. Here is an example of a coded message (Group 1's clue above), using an 'autokey cipher':

LPAVZ NOZ WBRAAZVQE WFA QHLS IJTA

This will make the learners pay more attention to each word of the message. See Appendix B 6.9 for suggested websites to help you code your messages automatically.

6.10 Ask the Internet

Main goals	Integrating reading and writing
Level	Pre-intermediate (B1) and above
Time	40–50 minutes
Learning focus	Integrating reading and writing
Preparation	None required
Technical requirements	A computer room, or class set of laptops/netbooks/tablets.

Procedure

1   Ask the learners to work in pairs to design a set of questions to 'ask the Internet' about a pre-selected topic (e.g. restaurants). Give them an example question, such as *Do people in (your country) eat out much?* Tell them they will be using the answers they find to write a guide on the subject.

2   Write the questions on the board. Examples may include:

What kind of food do people in (your country) like?
Which are the best / most popular restaurants in (your city)?
What's on the menu of a typical Chinese / French / Indian / Italian / Moroccan restaurant?
Are there any good restaurants near the school?
How important are the following factors when people go to a restaurant?
  • *variety of food?*
  • *friendliness of the staff?*
  • *comfortable atmosphere?*

3   Learners work again in pairs to research the Web, looking for answers to their questions.

4   When the learners have found their answers, ask them to talk to the whole class about what was mentioned (e.g. what was on the menu in the restaurants they looked at).

5   Tell the learners they are now going to design an online guide related to the subject they talked about (e.g. a guide to eating out or to setting up a restaurant or a menu for an invented restaurant), and they will have to make a number of choices. Ask them to predict what they think is important when designing the guide (in our example: choice of food / price / names of dishes / description of dishes / length / layout / photos of food / payment details).

6   When the learners have finished, print out and display the guides and/or use them for presentations or other tasks (e.g. in the example, role-playing restaurant situations).

6.11 Identifying text-types

Main goals	Identifying structure of different text-types
Level	Intermediate (B1+) and above
Time	40 minutes
Learning focus	Identifying specific text-types from structure and vocabulary
Preparation	Find links to a range of different examples of a text-type you choose (e.g. online newspapers in the example below), to give to the learners.
Technical requirements	A computer room, or class set of laptops/netbooks/tablets, with internet access

Procedure

1   Ask the learners to talk to their partner about the text-type you chose (e.g. news reports), and ask them to predict the features of that text related to overall organisation, layout, graphic features and choice of vocabulary, etc. For example, news stories generally say what the text is about in the first paragraph.

2   Ask the learners to turn the features they predicted into a set of questions. Examples may include:

Does the writer tell you what the text is about in the first paragraph?
Are there subheadings in the text?
Is the choice of vocabulary formal or informal?
Does the writer use the passive voice?

3   Tell the learners to use the Web to look for examples of the text-types, using the links you have provided, and to answer the questions.

4   While the learners are reading and taking notes, monitor and help with language.

5   Ask a volunteer from each group to give a short presentation to the class about the organisation of specific texts they have read.

Variation 1

Ask groups of learners to choose a different, but related, text-type (e.g. different kinds of narrative texts, such as fairy tales, jokes, stories, etc.) and compare the organisation and vocabulary. The texts should be more or less the same length.

Variation 2

Find a website (see this book's accompanying website, http://www.languagelearningtechnology.com, for suggestions) with funny examples of the type of text you want to focus on (letters, emails, etc.). There are lots of examples of funny letters of complaint, insurance claims, replies to spammers, etc.

Ask the learners to browse the texts on the site and choose one they like to explain later to the rest of the class. If using just one computer in the classroom, decide together which one(s) to read.

Once the class have read a few of the chosen texts, go back to them, and focus upon the form and language. Ask the learners to identify common features (e.g. vocabulary in a joke, organisation of text in an insurance claim, etc.) and example language that occur frequently in this type of text.

6.12 Big events

Main goals	Reading for information
Level	Intermediate (B1+) and above
Time	20 minutes
Learning focus	Summarising; newspaper language
Preparation	Find a number of newspaper websites to suggest to the learners (see Appendix B 6.12 for information and suggested websites).
Technical requirements	A computer room, or class set of laptops/netbooks/tablets, with internet access

Procedure

1 Tell the learners to work in groups, and ask them to choose a news story which is a 'big event'; in other words, something that happened that had an important impact and which was in the news over a long period of time (not just one day). Each group should choose a different event.

2 Ask the learners to work in groups of six to eight. They should choose their big event, talk about it and together remember as much as they can about it. Give them the form below, and ask for one volunteer to make notes, as their group members are talking, on eight or more relevant facts about the event.

3 Once the learners can remember no more details about the event, ask them to work in pairs on the computers and to find out more by going to news websites. They should read about their big event and revise their notes based on what they find.

4 After the pair work, the learners come back together and share what they have found, building a bigger picture of their event.

5 Finish with each group giving a short presentation to the class about their big event.

Variation

Narrow reading. Ask the learners to work in pairs, with each pair choosing a series of texts all related to the same topic (e.g. an evolving news story). Each individual or pair can choose to follow a story of their choice. As the story's 'schema' becomes reinforced, comprehension should be enhanced and vocabulary recycled at a higher rate. The learners can give a presentation of their topic, as above.

Big event _____

Event	What happened?
1	
2	
3	
4	
5	
6	
7	
8	
9	
10	
11	
12	
13	
14	
15	
16	
17	
18	
19	
20	
21	
22	
...	

6.13 Kids' storytelling

Main goals	Reading for pleasure
Level	Intermediate (B1+) and above (young learners)
Time	30 minutes
Learning focus	Reading aloud; pronunciation
Preparation	Find a website with stories for kids (see Appendix B 6.13 for information and suggested websites), and choose a story to read (or let the learners decide).
Technical requirements	One internet-enabled computer in the classroom, with a data projector (or IWB)

Procedure

1 Introduce the learners to the website, and choose a story to read together (or show them the one you have chosen – see example in Figure 6.2).

Figure 6.2: Story: http://learnenglishkids.britishcouncil.org/en/short-stories/spycat

2 Display and read the story to the learners. Once you have read the story, go back and read it again, this time asking learners to volunteer to read certain sections.

3 Return to the beginning again, and this time focus on the pictures, asking the learners to name vocabulary.

4 Finally, if the website lets you leave a comment, ask the learners what they thought of the story, and get them to write a comment about it.

Variation

If the website lets learners write their own stories, you can create one together with the class.

6.14 Interactive fiction

Main goals	Integrating reading and writing
Level	Upper-intermediate (B2) to Advanced (C1)
Time	30 minutes
Learning focus	Reading for information; reading for pleasure
Preparation	Find a piece of interactive fiction suitable for your class (i.e. a computer game where players type text in order to control characters), and print a copy of the *Beginner's Guide to Interactive Fiction* (free to download from the Web) for each learner (see Appendix B 6.14 for information).
Technical requirements	One internet-enabled computer in the classroom, with a data projector (or IWB), or a computer room or class set of laptops/netbooks/tablets, with internet access

Procedure

1 Tell the learners they are going to play a type of computer game (interactive fiction, or IF) that allows them to change the story depending on what they decide the characters do in the game.

2 Give each of the learners a copy of the *Beginner's Guide to IF*, which shows them the instructions they can type in to tell the character in the game what to do next (e.g. open wallet, go south, answer phone, etc.), and go through the vocabulary, making sure the learners understand it.

3 Choose an example story to demonstrate the game. Show the example you have chosen to the learners, and read the introduction to the story together (in the example in Figure 6.3, you play a character who wakes up one morning and can't remember what happened the night before).

Figure 6.3: IF game '9:05': http://adamcadre.ac/if/905.html

4 Next, read the description of the room together, and talk about the actions the character can do next (*answer the phone*, *go to the bathroom*, *open the wallet*, etc.). Decide together what the character should do, and type this in.

5 If the learners have access to computers, they can play in pairs, reading the story and writing what they want the character to do next. Otherwise, continue playing the game, asking the class to help you make decisions about what to do next. You could also invite volunteers to come up and write the instructions (*go east*, *take keys*, etc.).

6 When the learners come to the end of the game, ask them to compare how the story developed (if playing in pairs). You may also ask the learners if they want to try again to see if the outcome is different, because each time the learners play, the decisions they make will affect the outcome of the story (interactive fiction encourages re-reading in this way).

7 If the learners enjoyed the game, you could ask them to write their own branching story together (i.e. a story where readers' decisions lead to different outcomes). The story could be posted on a class wiki if you have set one up (see Chapter 2 *Building a learning community*).

Note

Thanks to Joe Pereira (http://www.theswanstation.com/wordpress) for promoting IF in ELT and for introducing me to '9:05'.

6.15 Fan fiction

Main goals	Promoting extensive reading; inferencing
Level	Upper-intermediate (B2) to Advanced (C1)
Time	30 minutes
Learning focus	Reading for pleasure; inferencing
Preparation	Find a fan-fiction website (see Appendix B 6.15 for information and suggested websites) that has writing that your learners are interested in. Select an example, and copy a short extract to show your learners.
Technical requirements	One internet-enabled computer in the classroom, with a data projector (or IWB), or a computer room or class set of laptops/netbooks/tablets, with internet access

Procedure

1   Ask the learners if they know what *fan fiction* is (fiction written by fans of a popular author's characters and world). Display an example on the board, or direct the learners to a fan-fiction website (if using multiple computers), and let them read some of the fan fiction. Ask the learners what they think of it (*Would they be interested in reading any / writing any?*).

2   If using multiple computers, let the learners explore the website and read some of the fan fiction for a book or TV series of their choosing. Ask them to explore some of the texts, and write notes about what they read (*Did they like it? Was it different from the original?* etc.). If you have only one computer, then choose one or two of the learners' suggestions and look at them together.

3   While the learners are reading, also ask them to infer what the author wanted to accomplish when writing the fan fiction (*Did the author want to extend or change anything related to the characters? Is the setting different – if so, then why?* etc.).

4   If there is sufficient interest, suggest to the learners that they could write a fan-fiction story, using the characters and setting they choose.

7 Writing

Writing is probably the skill most affected by the rise of the Internet. Apart from anything else, the last decade has seen the emergence, or rise in prominence, of important new tools such as blogs and wikis, and social-networking platforms that have seen our learners becoming more used to writing. In many cases, you will find that learners already write regularly online. One of the challenges for language teachers is to help learners extend their 'Internet world beyond their first language', and a way to meet this challenge is to use the Internet as a language-learning opportunity (Godwin Jones, 2008: 7).

The writing you will want to focus on will depend on the profile of your learners, and early on you should find out what kind of writing they are involved in now and may do in the future. In this chapter, there are activities that look at a range of different writing sub-skills, such as planning/generating ideas (7.6), writing more fluently (7.7) or more accurately (7.7), drafting and re-drafting (7.8, 7.9), concentrating on structuring of texts (7.10), writing paragraphs (7.1), increasing lexical range (7.11), reporting (7.14) and summarising (7.16), making text cohesive (7.5), and writing different genres (7.20) and text-types (7.13).

One of the areas you will want to examine is writing CVs (7.19), and another is email (7.13), especially if the learners are adults. The challenge with email for many learners is not only a linguistic one, but can also be related to unfamiliarity with a target language's cultural norms or values. Emails can often be a hybrid between spoken and written discourse, but you may find there are times when help with composing more formal email communication is required. Other areas looked at in this chapter include spelling, writing text messages, writing narratives, writing collaboratively, note taking, writing discursively and writing biographies.

The use of blogs (7.3, 7.4) can be encouraged with language learners, and the ease with which they can be published, and the potential they have for encouraging greater productivity, means they are attractive tools to introduce to language learners. Through writing a blog, a learner can develop a sense of voice, get lots of writing practice and learn to participate in a community of writers. How you introduce blogs to learners will depend very much on the time you have available, and your choice between the main three types – tutor blog, class blog and learner blog (Campbell, 2003) – will depend very much on what your aims are. Further discussion of these can be found in Activity 7.3 and in Chapter 2 *Building a learning community*.

Whichever type of blog you decide to use, experience has shown that it can be difficult to maintain momentum (Stanley, 2006), and some of the activities in this chapter have been written with this in mind. A key to successful use of blogs is to ensure that whatever is written by learners on a blog is related directly to what is happening in class. The teacher should work hard in the role of facilitator, responding to learners' posts promptly and writing short comments relating to content, rather than trying to correct learners' work online. The importance of audience should not be underestimated, as Warschauer (2010: 4) points out: 'Blogging can … be used to help students write for a social audience and hone their words in response to others, while becoming sensitive to both the benefits and risks of expressing themselves online.'

Collaborative writing can also be highlighted by the use of technology. Perhaps the best tool for this is the wiki (a simple website with content that can be easily added to and edited collaboratively). Whereas email, chat and blogs often accentuate informal and personal exchange, writing on a wiki (7.2) can be more formal and topic-based. Each learner can be made to feel they are contributing to a larger whole, although the process of developing collective knowledge is sometimes hard for learners to adapt to. One way of helping this transition to collaborative work has been suggested in an activity in this chapter: asking individual learners to become 'editors' of certain pages and to be responsible for the finished product (7.5). Apart from class wikis, teachers may also want to experiment with other projects such as the *Simple English Wikipedia* (http://simple.wikipedia.org), targeted at English-language learners. Collaboration on a project of this nature could be highly motivating for some learners.

Writing on social networks (7.1) is another area that should not be ignored. Social-networking sites, such as *Facebook* and *Twitter*, have become important to many of our learners' lives, and teachers may find that some of their learners are already using the target language to communicate with others on these sites. If this is the case, then using it in class could well be an option that will be popular with learners .

Collecting learner writing in electronic portfolios (e-portfolios) is another area which can be considered by the teacher. Gathering learner writing can be made an integral part of a learner's personal learning environment: the e-portfolio part of this process is further discussed in Chapter 11 *Assessment and evaluation.*

Apart from conventional writing skills, your learners may need to develop digital literacy skills, which is another reason for using digital tools. How much of this you do in the language classroom will depend on you and your learners, but there is much here to explore with learners: what information sources to use and how best to make use of them, the multi-modality of digital texts (i.e. combining text with images, included in activities in this chapter), writing in different digital contexts (e.g. using mobile phone text messages, or SMS, included in Activity 7.17), and the use of fonts and other design features, etc.

References

Campbell, A. P. (2003) 'Weblogs for use with ESL classes', *The Internet TESL Journal*, 9 (2). Available online at: http://iteslj.org/Techniques/Campbell-Weblogs.html [accessed May 2012].

Godwin Jones, R. (2008) 'Emerging technologies web-writing 2.0: enabling, documenting and assessing writing online', *Language Learning and Technology*, 12 (2), 7–13. Available online at: http://llt.msu.edu/vol12num2/emerging.pdf [accessed February 2012].

Stanley, G. (2006) 'Redefining the blog: from composition class to flexible learning', in E. Hanson-Smith and S. Rilling (eds.), *Learning Languages through Technology*, Alexandria, VA: TESOL, 187–200.

Warschauer, M. (2010) 'Invited commentary: new tools for teaching writing', *Language Learning and Technology*, 14 (1), 3–8. Available online at: http://llt.msu.edu/vol14num1/commentary.pdf [accessed July 2012].

7.1 Social-networking writing group

Main goals	Writing fluency
Level	Elementary (A2) and above
Time	15–20 minutes (homework)
Learning focus	Process writing; writing paragraphs
Preparation	Set up a writing group in a social network (see Appendix B 7.1 for suggested social networks), and invite your learners to join it. Keeping the group private will mean only your learners will have access. Alternatively, you can set up a special educational social network if you think this more appropriate.
Technical requirements	Learners should all have internet access from home and all be members of the same social network.

Procedure

1   Introduce the learners to the writing group or social network, and ask them to join it (you will probably have to send them invitations via email) and to introduce themselves (see example in Figure 7.1).

Figure 7.1: Private social-network group: http://www.edmodo.com. Image of Graham Stanley by Isabel de la Granja.

2   Tell the learners you want them to write a short paragraph every week about a subject of their choice. The paragraph could be about something they have done that day, reviewing a TV programme they have seen, talking about their job or school, writing about a person they know, etc. Be sure to choose topics appropriate to the learners' level. Remember, too, that although you can set a topic every week and ask the learners to write about it, the responses will be more varied and interesting if you encourage the learners to choose their own topics and write about something they are interested in.

3   Ask the learners to enter their paragraphs on the front page of the writing group, and make sure you respond, in the comments section, to what the learners say shortly afterwards (at least the same day or day after). Also, encourage the learners to write comments on the other learners' writing.

4   Respond on the content – don't correct the learners' language using the comments. Print the paragraphs and mark them up with corrections, according to a set of codes to give to the learners in class, or deal with a common mistake in an error-correction session together.

5   In class, be sure to talk about the writing the learners do on the website, creating a strong connection between what they write and what you do as part of the class.

7.2 Writing on a class wiki

Main goals	Drafting/re-drafting
Level	Pre-intermediate (B1) and above
Time	20 minutes
Learning focus	Collaborative writing
Preparation	Choose a wiki (a simple website) to use with the class (see Appendix B 7.2 for suggestions).
Technical requirements	One internet-enabled computer in the classroom with projector (or IWB)

Procedure

1 Plan a writing lesson that your class will do collaboratively in a wiki. In the example below, a story is used, but wikis are good for any writing projects that can be done collaboratively, such as recipes and biographies (as suggested in the Variation).

2 Go to the wiki you have chosen and set it up (you can do this before the lesson or, because it takes very little time, during the lesson). Ask the learners to join the wiki (you can get them to add their email addresses to the list of contributors during the lesson or later).

3 Create a new page, and show the learners how to start writing on a page and how to save their work. Next, show them that when someone adds something new to the page, a revised version of the wiki page is created, so someone can always go back to a previous version of the page if required. Show the learners how their entries will be identified by name when learners make changes to a wiki.

4 Tell the learners that because everyone's contribution to a wiki is recorded, and past versions saved, wikis are ideal for collaborative writing. Mention that this way of writing means that the learners can work together on a document, and you can see what each learner has contributed to a particular writing project.

5 Tell the learners they are going to write a story together, and split them into groups of three. Create a new page in the wiki for each group, and tell them that the person who starts will write the beginning of the story, the second person will continue with the middle and the third person will finish the story. Tell them also that each learner can edit/change anything the person who came before them wrote.

6 Look at the collaborative stories together next class, and use the history/revisions feature to examine who did what with each story.

Variation

For adults, give the writing a different focus and ask them to describe a process (such as a recipe for a dish that everyone in the group knows), or write a biography (in the style of a *Wikipedia* entry, for example).

7.3 Using learner blogs

Main goals	Writing fluency
Level	Pre-intermediate (B1) and above
Time	15 minutes
Learning focus	Process writing
Preparation	Choose a blogging platform you think your learners will find easy to use, and set up a *tutor blog*, which will connect to all of the *learner blogs* (see Appendix B 7.3 for more information and suggested blogging platforms). Alternatively, you and the learners can all write in the same blog (a *class blog*). See below for more information on these three types of blogs.
Technical requirements	A computer room, or class set of laptops/netbooks/tablets. Alternatively, you can demonstrate how to set up a blog and ask the learners to set up their blogs at home.

Procedure

1   Tell your learners that they are going to be writing on a blog, and show them the blogging platform you have decided to use. Demonstrate how easy it is to set up a blog by doing it there and then.

2   Make a decision (or ask the learners) whether you want the learners to each have their own blog (a learner blog) or if you are going to write together on the same blog (a class blog). Here are some things to keep in mind:

    Class blog. This is the easiest way to blog, and is recommended if it is the first time you are going to blog with learners. You administer the blog and ask each of the learners to sign up as writers (you can do this by entering their emails and inviting them to be writers on the blog). Having a class blog means there is only one blog for you to visit to read learner work, but it is less motivating for learners because they don't *own* the writing space.

    Learner blog. Giving each learner a blog is more motivating (because they own the writing space and can personalise it), but this makes it harder for you to manage because you have to visit each of the learners' blogs individually. If you decide to use learner blogs, be sure to add links from each of the learner blogs to your blog (the tutor blog), and see Appendix B 7.3 for more information on how to manage this way of blogging. A compromise, so that you don't have as many blogs to visit, would be to have groups of learners (three to four) set up their own blog.

    Tutor blog. This is the teacher's blog, which will act as a hub between the learner blogs. You can use it to post tasks (homework, etc.) and links for the learners. It is not necessary to start a tutor blog if you are not setting up learner blogs. Because learners will be accessing the tutor blog (to see tasks that you post), it is generally a good idea to post a list of links to the learner blogs on one side of the tutor blog, to make it easier for learners to find each other's blogs.

3   You can now ask learners to set up their own blog (a learner blog) or ask them to input their email addresses to the blog you set up previously (a class blog).

4   If you ask the learners to create their own learner blogs, get them to tell you the web addresses of their blogs. You can then add these web addresses to the list of blogs on your tutor blog, as mentioned.

5   Ask the learners to write their first individual blog post, introducing themselves. Ask the classmates that finish early to visit each other's blogs and leave a comment there. Tell the learners they will be using the blog for all of their writing homework.

7.4 Blogging summary

Main goals	Reporting/summarising; learner training
Level	Pre-intermediate (B1) and above
Time	15 minutes
Learning focus	Process writing
Preparation	Learners should each have learner blogs or access to a class blog (see Activity 7.3).
Technical requirements	A computer room, or class set of laptops/netbooks/tablets

Procedure

1 At the end of the class, tell the learners that you want them to summarise what they have learned in order to reflect on what was done and to tell you if they fully understood the lesson.

2 Get the learners to work in groups (on a class blog) or individually (if they have learner blogs). Ask them to answer the following questions in their summaries:

What did we do in class today?
What did you learn that was new?
Was there anything you didn't understand?
Would you like more practice?

3 Help the learners express themselves when they are writing. Tell them to concentrate on expressing themselves without fear of making mistakes. The important goals here are to encourage learners to express themselves in writing and for you to get feedback on what was done in the lesson.

4 Use the information the learners write, and act on it for the next class. If the learners want more practice on something you did last class, then work that into your lesson.

Variation

The blog can also be used for keeping a list of vocabulary that comes up, along with the context (example sentences).

7.5 Myths and legends

Main goals	Note taking and summarising; making texts cohesive
Level	Pre-intermediate (B1) and above
Time	20 minutes
Learning focus	Process writing
Preparation	You'll need to have set up a class wiki (see Activity 7.2).
Technical requirements	Learners should have access to the Internet from home. Alternatively, the second part of the activity below can be done in a computer room, or with a class set of laptops/netbooks/tablets (if available).

Procedure

1 Ask the learners to tell you the names of any myths and legends that are known to people either locally or the world over. Their examples may include:

Loch Ness monster	*Big Foot*	*Robin Hood*	*Count Dracula*
William Tell	*Trojan horse*	*Atlantis*	*Camelot*

2 Once you have a number of myths and legends written on the board (ideally there should be 8–10), ask the learners to form groups of three to four, and ask each group to choose a legend to discuss. Each group should choose a different one.

3 Ask each group to reconstruct the story of the myth they chose and to try to remember as much as possible about it. Learners should each make notes about the legend/myth their group chose, while the other members of the group talk about it.

4 Now tell the learners that you are going to create a section of the class wiki related to myths and legends, and that each group is going to write a page about the myth/legend they chose.

5 Tell the learners that they should aim to turn the notes into a text of two to three paragraphs. If they are doing this step from home, suggest one of the learners take the role of editor, in order to tidy up the group's text.

6 Set a deadline for the learners to finish, and check their progress. If any of the learners are having difficulties, tell them to look on the Web to see if they can find out information about the legend/myth they chose.

Variation 1
The learners can produce comic-strip or animated-story versions of their myths to go with their wiki entries (see the book's accompanying website, http://languagelearningtechnology.com, for suggestions).

Variation 2
Instead of myths or legends, the learners could talk about fictional characters and places from TV and films, etc.

7.6 Five-sentence photo story

Main goals	Planning / generating ideas
Level	All levels
Time	20 minutes
Learning focus	Narrative writing
Preparation	Choose a collection of photographs or an image search engine to use in class. I recommend you turn 'safe search' on before the learners come to class if you are using a live search engine, as this will avoid any embarrassing or inappropriate pictures turning up when you search. To see the options, enter a search word. See Appendix B 7.6 for tips on image searching and some suggested websites / collections of photos.
Technical requirements	One internet-enabled computer in the classroom, with a projector or IWB

Procedure

1 Tell the learners they are each going to write a story inspired by the same five photographs that you are going to choose together. Tell them that the stories should all have a clear beginning, middle and end, and that the class will finish by voting for the best one.

2 Go to the image search engine, and ask the learners what they would like you to search on. Encourage them to be descriptive, and search on very specific terms (e.g. instead of searching for *cat*, look for *black cat in the rain*, etc.). Tell them that they will decide on the best picture for the beginning together, and that they can take some time deciding which image they want.

3 After the learners have chosen the image they want to use, copy the image to a new IWB flipchart page (or paste it into a Word document if you don't have an IWB). Then give the learners two minutes to work in pairs to write the beginning sentence of the story.

4 Repeat the process until you have found five images in total. Learners may write one or several sentences to go with each. When the learners have finished writing, ask them to give their story a title, and then collect the stories and pin them on the walls of the classroom.

5 Ask the learners to walk around the classroom, to read all of the stories and then to choose their favourite one, writing the title on a slip of paper. Collect the slips of paper, count the number of votes and declare the winner.

6 Next, you can revise the language of the stories, dealing with any mistakes the learners have made. You could also ask the learners to take their stories and expand upon them for homework – they can add more detail, doubling the length.

7 When the learners give the stories back to you, make a classroom wall display, with the five photos as the centrepiece and the learners' stories surrounding them.

Variation

Alternatively, if the learners are using multiple computers, they can each choose five different images for their stories.

Note

Adapted from Levine, A. (2010) 'Five card Flickr': http://5card.cogdogblog.com

7.7 Speed writing

Main goals	Fluency / achieving grammatical accuracy
Level	All levels
Time	15 minutes (ongoing, weekly)
Learning focus	Personal writing
Preparation	Think of a subject for the learners to write about in class, or ask them to suggest one.
Technical requirements	A class set of laptops/netbooks/tablets and word-processor software

Procedure

1   Tell the learners that they are going to be speed writing for a short period in class, that the objective of this activity is to increase their writing fluency and that (over time) they will start making fewer mistakes.

2   Decide on a subject to write about and set the time limit (10 minutes is probably enough). Tell the learners that the objective is for them to write as much as they can in 10 minutes, rather than writing to a specific word limit, and start the clock.

3   After five minutes are up, tell the learners that they should be in the middle of their story (or whatever writing task they are doing). After eight minutes, tell them that they should be thinking about bringing their text to an end.

4   Once they have finished, ask the learners to count the number of words and to write this at the bottom of the text. When you correct the writing, circle each of the mistakes and subtract the number of mistakes from the total number of words each learner has written, creating that learner's score.

5   Make a note of the number of words and the score for each learner. Tell the learners that their objective is to write a little bit more each time they do the activity, and also to improve their score (i.e. make fewer mistakes). It is a good idea for the learners to look at the previous lesson's writing just before starting to write again.

Variation

As an alternative, learners can write narratives, and you can use one of the story-starter websites (see Appendix B 7.9 for suggestions).

7.8 Interactive story

Main goals	Drafting/re-drafting
Level	Primary/secondary (young learners) – all levels
Time	20 minutes
Learning focus	Narrative writing
Preparation	Try the software before the class, and familiarise yourself with the story elements.
Technical requirements	One internet-enabled computer in the classroom, with a projector, or IWB. Access to a story-telling website (see Appendix B 7.8 for suggestions)

Procedure

1 Tell the learners they are going to help you write a story, and start the story-maker software.

2 After deciding on the main character together, the class needs to set a goal (see the screenshot in Figure 7.2). 'Make friends' is a good goal to start with.

3 Once the goal has been set, you have an opportunity to change the background. Choose one with the class, and add any other elements (trees, sun, etc.) that are relevant to your story.

4 Optionally, you can click on the character and choose from a list of expressions: *happy, mad, normal, sad, sly, surprise, worry*. Don't worry about explaining these – when you click each one, the expression of your character will change.

5 You can also choose an action verb and the character will be animated. Choose from: *cheer, dance, eat, fall, fly, jump, look, play music, ride, roar, rub, sit, sleep, swing, talk, throw* and *wave*.

6 Now you are ready to begin. Work together with the learners and make up the story. The list of expressions and actions you have chosen should match the text; if they don't, you can go back and change them. Ask a volunteer to write the text as you edit the list of emotions and actions, or if you prefer, you can write the text.

7 When you have finished the first page, add another page and write the next part of the story. Continue adding new pages to the story until reaching a natural end. When you have finished, you can go back to the beginning, and this time the learners can take turns reading the story.

8 If you want, you can make copies of each page (by pressing the 'Print screen' button) and print out the story to make a wall display.

Variation

If the learners are older, then they can write their own stories, in pairs, on individual computers if they have access to them.

Figure 7.2: Storytelling website: http://www.carnegielibrary.org/kids/storymaker

7.9 Developing a story

Main goals	Drafting/re-drafting a story
Level	Pre-intermediate (B1) and above
Time	60 minutes
Learning focus	Narrative writing
Preparation	Choose a website that has a number of *story starters* or beginnings to stories (see Appendix B 7.9 for suggestions).
Technical requirements	One internet-enabled computer in the classroom, with a projector (or IWB)

Procedure

1 Tell the learners that they are going to develop a story, using a website with story starters to help them. Go to the website you have selected, and show the learners the possible story starters (see image in Figure 7.3). Ask the learners to choose one each, or choose one for the whole class.

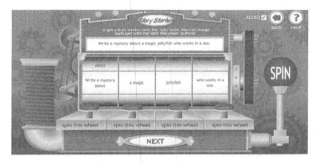

Figure 7.3: Story starter: http://teacher.scholastic.com/activities/storystarters

2 The learners now start planning what will happen next. When they have written a plan, ask them to present their ideas to a partner, and ask the partner to suggest improvements or changes if necessary.

3 Talk to the learners about structuring the story into three clear parts – beginning, middle and end. Tell them that the beginning should contain the background (who the characters are, where the story is set); the middle can be about what happens (is there a problem? Do the characters need to get something? etc.); and then the ending can be about the solution to the problem, or what happens when the characters get what they want, etc.

4 Now ask the learners to write a very quick draft of the story. Set a time limit (20 minutes or so), and tell the learners not to worry about paragraphing or details but to get the main story down onto the page.

5 Ask the learners to swap stories with their partner and to give advice to each other about how to make the stories better.

6 Finally, the learners write the finished draft of their stories in class or for homework.

Variation

After the learners have written their stories, they could turn them into animated films. See Appendix B 8.12 for suggested animated-film websites.

7.10 Crazy stories or poems

Main goals	Structuring texts; writing and editing with grammatical accuracy
Level	Pre-intermediate (B1)
Time	20 minutes
Learning focus	Narrative writing
Preparation	Choose an automatic text generator suitable for your class (see Appendix B 7.10 for suggestions) which lets you input different parts of speech (nouns, adjectives, verbs, etc.), and then generates a story or poem automatically. The term 'crazy story' is used here because the results can be funny or crazy, depending on which verbs, adjectives, etc. the learners use.
Technical requirements	A computer room, or class set of laptops/netbooks/tablets. Alternatively, you can use just one internet-enabled computer in the classroom, with a projector.

Procedure

1 Tell the learners they are going to automatically generate a crazy story (or poem, depending on the website you have selected – some websites generate stories with the words and others poems). Tell them the result will be crazy or funny, depending on which words they select.

2 If the class is using multiple computers, send them to the website to generate their own texts. Otherwise, display the website and ask the learners to suggest the parts of speech that need to be entered (see example in Figure 7.4).

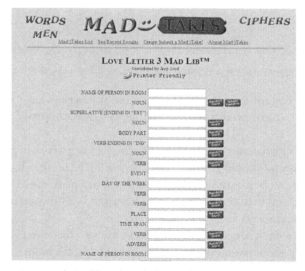

Figure 7.4: Automatic text generator: http://www.madtakes.com

3 The learners input the words in the table, as suggested by the labels. As they can enter any word they want, while they are doing so monitor and make sure they write the parts of speech as labelled.

4 Once the learners have generated a story, look at it together (or the different stories if they are doing the task individually), and focus upon the words the learners have entered. The nature of this type of site means the result is likely to be funny or silly. Ask the learners if changing the words they entered would create a funnier result.

5 Now focus on the randomly generated part of the texts. Ask the learners to notice the tenses and linking words (if it is a story), or number of words and descriptive language (if it is a poem). If looking at a story, make sure that they notice the beginning, middle and ending, and ask them to take note of the information that appears in each part. Also ask them to make a note of how the text is structured.

6 Try another automatically generated text from the same website. Repeat Steps 2 to 4 above, and then compare the two texts. Look at what is different and what is similar about the way the texts have been structured, the tenses that have been used, etc. The stories will be different depending on the different parts of speech that the learners have been asked to input.

7.11 Art stories

Main goals	Writing narratives; increasing vocabulary
Level	Pre-intermediate (B1) and above
Time	20 minutes
Learning focus	Descriptive writing
Preparation	Choose a website that has images of paintings that your learners can use (see Appendix B 7.11).
Technical requirements	A computer room, or class set of laptops/netbooks/tablets. Alternatively, the learners can choose the paintings they want to use at home.

Procedure

1   Ask the learners to work in groups to discuss the following: *What makes a good story?* Here are some discussion prompts to help:

   Structure: *How important is a strong beginning, middle and ending?*
   Characters: *A good story needs strong characters. True or false?*
   Setting: *The place of the story needs to be described well. Do you agree?*

2   After the learners have finished, ask them to share their ideas with the rest of the class and write their main ideas on the board.

3   Next, tell them they are going to work in pairs to create a story from a series of paintings that they find on the Web. Give the learners links to suggested website(s); tell them that the images they select must all be paintings (not photographs), and that there must be at least one image representing the setting of the story. The paintings can be related (by theme, period, etc.) or can be entirely different.

4   The learners find and copy and paste the images into the top half of a Word document and write their stories below.

5   When the learners have finished, ask them to look at each other's stories and to make suggestions about how they can be improved (adding or changing adjectives, etc.). While they are commenting on each other's stories, monitor the learners and make suggestions, too.

6   Finally, the stories can be printed out and a class booklet published, with copies given to the learners. Alternatively, the stories can be published online (in a class wiki or blog, for example).

Note

Adapted from Saumell, V. (2012), an idea presented at the 2012 IATEFL conference in Glasgow, Scotland.

7.12 Do you dream?

Main goals	Multimodality
Level	Intermediate (B1+) and above
Time	20 minutes
Learning focus	Descriptive writing
Preparation	Use an image bank and a dream dictionary (i.e. an A–Z reference guide to interpreting the meaning of images that occur in dreams). See Appendix B 7.12 for suggestions.
Technical requirements	Access to word processors, using a class set of laptops/netbooks/tablets, or a computer room, with internet access

Procedure

1 Ask the learners to talk in pairs about sleep and dreaming. They can use the following questions to help them:

How many hours do you sleep?
How many hours do people need to sleep?
Have you ever sleepwalked?
Do you remember what you dream about?
How often do you dream?
Have you ever had a recurring dream?
What about nightmares?
Do you ever daydream?

2 After the learners have shared what they talked about in pairs with the rest of the class, tell them they are going to write a dream and then interpret it. The dream they write could be one they have actually had, or a combination of different dreams or one they have made up (if they can't remember any dreams). Tell them that although they can make up a dream, the interpretation will probably be more interesting to them if it's about a real dream they have had.

3 Monitor and help the learners with language as they write. As some of the learners finish, you can encourage them to illustrate their dreams, using images from the Internet.

4 Introduce the learners to the dream-dictionary website, and show them how to search for the elements of their dream (e.g. falling and waking up before hitting the ground).

5 When all of the learners have finished writing, ask them to take turns to tell each other their dreams while their partners use the dream-dictionary website to interpret them.

6 Finish by asking the learners what they thought of the interpretations. Did they think they were accurate?

Variation 1

If multiple computers are not available, but you have one computer in the classroom, the learners can write on paper, and you can take turns interpreting their dreams, using the dream dictionary.

Variation 2

You can always ask the learners to start from the dream dictionary: choose some of the entries written there before the learners write the interpretations into the description of a fake dream.

7.13 **Message from the past**

Main goals	Writing different text-types (email)
Level	All levels
Time	20 minutes
Learning focus	Personal writing
Preparation	Access and set up an account with a 'future email' website (see Appendix B 7.13 for suggestions) – a website that allows you to write and then 'freeze' an email for a length of time (one month, a year, 10 years, etc.).
Technical requirements	One internet-enabled computer in the classroom, with a projector, or a computer room or class set of laptops/netbooks/tablets

Procedure

1 Ask the learners to imagine what their lives will be like in a) one year's time; b) five years' time and c) 10 years' time, and to work in pairs or small groups to make predictions. As well as telling each other their predictions, they should also make a note of them. While doing the activity, the teacher should monitor and correct mistakes, etc. With advanced levels, this activity is ideal for asking the learners to use examples of the future perfect or future continuous.

2 Tell learners to go to the future email website. If there is only one computer, you can write a class email to a learner the class chooses.

3 Assuming each learner has access to a computer, ask the learners to write an email addressed to their future selves (see example below), and add the future date that the emails should be sent (in one year's time, five years' time, and 10 years' time).

> **Dear older Sophia (2023)**
>
> When you get this email (in 2023), you will be 31 years old. I imagine you now will have finished studying and will be working as an architect. Will you have started the business you thought you wanted to set up in 2013?
>
> What about your personal life? I think you now will be married, and you will have the two children you wanted. Will they be a boy and a girl?
>
> Well, I hope all is well with you. Please send a letter to me from the future, and let your past self know how you are.
>
> Best wishes
> Younger Sophia (2013)

Variation

Instead of writing letters to their future selves, or as a follow-up to this activity, ask the learners to write an email or letter to their younger (i.e. past) self. Tell them to imagine that a time machine exists, and they can give their younger self some advice.

7.14 Report writing

Main goals	Reporting/summarising; formal language, etc.
Level	Pre-intermediate (B1) and above
Time	20 minutes
Learning focus	Professional writing
Preparation	This activity works best as a collaboration between different classes, either at the same institution or as part of a collaborative project with another organisation (see Chapter 10 *Project work* for ideas how to organise this). Choose a website which allows learners to create survey questions (see Appendix B 7.14 for suggestions).
Technical requirements	A computer room, or class set of laptops/netbooks/tablets. If your class doesn't have access to a computer for each learner, part of the activity could be done by the learners at home.

Procedure

1   Tell the learners they are going to write a report about something which interests them or an issue that concerns them. First of all, they should think about an overall question for their topic. Some examples could be:

What makes a successful film?　　　　　*How can we stop global warming?*
Should we all become vegetarian?　　　　*What is the best job in the world?*
What changes does our town need?　　　　*What are the advantages of being famous?*

2   Once the learners have decided their overall question, ask them to break it down into specific or related questions, the answers to which will help them answer the main one. Examples for *Should we all become vegetarian?* could be:

Do you like animals?　　　　　　　　　*Is eating meat healthy?*
Could you survive without meat?　　　　　*Are vegetarians less or more healthy?*

3   Tell the learners that after they have asked each other the questions in groups, or as a class survey, they will need to interpret the answers and transform them into sentences that they can use in the report. For example, if most learners say they think vegetarians are very healthy, then this translates to: *Most people think vegetarians are very healthy, so we should stop eating so much meat.*

4   Tell the learners they are now going to create a written survey online, using a website that creates survey questions, and introduce them to the website. When the survey is complete, explain that you are going to ask a different class to complete it. Then next class (after the other class has responded to the questions), the learners look at the results and start writing the report.

5   Ask the learners to start their report by drawing conclusions, based on the answers to their survey, and then to report the details. The learners can write sentences analysing the statistics, and they can finish by saying what their opinion is and whether they think the report reflects what people think in general, or if it only reflects the opinions of the particular group of people who completed the survey.

7.15 Sensationalist reporting

Main goals	Writing different genres/text-types
Level	Pre-intermediate (B1) and above
Time	20 minutes
Learning focus	Professional writing (B1)
Preparation	Find an online newspaper website to show your learners, or use the paper version of a newspaper if you have access to an example (see Appendix B 7.15 for suggestions).
Technical requirements	Learners should each have a digital camera (or their mobile phone camera) to use outside the classroom. In class, an IWB, or computer with projector, is necessary to display the learners' work.

Procedure

1 Write the word 'sensationalism' on the board, and ask the learners if they know what the word means. Show them the cover of a sensationalist newspaper (or find one on the Web) to demonstrate the types of stories that make the front page.

2 Ask the learners to look at some of the sensationalist news articles to get an idea of the format. Tell them that usually a news article has the following parts:

Headline: a short, attention-getting statement about the event
Lead paragraph: usually contains the *who, what, where, when, why* and *how* of the event
Explanation: any details the reader might want to know, including direct quotes from witnesses
Additional information: the least important information, including reference to similar events, which goes at the end

Tell them that whereas a standard news article is concerned with reporting the facts, a sensationalist news article is all about making the story more interesting, even if the writer has to exaggerate or make up some of the facts.

3 Tell them that their homework assignment is to write a sensationalist story, based on some photographs they take outside the class.

4 Ask the learners to write their story and then to send it to you before the next class.

5 Display the stories on the IWB, or using the projector, and role play being the editorial board of a sensationalist newspaper. Should you publish the story? Or would you get into trouble if you did? Do the same role play for all of the stories, and also decide which of the stories should go on the front page.

7.16 Biographies

Main goals	Writing biographies; summarising
Level	Intermediate (B1+) and above
Time	20 minutes
Learning focus	Professional writing
Preparation	Find an example timeline on a timeline website that your learners will like (see Appendix B 7.16 for suggestions), and create a class account on the website.
Technical requirements	A computer room, or class set of laptops/netbooks/tablets. Alternatively, the learners can do the activity for homework.

Procedure

1 Ask the learners if they know what a 'timeline' is, and then show them an example (see Figure 7.5).

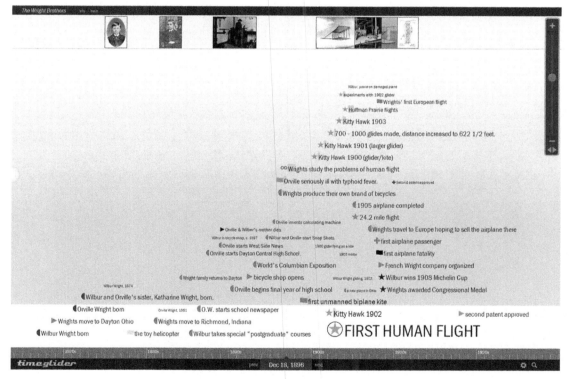

Figure 7.5: A timeline created with http://www.timeglider.com

2 Tell the learners to work in pairs and think about a subject they would like to write a timeline for (a famous person, someone from history, a character from a book, a company, sport or hobby, etc.).

3 Once the learners have decided on their subject, ask them to go to the website you have chosen and to log in with the class account. Tell them they will use the website to start creating their timeline.

4   Tell the learners to use the Web to research their subjects. They will need to read about the topic and then summarise each key moment in their timelines with a title and a short paragraph to go with the title.

5   Tell the learners they can also add photos and videos where appropriate.

Variation

Instead of a specific biography site, you could take advantage of the class wiki (Activity 7.2), if you are using one, and get learners to write their biographies there.

7.17 Translate to SMS

Main goals	Spelling
Level	All levels
Time	20 minutes
Learning focus	Spelling and language for texting
Preparation	Use a website that shows and translates standard English to SMS messages. See Appendix B 7.17 for more information and suggested websites.
Technical requirements	One internet-enabled computer in the classroom, with a projector (or IWB)

Procedure

1 Ask the learners if they know any of the typical abbreviations used when sending SMS (text messages) in English using a mobile phone, or, alternatively, you can offer some abbreviations. Here are some examples:

CUL8R (= see you later)   *THNX (= thanks)*   *LOL (= laugh out loud)*
2day (= today)   *B4 (= before)*   *k (= OK)*

2 Ask the learners to think of some other English examples, and translate them into SMS on the website you have chosen earlier.
3 Give the learners a paragraph of standard English, and ask them to abbreviate it for an SMS message. When they have finished, check the text using the SMS translation website.

Variation

Instead of giving the learners a standard English text to translate into SMS, do the reverse, and get them to translate an SMS text (or texts) into standard English.

7.18 Pros and cons

Main goals	Writing different genres/text-types
Level	Intermediate (B1+) and above
Time	20 minutes
Learning focus	Argumentative essay (writing about pros and cons)
Preparation	Use a website with lists of pros and cons (see Appendix B 7.18 for suggestions).
Technical requirements	A computer room, or class set of laptops/netbooks/tablets, with internet access

Procedure

1 Write the phrase *pros and cons* on the board, and ask the learners if they know what it means. Tell them that it can also be expressed as *for or against* and *advantages and disadvantages*, and show them some examples of pros and cons (see Appendix B 7.18).

2 Ask the learners to work in pairs and think of something they are interested in that has pros and cons. Write some examples on the board to help them:

Plastic surgery   *Owning a dog*   *Changing jobs*   *Living abroad*

3 Once the learners have chosen a subject, ask them to make two lists, one of pros and one of cons, either on the website you have chosen or in Word.

4 Once the learners have made their lists, ask them to evaluate the results and then decide how best to present the information in an essay. You can also ask the learners to look for examples of this type of argumentative essay online and to examine the features of these essays before they write one themselves.

5 After the learners have completed Step 4, they can write the essay in class or for homework.

7.19 Social network CVs

Main goals	Writing different text-types (e.g. a CV)
Level	Intermediate (B1+) and above (especially Business English learners)
Time	20 minutes
Learning focus	Professional writing
Preparation	Ask the learners to set up an account with a social network that is professionally focused, where members post their curricula vitae (see Appendix B 7.19 for suggestions). Start by creating an online CV for yourself, and fill in your professional experience.
Technical requirements	One internet-enabled computer in the classroom with a projector (if the learners are to do the activity at home), or a computer room or class set of laptops/netbooks/tablets

Procedure

1   Open the social-networking site, and show the learners your professional profile. Tell them that this activity can help them build an online CV that they can share with potential employers.

2   Ask the learners to look for some examples of online CVs by people who are in the same field/line of work as they are in now, or hope to be in one day. Ask them to make note of any vocabulary/ language that these people have used that they think they could use when writing their own CVs / professional profiles.

3   Ask the learners to have a go at writing their own CVs, using the site. If learners are not yet working, they can create an imaginary CV. Once they have done this, in the next class look at what the learners have written, and give suggestions as to how their CVs could be improved.

4   Finish with the learners playing the role of career advisers, looking at their classmates' CVs and suggesting different jobs that might be suitable. Help them with vocabulary for professions they may not know.

7.20 Academic writing

Main goals	Writing an example text of a specific genre, e.g. an academic abstract for English for Academic Purposes (EAP); choosing the right register/style
Level	Upper-intermediate (B2) and above
Time	20 minutes
Learning focus	Academic writing
Preparation	Choose a website that has a selection of texts of the genre you have chosen (e.g. for academic abstracts, either a conference website or an academic journal would be suitable, depending on your learners' needs).
Technical requirements	One internet-enabled computer in the classroom, with a projector, or a computer room or class set of laptops/netbooks/tablets

Procedure

1 Present a specific genre of text the learners may need to write (e.g. an academic abstract) and explain what it is (e.g. an abstract is a short summary of an article).

2 Tell the learners what information is required when writing this specific genre of text, and write a list on the board of the generic features of the text-type. For instance, for an academic abstract:

Problem statement: *What is the problem your research tries to solve?*
Approach/methods: *What did you do to get the results? What was the procedure?*
Results: *What were the findings of the research? What did you learn?*
Conclusion: *What are the implications of your findings?*

3 Ask the learners to write a text of the specified genre, and then get them to compare what they have written with a partner.

4 Go to the website you have selected earlier, and find examples of the formal features of the text-type (length of text, register, type of language used, structure, etc.) from actual examples (in this case, abstracts). The learners can do this step on their own if you have access to multiple computers.

5 If you have set up a class wiki (see Activity 7.2), then you can ask the learners to select good examples (i.e. ones they think are well written) and copy and paste them into the wiki in order to use them as class models.

6 Once you have some examples the learners are happy with, look together at the features of the text-type, and ask the learners to make some generalisations which will help them write similar texts.

7 Ask the learners to edit the texts they wrote earlier. When they have finished, share the texts with the rest of the class, and ask for comments and corrections.

8 Speaking

For many years, the computer had generally been more associated with applications in the area of written language than spoken language (Pennington & Esling, 1996: 153), but with new developments in Web 2.0 and teachers' and learners' increased access to the Internet for language learning and teaching, this focus has been changing.

Taking advantage of the expanded application of computers, this chapter includes both activities that use technology as a stimulus for discussion and others that suggest recording learners using Web 2.0 tools, which is one of the best ways technology can help learners improve their speaking skills. Nowadays, it is easy to record learners speaking, as most mobile telephones have built-in voice recorders, and there are many free web tools that enable you to do such recordings, as well.

There are many advantages to recording learners speaking. To begin with, as it is difficult for a teacher to listen to learners in a crowded classroom, asking learners to make recordings makes it easier for a teacher to assess how well a learner is speaking and to help them improve. When learners record themselves speaking, they can also listen to how they sound, and this should help them understand how well they speak English and what they need to do to get better. The fact that they are being recorded also makes it more likely that they will want to perform at their best, and many will practise what they say or record themselves several times before they are happy with the result. This means they spend more time thinking about how they speak. In particular, setting these types of tasks for homework can be a very rewarding way of using technology.

When the computer is being used as a tool, Levy (1997) suggests that the teacher will most likely be involved in some learner training; that is, part of the teacher's time will be spent showing the learners how best to learn with the tool. These tools are often asynchronous (i.e. communication does not take place at the same time that the learner is recording) and can show improvements in speaking confidence and quality of output 'through preparation, repetition and re-recording' (Pop, 2011: 114).

Computer Mediated Communication (CMC), which happens when two or more networked computers are used for communication, is also a feature in this chapter. CMC, using voice, is an ideal medium for collaborative learning and is perhaps one of the most exciting possibilities that technology can offer the language teacher and learners. With the Internet entering more classrooms, free tools such as *Skype* (http://www.skype.com) now make it possible for teachers to break out of the four walls and invite others to participate. Activity 8.8 takes advantage of such tools, and there are more ideas in Chapter 10 *Project work*.

Most of the activities in this chapter deal with fluency (8.3, 8.5–8.10, 8.12, 8.13), accuracy (8.3, 8.5, 8.8, 8.11, 8.13), pronunciation (8.2, 8.3, 8.5, 8.8, 8.13) and learner autonomy (8.1).

The chapter includes ideas for using technology to encourage speaking practice, both in class and at home. There are both speaking as monologue activities and interactive speaking activities. The former include such areas as reading aloud, and rehearsed and improvised monologue, while the latter include scripted and unscripted dialogue.

Access to internet-enabled computers with a headset or separate microphone is among the most useful tools for these activities. The technology that can be used also includes audio-editing software, voice recorders and audio-recording websites, internet telephony, mobile phones, webcams, video-interview websites, computer games and virtual worlds.

As I hope to show, there are now many tools available, and many ways in which technology can be used to enhance speaking. Hopefully, this chapter will help you to help your learners improve their speaking through the use of appropriate technology.

References

Levy, M. (1997) *Computer-Assisted Language Learning*, Oxford: Oxford University Press.

Pennington, M. C. and Esling, H. (1996) 'Computer-assisted development of spoken language skills', in M. C. Pennington (ed.), *The Power of CALL*, Houston: Athelstan, pp. 153–89.

Pop, A. (2011) 'Integrating asynchronous writing and speaking tools for EFL optimisation', in T. Pattison (ed.), *IATEFL 2011 Brighton Conference Selections*, Canterbury: IATEFL, pp. 113–15.

8.1 Spoken journals

Main goals	Encouraging learners to keep a spoken dialogue journal, reflecting on their language learning in class
Level	All levels
Time	10 minutes
Learning focus	Learner autonomy
Preparation	Give your learners your email address so they can send you an audio file, and introduce them to a simple audio-recording tool (see Appendix B 8.1 for suggested websites).
Technical requirements	All of the learners need an internet-enabled computer (with a microphone) to use from home.

Procedure

1 Explain to the learners that they are going to reflect on their learning by keeping a spoken journal, and introduce them to the website you have chosen, showing them how it works by making a short recording and playing it back.

2 Hand out some questions you would like them to answer. The questions could be about what you have done in class or about their experience of learning the language. Here are some examples:

What things did you find useful / did you like doing in class today?
What things didn't you find useful / didn't you like doing in class today?
In general, what part of learning the language do you find most difficult?
What do you think you need help with now?
Are there any questions you want to ask me?

3 Tell the learners that each of them should record themselves at home and send you an email with the link to the recording (the website automatically stores the audio recording online). Let the learners know that the journal will be a private dialogue between you and them, and that you will record an answer and send the link to the audio recording back to them.

4 When you receive an email from a learner, with the link to an audio file, listen to the recording and then record and send a reply, without too much delay. Like written dialogue journals (see Chapter 7 *Writing*), the focus should be on meaning, rather than form, when you record your reply, although there's nothing to stop you taking a note of language that each individual learner needs to work on.

5 The spoken journal does not always have to be about the learners' language learning. The next time you decide to do this activity for homework, ask the learners to respond to different questions (e.g. about what they did at the weekend, etc.).

6 Persuade the learners to record their journals on a regular basis (once weekly, for instance); doing so should build their confidence in speaking and encourage learner autonomy. Because the learners are able to listen to themselves, too, they will usually try to improve their spoken performance and should become more fluent and accurate over time. Remember that the questions you ask them to answer can be modified to reflect specific activities in class, or specific needs of the learners.

Variation 1
If learners all have smartphones, you can use an app, such as http://audioboo.fm/, instead of the web-based tool suggested above. If you want to add video, then http://mailvu.com/ can be used.

Variation 2
Use the audio-recording tool for spoken homework assignments, and instead of making it private between teacher and learner, publish the links to the learners' voice recordings on a class wiki or blog (see Chapter 2 *Building a learning community*). Then encourage the learners to listen to each other.

Variation 3
Apart from using the audio journal for teacher-to-learner communication, you can encourage learner-to-learner interaction. Get the learners to ask each other questions for homework about a topic the teacher (or the learners themselves) decides on, and to respond to each other. If you use this option, ask them to include you when they send the email with the link to their recording. You can also make the recordings public, as in Variation 2.

Variation 4
For ESP students, you can ask them to do certain tasks specific to the subject / area of interest (e.g. tourism students can leave a message replying to a customer complaint, etc.). If the learners decide on the task themselves, make sure they give you a copy of the task so that you know what the recording is in response to.

8.2 Speaking pictures

Main goals	Monologue; pronunciation
Level	All levels (young learners)
Time	20 minutes
Learning focus	To encourage speaking and work on pronunciation, and to share young learners' work with parents
Preparation	Set up a class account at a website that allows you to upload images and record audio files to go with them (see Appendix B 8.2 for suggestions). These websites allow you to upload a photo, or drawing, and to record an audio description, etc. of the photograph (see Variation below for older learners).
Technical requirements	A voice recorder, or computer with microphone, the learners can use either in class or at home. The teacher also needs access to a digital camera, or document scanner, to capture the learners' drawings after the classroom activity. The teachers will then upload the audio files and photographs (or scanned documents) to the website.

Procedure

1 Although you don't need a computer in the classroom for this activity, if you do have one, then you can play an example video on the audio/image website and tell the learners they are going to do an activity where they animate a photo or a drawing. The website in Figure 8.1 lets you upload a photograph (or drawing) and an audio file, and then it automatically animates the mouth of a character to the recorded audio, with a fun result.

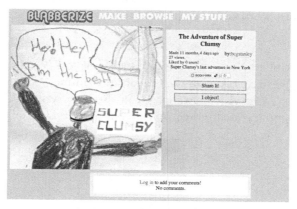

Figure 8.1: Learner work in Blabberize: http://blabberize.com

2 Give out sheets of paper, and ask the learners to work in pairs or small groups to write a story in their notebooks. Then get them to work together to draw a picture illustrating it. The story can relate to whatever you have been doing recently in the classroom with the learners, or if you want something different, then you can use one of the story starters below:

a) *Scientists have recently discovered a talking animal in the jungle, and they bring it back to the city, but it escapes as they are taking it to the zoo. What happens next?*

b) *Last weekend, you were out riding your bicycle when you saw a strange light in the sky. The light became bigger, and then you saw it was an alien spaceship. The spaceship landed and a door opened. What happened next?*

c) *You go to the beach with your friends and find a map showing hidden treasure. The map leads you to a cave on the beach. You go inside. What happens next?*

3 While the learners are writing their stories, help them with vocabulary and ideas (e.g. with an animal story, help them with the names of animals, verbs of motion, etc.). When they have written the basic story, give them coloured pencils and, using a sheet of paper (per group), ask them to draw the story with different frames, as if it were a comic strip.

4 Before recording the stories, ask each group to rehearse them, and help the learners with their pronunciation. Then record the stories when you and they are happy with their performance. Each learner in the group should play a part if his/her drawing/story involves multiple characters, but if not, ask each learner to take turns saying a sentence.

5 If you are using a voice recorder in the classroom (this could be your mobile phone), while the learners are drawing their stories, you can take each group aside and ask them to record their stories. Then upload this file, with their drawing, later. Alternatively, take each group to the computer to record the audio.

6 After class, scan the pictures, or take a photo of each one with a digital camera and upload each picture, along with the learners' accompanying mp3 audio file. When the picture is uploaded, you will be prompted to identify any mouths in the learners' drawings: the result will show the characters 'talking' along to the recording (i.e. the mouths in the pictures will move).

7 Watch and listen to the finished stories next class, and give the learners the link to the webpage so that they can share their work with their parents, too.

Variation

With older learners, you can use a more serious tool such as *VoiceThread* and ask them to talk about a favourite photograph they have taken, or their favourite painting. With this tool, you can upload multiple images, and people who visit the webpage can also leave written, audio and video comments. *VoiceThread* also has an application for the *Apple iPhone* and *iPad* (see image in Figure 8.2).

Figure 8.2: Image of the http://www.voicethread.com app for the iPod Touch/iPhone

8.3 Reading aloud

Main goals	Reading aloud
Level	All levels
Time	Several classes (30–35 minutes per class)
Learning focus	Fluency; accuracy; pronunciation
Preparation	Ask the learners to come to class with their mobile phones (to use as voice recorders). Choose a text, or part of one, for the learners to read. Alternatively, if you have learners who are preparing for a formal presentation (e.g. for business), they could use their presentations.
Technical requirements	One voice recorder for each group of learners (mobile phones can be used)

Procedure

1 Tell the learners they are going to be recording themselves reading aloud, and so they should try to sound as natural as possible while they do so. Give them the texts they are to use, and ask them to read them aloud, rehearsing the pronunciation.

2 Ask the learners to divide the text into tone units (i.e. the strings of words between pauses) by marking with a line where the pause will be. Encourage them to ask you when they want help with pronunciation. If you are a non-native speaker and would like a native model for learners, you may wish to ask a native speaker to record the text for you before the start of the class.

3 Split the learners into groups, and ask them to take turns reading aloud (e.g. a paragraph each). The learners should practise their recordings until they are ready to record them. When the learners are recording, encourage them to listen to themselves and re-record if they are not happy with the results.

4 When the learners have finished, ask them to play the recordings back and to tell you what they thought of the activity (did it help them with pronunciation, etc.?). You could also formalise the activity, giving points for clarity, fluency (e.g. lack of hesitations) and communicative effectiveness.

8.4 Unscripted and scripted dialogues

Main goals	Dialogue; interactive
Level	All levels
Time	30 minutes
Learning focus	Fluency; accuracy; pronunciation
Preparation	Choose an audio website to use for this activity (see Appendix B 8.4 for suggestions), unless you choose to use voice recorders (on mobile phones, for example).
Technical requirements	A computer room, or class set of computers. Alternatively, use voice recorders (e.g. learner mobile phones).

Procedure

1 Ask the learners to work in pairs and have a conversation about a particular subject that interests them (e.g. what they did at the weekend, where they are going on holiday, etc.). Tell them to speak for about a minute or so and to record themselves using the audio software, or voice recorders.

2 Now ask the learners to listen back to the conversation and to transcribe it, writing exactly what they said.

3 Once the learners have the written record, ask them to rewrite it to make it better (i.e. with fewer errors / expanded content). They can exchange their transcripts with other pairs to get a second opinion, or the teacher could code the text for self-correction.

4 When the learners have finished rewriting their conversation, get them to record this scripted version.

5 Finally, ask the learners to listen to both versions of their recording and to decide which one they prefer, and why.

8.5 Mobile circle game

Main goals	To encourage learners to get to know other classmates by sharing information and talking about what they use their mobile phones for
Level	All levels
Time	10 minutes
Learning focus	Fluency; personal information; mobile-phone vocabulary
Preparation	Teachers should adjust vocabulary, and questions, to the learners' level.
Technical requirements	Mobile phones (optional)

Procedure

1   Sit the class in small circles (of about four or five), and tell the learners they are going to use their mobile phones to talk about themselves and their lives.

2   You can begin by modelling the activity. Take out your mobile phone, and introduce yourself by saying, for example, 'I'm Julia, and I don't make many calls on my mobile. I do send lots of text messages, though.'

3   Encourage the next learner in the circle to repeat some of the information and respond to it: 'You're Julia, and you send lots of text messages. I'm Roger. I also send lots of text messages, but I mainly use my mobile for playing games.'

4   The third learner repeats and responds to something the second learner said, and so it goes on. Ask the learners to keep the conversation going, talking about different topics related to their mobile phone. You can write some of these prompts on the board to help them:

calls　　*text messages (SMS)*　　*alarm clock*　　*games*　　*apps*　　*dictionary*
camera　　*social networking*　　*Internet*　　*video*　　*music*　　*news*

5   Finish the activity with a class discussion about mobile phones. Here are some question prompts to help you:

How important is a mobile phone to you?
Do you ever leave the house without it?
How often do you switch your mobile off?
Do you know anyone who doesn't have a mobile?
What's the most important feature on your mobile?
Is there anything your mobile doesn't do that you wish it did?

Note
Include yourself in the class discussion, in order to encourage a communicative atmosphere in your classroom.

8.6 Guided tour

Main goals	Monologue; giving information to a visitor about places to visit
Level	All levels
Time	40 minutes
Learning focus	Fluency; describing the features of places and why people should visit them
Preparation	Choose and register with an audio-guide website (see Appendix B 8.6 for suggested websites), and create an example. If appropriate, download an audio-guide app on your smartphone if you have one, and it's available.
Technical requirements	A computer in the classroom, and a voice recorder if possible. If you want learners to record directly to the website, then a computer room, or class set of tablets/netbooks/laptops, with internet access and microphone/headsets, will be needed.

Procedure

1 Ask the learners if they have ever had to show a visitor around. If so, where did they take the visitor? Tell the class that they are going to choose three places (famous sights, or ones that are culturally interesting) to recommend to a visitor on a day-trip to their home, and then they are going to each record a brief general description about the place for an audio-guide website. Tell the learners that they will then put the places in order to create an itinerary for a visitor.

2 Introduce the learners to the website, and choose one or two real examples that people have recorded about a place they might want to visit some day. Tell them that if they have a smartphone, then visitors can listen to these recordings using an app. The app lets a visitor listen to a description of a place during the visit itself. If you and any of the learners have smartphones, you might want to download an audio-guide app to see how it works.

3 Ask the learners each to pick a place in their hometown. If they come from the same town or city, don't let them choose the same place to speak about, and make sure you have a good range of places that a visitor might want to visit. The learners can use the Web to research the places and find information about them: they can look for the official websites of the place they have chosen and/or online tourist guides with information.

4 Ask the learners to write notes about the place they have chosen, including the main features of interest, and anything surprising about the place that locals may know.

5 Now ask the learners to turn these notes into a text that they can record, and which will become their contribution to the website. Encourage the learners to rehearse their texts (not to read them aloud) and speak directly from notes, because they will sound more natural this way. Help the learners with any language they may need during this stage, and help them correct any errors, and their pronunciation, while they are rehearsing what they will say.

6 Once learners have thoroughly rehearsed what they will say, you can ask them to record into a voice recorder. If possible, they can do this alone in another room. Alternatively, you can take the class to a computer room to record directly to the audio-guide website, using the class account that you set up earlier.

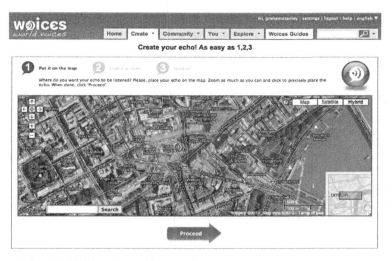

Figure 8.3: Audio-guide website, World Voices: http://www.woices.com

7 On the website, learners (or the teacher if you are not using multiple computers) can find the places they recommended on the map, and then put a place-marker on each (as in the image in Figure 8.3) and upload the audio file to go with the map.
8 Each of the recordings needs to be either uploaded or recorded directly to the website. Once finished, back in the classroom, you can connect the recordings that are in the same city or town together in logical order, as a guided tour (i.e. an itinerary for the visitor), and then listen to the learners' work as a class.

Variation 1

Make the activity more fun for younger learners by designing a treasure hunt, with audio clues through a particular city they live in or know.

Variation 2

This activity works well as part of a longer project with another class in a different country. Each class prepares an itinerary for the learners in the other class, telling them more about the city or town they live in. See Chapter 10 *Project work* for more ideas on how to organise this option.

8.7 Virtual-world tourists

Main goals	Motivating speaking
Level	All levels
Time	30–40 minutes
Learning focus	Fluency; accuracy; pronunciation
Preparation	Choose an online 3D virtual world (i.e. a computer-based simulated environment where users can interact with each other), and create an account. Before doing this, make sure you can install the required software on the computer in the classroom. Choose an area of the virtual world that is similar to a country in the real world. See Appendix B 8.7 for suggestions of virtual worlds and areas to visit.
Technical requirements	One computer in the classroom, with a set of speakers and microphone, and a voice recorder to record the learners speaking

Procedure

1 Tell the learners that you are going to visit a virtual world and you want them to take turns to describe what they see to the class, imagining that they are visiting the place on behalf of a virtual-world travel agency.

2 Ask one of the learners to control the *avatar* (i.e. a 3D representation of a person in a virtual world). As the learner moves the avatar, you will see different aspects of the place you are visiting. Start recording and describe the place, talking aloud, as it is revealed to the class. After a minute or so, ask the learner to continue with the description, and ask for a volunteer to control where the avatar goes.

Figure 8.4: Image of virtual world

3 You can choose to visit cities, either ones based on real-world cities (see image in Figure 8.4 above) or fantastical places that only exist in the virtual world.

4 Continue recording the learners speaking, and when the tour is over, or in the following class, listen back to the recording and focus upon parts of it that could be improved upon. Ask the learners to transcribe parts of the recording and then rewrite them, improving upon what they have recorded.

5 Follow up the virtual visit by asking the learners to write about their visit. They can imagine they are writing an article for a travel magazine or website, or they could write an email to friends, recommending that they visit the same place, too.

8.8 Talk-radio speaking

Main goals	Interactive speaking
Level	All levels, particularly young learners and teenagers
Time	Several classes (40–60 minutes per class)
Learning focus	Fluency; accuracy; pronunciation
Preparation	Be prepared to record a complete radio show with learners, unless you have time and are competent with audio-editing software (see Appendix B 8.8 for suggested websites).
Technical requirements	One computer in the classroom, with a set of speakers and a microphone. Alternatively, multiple computers can be used.

Procedure

1 Tell the learners that they are going to create a 'talk-radio' show, and ask them if they know what one is (i.e. a radio show based on information, rather than music).

2 Ask the learners to predict what sections the radio programme includes. Some suggested answers include:

news   gossip   interviews   weather   sports   horoscope   politics

Confirm with the learners which sections to include in the programme (e.g. three to four different ones), and, to help them, decide on the order in which they will appear.

3 Tell the learners they are going to work together to prepare their section of the talk-radio show, and ask them to work on the script. If they are responsible for the news, ask them to write brief summaries about two to three news events (real or made-up). If writing the script of the gossip section, they could write an interview with a famous celebrity. While they are preparing their scripts, monitor and help with language, as needed.

4 In the next class, when the learners have their finished scripts, decide on an order for the show, and start to record the sections of the programme, in order. Ask the other learners to be quiet while each group records their part. Continue until the recording has finished.

5 You can finish by playing back the complete radio show (or wait until the next class to do so).

Note

See Chapter 5 *Listening* for ideas on how to use this programme with other skill areas.

8.9 Current affairs

Main goals	Interactive speaking
Level	All levels
Time	10 minutes
Learning focus	Questions and answers; stimulating a discussion about current affairs
Preparation	Create a class account on a website where it is possible to do video interviews (see Appendix B 8.9 for suggested websites).
Technical requirements	An internet-enabled computer in the classroom. If you want the learners to respond in class, then you will need a computer equipped with a webcam and microphone. Otherwise, you can ask them to respond for homework, but they will need a webcam.

Procedure

1 Tell the learners that they are going to create questions that will be used to poll the class on a given topic and record a video response to each other's questions, role-playing a TV interview.

2 Ask the learners if they have ever been approached by a TV or radio reporter for an opinion about something topical / in the news. If anyone has, get them to tell the rest of the class about the experience. If nobody has, then ask them to imagine the kinds of questions that the TV or radio reporter would ask, and write the questions on the board. Here are some example questions on the subject of education:

Do you think it is easier or more difficult to be a learner nowadays?
Do learners have to work harder in order to be successful these days?
What do you think about the proposed changes to the education system?

3 Tell the learners that they are going to be interviewed about their opinions on a particular subject / something in the news, and decide together what that subject will be.

4 Ask the learners to work in small groups to brainstorm the questions about the subject, and then decide together a small number of these (four or five) that seem to be the best ones.

5 Log into the class account on the video-interview website, and create the poll, writing in the questions that everyone agreed on. On this type of website, the questions are usually written and the responses are video recordings.

6 If you have a webcam and want the learners to answer the questions in class, then ask for a volunteer to play the role of the person being interviewed on TV. Record their responses to the questions they are happy to answer. Tell them they do not have to record an answer to every question.

7 Continue with other volunteers from the class. After each person has spoken, ask the learners if they agree with the various opinions expressed on the topic. Be prepared to let the discussion continue if it is interesting, at the expense of recording more learners (the activity can always be continued for homework).

8   If you run out of time, then suggest the learners add more video responses to the questions from home.

9   As a follow-up, you can watch some of the video recordings next class and look at the language the learners used, helping them to improve upon it and asking them to notice any particularly good use of English.

Variation 1

Use this activity as part of a longer project with another class in a different country, with your learners asking the other class questions and then answering the questions the other class asks. See Chapter 10 *Project work* for more ideas on how to organise this option.

Variation 2

If the learners are younger, instead of focusing on current affairs you can ask about something more suited to their lives and interests (how they feel about exams, homework, etc.).

8.10 Train or coach?

Main goals	Comparing train and coach journey planners, and deciding which is best
Level	Elementary (A2) – Upper-intermediate (B2)
Time	20–30 minutes
Learning focus	Fluency; language used for planning a trip; language of comparison (*Going by train is faster*; *The coach is the cheapest way*, etc.)
Preparation	Choose two journey-planning websites that are in English, one with a timetable for coach transport and another for train transport. In the example in Figure 8.5, the UK's National Express website has been used, but any travel website with similar journey planners can be used. As this activity relies on learners knowing something about the places to visit, it works well as part of a project about a particular country (see Variation 1).
Technical requirements	A computer room, or class set of tablets/netbooks/laptops, with internet access

Figure 8.5: National Express coach and train journey planners: http://www.nationalexpress.com

Procedure

1   Ask the learners to work in pairs, and tell them to imagine they are all on holiday in a particular country (e.g. the UK) and about to go on a journey somewhere else in the country.

2   Tell them they have to decide how they are going to get there – by coach or by train – and their decision will depend on their own preferences (how much it costs, how long it takes, etc.). The learners should choose a place they know so they don't have to research basic information (such as how far away it is).

3 Generate and ask questions based on the order of the information required in the journey-planning website. Give each pair of learners time to decide the answers to the questions, and ask one of them to write down their decisions. Some example questions could be:

Where are you exactly? (i.e. which city/town?)
Where do you want to travel to?
When do you want to leave? (i.e. the date)
What time do you want to arrive?
How long are you staying for?
When are you coming back?

4 Now with the computers on, hand out a teacher-created *Journey-comparison worksheet* (like the example below) to each pair of learners, and ask half of them to go to the travel website for the coach and the other half for the train, writing down travel information for either train or coach.

Journey-comparison worksheet

From:
To:
Date:

Train	Coach
Departure time:	Departure time:
Arrival time:	Arrival time:
Duration:	Duration:
Transfers:	Transfers:
Cost:	Cost:

From *Language Learning with Technology* © Cambridge University Press 2013   PHOTOCOPIABLE

5 Once the learners have finished, ask them to form a group with those who researched travel in a different way and to share their information. The purpose is to decide whether they are going to travel by train or coach. Ask a spokesperson for each group to report their decisions to the class, along with the reasons for their choices.

Variation 1

Use the above activity as part of a longer project about travelling to a particular country. After researching places to visit, the learners plan a tour of the country and then check the dates/times of coaches and trains to a number of destinations. See Chapter 10 *Project work* for more ideas on this option.

Variation 2

Learners role play a travel agency and work in pairs, with one learner (the travel agent) using the computer to ask questions, and the other (the customer) using the journey-comparison worksheet. The learner playing the travel agent uses the website to find the information, and the traveller decides which option to book.

8.11 Discussions of interest

Main goals	Dialogue; engaging learners in discussion
Level	Pre-intermediate (B1) and above
Time	30–40 minutes
Learning focus	Fluency; learners start a discussion about something that interests them and respond to their classmates' discussions.
Preparation	Choose an *audio-voice forum* website (this is similar to an internet forum where people ask written questions and leave answers). See Appendix B 8.11 for suggested websites.
Technical requirements	A computer room, or a class set of tablets/netbooks/laptops, with internet access, and headsets (or microphones and earphones). Learners need to have email accounts.

Procedure

1 Tell learners they are going to record their opinions on a website and that first, they are going to listen to a few examples done by other speakers.

2 Introduce the learners to the audio-voice forum, and ask them to find a subject that interests them in one of the forums and to listen to what people have to say. Alternatively, you can pre-select a few discussions you think will interest the learners, and direct the learners to them. In the example shown (see Figure 8.6), you can see a talk group that has been set up specifically for language learners. The learners click on one of the titles (e.g. *Your future*) and then are able to listen to a number of different speakers talking about the topic.

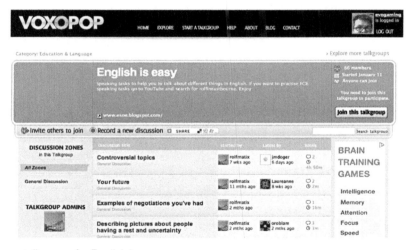

Figure 8.6: Voxopop talk group for English learners

3   After the learners have had a chance to listen to some discussions, stop them, and ask if there were any they found particularly interesting. At this point, you can play one or two of the discussions for the whole class. The purpose is to show the learners how the software works, and it is a warm-up to the learners recording themselves, speaking on the website.

4   Ask the learners to work in pairs, and for one of them to register and create an account on the site. Tell them they are going to create their own discussion. Ask them to think of a topic they would like to ask people to talk about. If any of them are stuck for ideas, you can suggest one of the following:

A TV show / film I've watched recently *The best place in the world*
My first day at school/university   *The best day of my life*
My favourite food   *A typical weekend*

5   Ask the learners to start the discussion off, with each of them recording their opinions. Tell them to finish by asking what other people think, as in the example below.

Please, could you tell me what your favourite food is?
The food that I like best is vegetarian because I don't eat meat. I love pasta made with courgettes and cream-cheese sauce. What about you? (Isabel, Barcelona)

6   When the learners have finished, ask them to choose one or two of their classmates' discussions and add their own ideas, recording replies. Finish the activity by asking the learners to summarise what they asked and the responses they received.

8.12 Animated film

Main goals	Dialogue; creating a spoken narrative
Level	Pre-intermediate (B1) and above; teenagers/adults
Time	40–50 minutes or more (best done over two separate classes)
Learning focus	Accuracy; narrative tenses
Preparation	A class account for an animated cartoon website (see Appendix B 8.12 for suggested websites) that allows the uploading of recorded audio. This activity works well if it is used to revise work on narrative tenses.
Technical requirements	A computer room, or a class set of tablets/laptops/netbooks, with internet access and headsets (or earphones and microphones). Alternatively, the learners can do this part at home.

Procedure

1   Tell the learners that they are going to work in pairs to create an animated story with a strong beginning, middle and end. Choose a theme (e.g. a local legend, a ghost story, etc.), and ask them to brainstorm ideas for the story and to write a couple of sentences for each part.

2   When the learners have their basic ideas, ask them to report them to the class, using verb forms in the past. Encourage feedback from the rest of the class, and help the learners make their stories better.

3   Tell the learners they are going to create an animated version of the story they have written, and get them to go to the animated cartoon site to begin to create the story. In the cartoon site, they can choose the background and characters from a library and then write the dialogue in cartoon bubbles.

4   Once the learners finish one scene, they start on the next, until they have finished telling the story. Set a time limit on them finishing their basic cartoons. Those who don't finish should complete the cartoons at home.

5   Next class, ask the learners to record audio for their cartoon stories. Before they do the recording, encourage them to rehearse it a couple of times until they are happy with the way it sounds. While they are rehearsing, monitor the class, and offer help to the learners who need it.

6   When the learners have finished their animated films, hold a film festival and ask the class to vote for the best film (see Chapter 10 *Project work*).

Variation

If you are short of time, ask the learners to create animated films of a joke rather than a story.

8.13 **World issues**

Main goals	Interactive speaking
Level	Intermediate (B1+) – Advanced (C1)
Time	15–20 minutes
Learning focus	Fluency; debating; negotiating and giving advice (*would, should, could*). Stimulating group discussion and debate about a real social issue, and giving the learners practice expressing their views and opinions.
Preparation	None required
Technical requirements	A connected classroom (an internet-enabled computer and data projector) and access to the game *Stop disasters* (http://www.stopdisastersgame.org), which is a simulation of what it is like to be a farmer with a family in a country where disaster strikes

Procedure

1   Tell the learners they are going to help you play a game set in a place where there is a risk of a natural disaster (e.g. *Stop Disasters*, Figure 8.7). Choose the disaster you want to avoid in the game (e.g. flood, tsunami, earthquake, etc.). Then ask the learners to talk together to imagine the difficulties someone might face in a place where a natural disaster such as this is likely, as well as the resources they would need to overcome it. If you feel some input is necessary beforehand, then look for a recent news article about the subject before you play the game, in order to give your learners some background information.

2   Write up the learners' ideas on the board in two columns (*resources* and *difficulties*). Once you start playing the game, you can add to these lists as new information is revealed.

3   Start the game, and explain the objectives (to prevent a natural disaster being a catastrophe by investing in measures to improve the situation, such as early warning systems). Go through the options with the learners (look at the choices available on the menus), making sure they understand the meaning of the vocabulary there, and the differences between choosing one option over another (price, etc.).

4   Ask the learners in groups to decide what they would spend their money on if they were in the situation you have chosen to face (i.e. a flood, tsunami, earthquake, etc.), and give them a minute or two to make their decision. Write the following sentence frames on the board to help the learners:

We would spend our money on ... because we think ... is more important than ...
We have decided to ... because we think that ...

5   If there are any disagreements, encourage the learners to debate the pros and cons (i.e. advantages and disadvantages) of spending money on one thing rather than another, and to defend their decision. If necessary, take a vote, or take an executive decision based on the best argument.

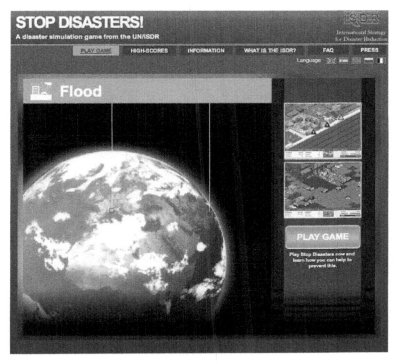

Figure 8.7: Stop Disasters: http://www.stopdisastersgame.org

6 Continue playing until time runs out (usually 20 minutes or so) and the disaster actually strikes.
7 After the disaster is over, look at the damage caused, and evaluate the decisions taken by the learners. Should they have chosen to spend their money on something else? What? How would things be different if they had done so? Continue encouraging group discussion and debate, and make sure you focus on the event, asking what the learners could have done differently from what they chose to do.

Variation 1
Instead of doing the activity in the classroom and encouraging a discussion, you can use the website with a class set of laptops/netbooks, or you can do the activity in a computer room. If you use this option, ask the learners to take careful note of what crops they buy and what happens (how much money they make or lose), and to write a summary of what the event is. After playing for 15 minutes or so, stop the activity, and ask the learners to compare how well they survived in the game. Finish by asking the learners to write a narrative of what happened to their family.

Variation 2
Similar games that you can play with the class, but which focus on other topics, include *Spent* (http://playspent.org) and *Against all odds* (http://www.playagainstallodds.com), which are online games that deal with real-world issues.

9 Pronunciation

Pronunciation is an area of language teaching that is often overlooked. Many teachers lack the training or confidence to teach it, or don't appreciate the importance of this area and choose not to spend much time focusing on phonology. Although, as Pennington and Richards say, it is often viewed as having 'limited importance' in communicative curricula (1986: 207), it is in fact often the main barrier to understanding. Helping learners with their pronunciation can also help them with listening skills, in particular with features of connected speech.

While often neglected, pronunciation teaching is the one area of language teaching where technology has often played a key role, from the days of long-playing records that modelled native-speaker accents to the endless imitation drills on tapes in the golden age of the language lab in the 1970s. More recently, many tools and websites have been developed to help the teacher and learners with pronunciation.

This chapter deals with general pronunciation (9.3, 9.11), including raising awareness of phonetics (9.7) and of common pronunciation errors (9.4); and more specific areas, such as word stress (9.1), features of connected speech (9.5), use of phonemic script (9.12), vowel and consonant sounds (9.2), stress and intonation (9.12, 9.14), chunking (9.12) and minimal pairs (9.4).

There are activities that are designed to work on sensitisation and ear training: skills for understanding speech that help learners identify and distinguish between different sounds, or help them with the decoding of connected speech. For these activities, we will use pronunciation resources found on video websites (9.9, 9.10, 9.14), talking pronunciation dictionaries (9.1), and phonemic charts and other tools found online (9.2).

As far as productive skills are concerned, technology for recording is so commonplace that it seems negligent not to take advantage of it in the classroom. For production, activities use computers with headsets or stand-alone microphones (such as 9.8), mobile phones (9.4, 9.11), podcasting websites (9.1, 9.8), voice recognition software (9.8) and a teleprompter, i.e. the device used in television to show an actor the script line-by-line (9.5).

Recording learners can help in different ways. Learners become more aware of how they sound to others, and this can lead to their becoming more comprehensible when speaking. Although learners will need time to develop this awareness, intelligibility can arguably be improved by first listening to oneself.

When computers play a part in helping learners with pronunciation, this is usually referred to as *computer-aided pronunciation* (CAP), and although CAP can help by increasing learners' awareness of their pronunciation performance, it is through recordings that learners can more clearly understand other varieties of English and how they differ. Through the use of audio diaries (9.3), or creating speech samples for assessment (9.4, 9.8), focus can be directed towards specific features of pronunciation, and these features can be more easily worked on in class.

Podcasting (9.1, 9.8) is one example of how technology can be used to support pronunciation, in and out of the classroom. Podcasts are easy-to-create audio files that can be subscribed to and downloaded from the Internet. Learners can also be encouraged to create audio files and upload them. Although it is not strictly necessary to upload the files, doing so provides learners with a sense that there is an audience (beyond the teacher) out there listening, and uploading learner audio can be motivating and lead to increased performance.

Some of the activities in this chapter make use of voice-recording software or voice recorders (9.2–9.4, 9.6) that are now normally found in every mobile phone. Introducing learners to this frequently overlooked tool can lead to their using it more often outside of the classroom, and this encourages learner autonomy.

I hope the activities here will help you rethink your own teaching and provide ideas on how to integrate technology into your classroom to help your learners with pronunciation.

References

Pennington, M. C. and Richards, J. C. (1986) 'Pronunciation revisited', *TESOL Quarterly,* 20, 207–25.

9.1 Class-vocabulary audio notebook

Main goals	Pronunciation of class vocabulary
Level	All levels
Time	10 minutes
Learning focus	General pronunciation
Preparation	Choose a podcasting website that allows you to create short recordings (see Appendix B 9.1 for suggestions), and create a class account.
Technical requirements	One internet-enabled computer in the classroom with a microphone, or a class voice recorder (a mobile phone can be used). Alternatively, learners can use their own mobiles with voice recorders.

Procedure

1   As the class encounter new words and phrases that are difficult to pronounce, ask volunteers to record them. They can do so by coming to the computer and recording directly to the podcasting website; alternatively, you can use a mobile phone with a voice recorder and upload the vocabulary sound file afterwards, or ask the learners to take responsibility for their words and phrases, record them on their phones and upload them to the podcasting site for homework.

2   Refer to the recordings from time to time in class. Use them when looking at pronunciation issues (vowel sounds, minimal pairs, etc.), and as home-made examples of pronunciation when looking at the phonemic chart.

3   Inevitably, pronunciation will vary, and some of your learners may record pronunciations that do not correspond to the phonemic chart. For this reason, you should tell the learners that the phonemic chart is meant as a helpful guide, and that they should not be discouraged by less than perfect pronunciation.

Variation

With enough examples, you could create your own pronunciation page / phonemic chart on a class wiki.

9.2 Phonemic dialogues

Main goals	Production; awareness of phonemic script
Level	All levels
Time	20 minutes
Learning focus	Phonemic script; general pronunciation practice
Preparation	Find a website that helps translate into the International Phonetic Alphabet, or a phonetic alphabet recognised in your country (see Appendix B 9.2 for suggestions), and take a short dialogue and convert it.
Technical requirements	A computer room, or class set of laptops/tablets/netbooks, with internet access

Procedure

1   Present the phonetic alphabet and make sure learners are familiar with all of the symbols.
2   Give the learners the dialogue in phonemic script, and ask them to work in pairs and read it aloud.
3   Introduce the learners to the phonemic-script website, and tell them that it will automatically convert what they write into phonemic script and that this can help them with the pronunciation of anything they want to read aloud. Ask them to try the website using a previously written dialogue, or write one specifically for this class and ask learners to convert it using the website.
4   Once the learners have finished converting the dialogue, they practise reading it aloud.
5   Next, ask the pairs to write and convert other dialogues. They then swap computers and read out another pair's dialogues, written in phonemic script.

Variation 1
Learners can take the lyrics of a song they know and convert them into phonemic script. As they know the song, this should make it easy for them to relate the script to the sounds. You can also use songs to focus on a particular feature of pronunciation (e.g. connected speech).

Variation 2
Poems can be used instead, and, after transcription, the learners can use the scripts and record themselves with audio software (see Appendix A, *Audio recording and editing* for suggestions), or the voice recorders on their phones.

9.3 Howdjasayit?

Main goals	Production; word stress
Level	Elementary (A2) – intermediate (B1+)
Time	20 minutes
Learning focus	Pronouncing difficult words; stress
Preparation	Choose a talking pronunciation-dictionary website (see Appendix B 9.3 for suggestions), and select a number of word families (as in the examples below).
Technical requirements	A computer room, or class set of netbooks/laptops/tablets, with internet access

Procedure

1 Give the learners a selection of related words, such as:

photograph	*photographer*	*photography*	*photographic*
economy	*economics*	*economist*	*economical*

2 Ask the learners to work in pairs and try to pronounce the words on the list, focusing upon the stress patterns:

e.g. Oooo (ecȯnomy), (ecȯnomist), (econȯmics), etc.

3 Now ask the learners to use the pronunciation-dictionary website to check the pronunciation of the words, focusing particularly on the stress.
4 Ask the learners to work in pairs to produce sentences using the words.
5 When the learners have finished, ask for volunteers to say some of their sentences aloud to the class.

Variation

Turn the activity into a game. Ask half of the class to find the pronunciation of one set of words, and the other half to do the same with a different set. Then learners change partners and present three different pronunciations of each word, asking their new partner to guess the correct one. Learners get a point for choosing the correct pronunciation.

9.4 Schwa what?

Main goals	Receptive; awareness raising
Level	Elementary (A2) and above
Time	15 minutes
Learning focus	Selected vowel or consonant sound
Preparation	Choose a sound – a vowel or consonant that you want to target, and prepare some sentences where this sound is frequent. Choose an online phonemic chart to use (see Appendix B 9.4 for suggestions).
Technical requirements	One internet-enabled computer in the classroom, with projector. Learners should have access to voice recorders (almost all mobile phones have these built into them now) – one per group of three to four learners should be enough.

Procedure

1 Tell the learners that you are going to say some sentences that illustrate a particularly high-frequency vowel or consonant sound, and that you want them to record you speaking and guess what the high-frequency sound is.

2 When the learners are ready, say the sentences at a natural pace, and then let them replay the sentences and work out a) what the sound is and b) how many times it occurs.

3 Once the learners have identified the sound and its frequency, check their answers, and then ask them to compose some different sentences per group, with the same sound, and to record the sentences.

4 Now display the phonemic chart and look at the sound in question. Play the example sentences and ask the learners to play their examples.

Variation

If the learners have access to computers in the classroom, or for homework, you can ask them to transcribe what you said first (or part of what you said if it's too long), using the phonemic-script website (see Activity 9.2), before identifying the sound, using the phonemic chart.

9.5 Phonetic games

Main goals	Raising awareness of phonetics and phonemic spelling
Level	Elementary (A2) and above
Time	10 minutes (ongoing)
Learning focus	Phonetics (various)
Preparation	Choose a website with lots of phonetic games (see Appendix B 9.5 for suggestions), and select a particular game to play, or let the learners choose one.
Technical requirements	One internet-enabled computer in the classroom with projector (or IWB) and speakers

Procedure

1 Towards the end of class, go to the website with lots of phonetic games on it. Choose a game that you think your learners would benefit from playing. This could be a game where learners have to find the last phoneme (i.e. individual sound) in a word that links it to the next word or have to match the halves of the phonemic spelling of a particular word, or a game of phonetic Pelmanism (i.e. matching the real spelling of a word with its phonetic spelling). Alternatively, ask the learners to choose one of the games on the website.

2 Split the class into teams, and let volunteers from each team play the game. Keep track of scores, and declare the winning team 'Phonetic class champions'.

3 After the learners play the game, discuss the specific pronunciation features that the game practised, and ask the learners what they learned about phonetics. If they played a game that used phonemic script, make sure you have a phonemic chart handy (either on the wall of the classroom or online) to refer to, if necessary.

9.6 Minimal-pair poems

Main goals	Production; awareness of common pronunciation errors
Level	Pre-intermediate (B1) and above
Time	20 minutes
Learning focus	Minimal pairs
Preparation	Find a website with pronunciation help for minimal pairs (see Appendix B 9.6 for suggestions).
Technical requirements	Voice recorders (learner mobile phones, mp3 players, etc.), or multiple computers with audio software installed (see Appendix A, *Audio recording and editing* for suggestions).

Procedure

1   Tell the learners that they are going to find minimal pairs, i.e. two words that differ in only one sound. Ask them to go to the website that offers help in this area and to look at some of the minimal pairs. Alternatively, print out a list of minimal pairs you want the learners to focus on. They work in pairs and practise their pronunciation.

2   Ask the learners to choose a number of these pairs and to produce a nonsense poem to practise them, underlining the minimal pairs. Use this one as an example:

As you <u>sit</u> on the <u>seat</u>
Your <u>feet</u> don't <u>fit</u> and
When you <u>walk</u> to <u>work</u>
The <u>birds</u> are <u>bored</u>
Though you <u>saw</u> they sang <u>so</u>
Beautiful a <u>note</u> – <u>not</u>
A <u>thing</u> you <u>think</u> you'll
Hear ever again

3   If you think writing a poem is too difficult, then just ask the learners to write sentences with the minimal pairs. When the learners have finished, ask them to test their classmates by getting their classmates to read the poem or sentences to see if they can pronounce them correctly.

4   When the learners have finished, ask them to record their poems, using the voice recorders (in their mobile phones).

5   You can share the recordings online if you have a class wiki, blog or website.

9.7 Newsreader

Main goals	Production; features of connected speech
Level	Pre-intermediate (B1) to Upper-intermediate (B2)
Time	20 minutes
Learning focus	Tone groups (connected speech and pausing)
Preparation	Choose a teleprompter website or software (see Appendix B 9.7 for suggestions) that you can use with your learners in class. A teleprompter is a device used in television to produce a line-by-line reproduction of a script. You also need a number of suitable news texts for your learners to read (copied to a word-processor document). Find a video clip of a newscaster reading the news to show in class, as well, and make a transcription of it, with a copy for each learner.
Technical requirements	One internet-enabled computer in the classroom, with a projector

Procedure

1 Establish the meanings of 'teleprompter' and 'autocue', i.e. machines *that help TV news presenters say what they need to say, without memorising, by displaying what they have to say line by line.* If necessary, search on the word 'teleprompter', using *Google Images* search, and show the learners pictures. Tell the learners that there are software and websites that do the same thing, and that they are going to try this software today.

2 Show the class a video clip of a newscaster reading from a teleprompter. The first time you show them the video clip, ask them to listen for the gist of what is being said, and check comprehension by asking some general questions.

3 Play the video clip again, and this time, give the learners the transcript. Ask them to focus on the pausing and rhythm of what is being said, marking it on the transcript. Ask them if they think they could mark pausing and rhythm if they were reading from a teleprompter.

4 Hand out the first news text, and copy and paste it into the teleprompter software. Ask the learners to listen to you reading it and to underline the words you stress, and also to mark the places where you pause, with stress underlined and pauses marked with the symbol **/** (see below for an example of a marked-up script).

Encyclopaedia Britannica ends print edition

Encyclopaedia Britannica, the world's most famous set of reference books, has decided to stop printing its 32-volume collection. / The decision ends a 244-year history of the iconic printed edition. / Instead, it will focus on its online version and try to fend off competition from other web-based encyclopaedias. / Officials said the end of the physical books had been foreseen for many years, although they played down the impact of Internet sites. / Britannica president Jorge Cauz said:/ 'This has nothing to do with Wikipedia or Google ... / This has to do with the fact that now Britannica sells its digital products to a large number of people.'

Adapted from http://www.breakingnewsenglish.com

---

5 Invite some of the learners to try the teleprompter and to read the text aloud using the same stress, rhythm and pausing that you did. The advantage of using a teleprompter is that it makes it easy for learners to mark stress and pauses, and it is also highly motivating.

6 After a couple of learners have tried reading the text and have been given feedback, hand out the next text, and ask the learners to work in pairs to decide which words they would stress and where they would pause. Encourage them to read the texts out loud and to be more expressive than they would usually be when reading.

7 Ask for a volunteer to read the new text from the teleprompter, and then give feedback on how they did.

8 Continue the steps above with a third text.

Variation 1

Use a voice recorder or audio software (see Appendix A, *Voice recorders* for suggestions) to record the learners when they read from the teleprompter, and use the recording as the basis for pronunciation feedback in a later class.

Variation 2

Instead of using news articles, try other types of texts (jokes, adverts, film trailers, etc.), or experiment with dialogues (learner-written 'radio plays', etc.).

9.8 Tongue twisters

Main goals	General pronunciation; for fun
Level	Pre-intermediate (B1) and above
Time	20 minutes
Learning focus	General pronunciation
Preparation	You will need a class account with a podcasting site.
Technical requirements	One internet-enabled computer in the classroom, with a microphone

Procedure

1   Introduce the learners to a number of different tongue twisters or limericks, and ask them to practise them. Give them help with pronunciation, as needed. Here are some tongue twisters you can use:

Pirates' private property
World Wide Web
Black background, brown background
Seventy-seven benevolent elephants
I scream, you scream, we all scream for ice cream
I saw Susie sitting in a shoeshine shop, where she sits and she shines

2   Once the learners are confident, ask them to come to the microphone and record a chosen tongue twister. Upload the recording to the podcasting website, and share it on the class blog or wiki, if you have one.
3   If appropriate, use these recordings to identify sounds which are difficult or problematic for the learners, and work on these sounds next class.

Variation

Learners could also record their favourite tongue twister in their own language and then translate it into English for the class.

9.9 Voice recognition

Main goals	Using voice-recognition software; just for fun
Level	Pre-intermediate (B1) and above
Time	15 minutes
Learning focus	General pronunciation
Preparation	Choose voice-recognition software to use, either on the computer, learner smartphones or a website (see Appendix B 9.9 for suggestions).
Technical requirements	One internet-enabled computer in the classroom, and projector, with speakers and a microphone. Alternatively, you can use the voice-recognition software on learner smartphones (it's usually an app that comes with the phone, or which can be downloaded).

Procedure

1   Write the letters VRS on the board, and ask the learners if they know what they stand for. Tell them the answer (voice-recognition software), and ask if anyone has ever tried to use it, and if so, what for. Some examples are:

On a mobile, to search the Internet and use other applications
In a car, to give instructions for the heating system, music, etc.
On a computer, to replace the keyboard when writing
On a games console, to play without using a controller

If any of the learners have smartphones with VRS, you could then ask one of them to demonstrate it and show the class how it works, and what it is useful for.

2   Access the VRS on the computer, or website, and ask the learners to take turns trying it out with some dictation. Ask them to choose a text from their book and try reading parts of it, in turn. If the software doesn't understand some of the learners, tell them not to worry: it takes time for VRS to get used to a voice, and for someone to get used to VRS.

3   You could also test the voice-recognition software and the learners' own pronunciation with the minimal-pairs poem (9.6), or tongue twisters (9.8), or other examples you have at hand. Try reading these, and see how accurately the VRS turns the learners' words into text.

4   Finish the activity with a discussion:

Who might benefit most from VRS? Office assistants? Writers? Taxi drivers?
Are there any potential problems with VRS? You can't, for example, use it in a car, to replace driving – it would be too dangerous.
Will we have VRS in our homes in the future? If so, for what? For example, to open doors, and turn on lights and the TV?

9.10 Smartphone app

Main goals	General pronunciation; learner autonomy
Level	Pre-intermediate (B1) and above
Time	20 minutes
Learning focus	General pronunciation
Preparation	Find an English pronunciation app that will work on your learners' smartphones. See Appendix B 9.10 for suggestions.
Technical requirements	Your learners need to have smartphones for this activity to work. One smartphone per group of three learners is sufficient.

Procedure

1   Introduce the learners to the smartphone app, and ask them to try out some of the different features of it. These may include: a phonemic chart, the ability to listen and record, a game matching phonetic spellings to symbols, etc. Teachers should explain and demonstrate some of the features of the different apps to the class.

2   Once the learners have had a chance to look at all of the features, ask them to work in groups of three and brainstorm how they can use this app to support their learning, in and outside of class. These questions may help them:

How can this app help you with your pronunciation?
How do you think playing the matching game helps you?
Which features of the app did you find most useful?
How, and when, would you use these features?
Are there any features of the app you think you wouldn't use? Why not?

3   Ask the learners with smartphones to use the app for a week, and practise at home or on their way to work or school. After a week, ask them again what they think of the app, and if they are going to continue using it.

9.11 What's the intonation?

Main goals	Awareness of intonation and stress
Level	Pre-intermediate (B1) and above
Time	20 minutes
Learning focus	Intonation and stress
Preparation	Use a website with recordings of a variety of people speaking, where the stress and intonation are apparent (see Appendix B 9.11 for suggested websites).
Technical requirements	A computer room, or class set of laptops/tablets/netbooks, with audio software installed (see Appendix A, *Audio recording and editing* for suggestions)

Procedure

1 Ask the learners to work in pairs, go to the website you have chosen and select a recording to listen to. Alternatively, guide the learners to a particular recording that you know contains interesting examples of stress and intonation.

2 Encourage the learners to notice the intonation and stress when they listen to the recording(s).

3 Ask the learners to choose five short utterances from the recording (maximum eight words per utterance) where there is a distinctive change of pitch (because of emphasis or emotion or because the speaker has asked a question, etc.). Then ask them to transcribe the utterances, marking the intonation and stress.

4 Ask the learners to repeat the phrases with similar intonation and stress.

5 When the learners are happy with their pronunciation, they read out the phrases in front of the class, imitating the stress and intonation, as best they can. If they record themselves, too, they can listen back to see how well they did.

9.12 Different accents

Main goals	Receptive; awareness raising
Level	Intermediate (B1+) and above
Time	20 minutes
Learning focus	Awareness of varieties of English
Preparation	Find a website that has examples of people speaking English with different accents. There are also lots of videos available on *YouTube* and other video-sharing websites. See Appendix B 9.12 for suggestions. Find two to three short videos (three to five minutes) of people talking English with a few different accents. Be sure to choose those your learners will understand: it will help (especially with lower levels) if you have a transcript of the video.
Technical requirements	One internet-enabled computer in the classroom, with a projector. Optional: one voice recorder (learners' mobile phones will suffice) per pair of learners

Procedure

1   Ask the learners if they think they can tell the difference between different English accents. Ask them to name some of the different accents, and write these on the board. Ask if anyone can imitate accents.

2   Tell the learners you are going to play some recordings, and they are to listen and then say which accents they have heard. Play a recording, and then ask the learners to identify the accent(s). Repeat a few times. Which accent did they find easiest to understand? Which was the most difficult?

3   Now tell the learners you want them to imitate the accent that you play. Give them the transcript of the video, if you have it. Tell them to repeat and try to imitate the sentence. Play just a part of the recording. If you have access to voice recorders, ask the learners to record themselves, imitating the accent.

4   If the learners like this, you could ask them to do the same for homework and to record themselves imitating an accent. Ask them to make the recording available to the class so you can listen to it next time. See Appendix A, *Audio recording and editing* for suggested tools for recording audio.

5   Finish with a discussion about accents. Use the questions below to help the learner discussion.

> *What is your accent when speaking your first language?*
> *Can you change your accent to that of a different city or region?*
> *How close do you think your accent is linked to your identity?*
> *How important is accent when speaking another language?*
> *Do you think you have adopted the accent of an English-speaking country or region when you speak English? Do you think this is a desirable goal to achieve?*

Variation

Instead of focusing on accents related to national, or other geographical, boundaries, you can play other types of accents (e.g. non-native speaker accents / famous people's accents), and ask learners to imitate / comment on these.

9.13 Guess the language

Main goals	Receptive; awareness raising
Level	Intermediate (B1+) and above
Time	20 minutes
Learning focus	Focusing upon visual cues to pronunciation (e.g. lip rounding, jaw tension, etc.)
Preparation	Go to a video-sharing site and select a number of videos of (non-famous) people speaking different languages, including the learners' language(s) and English. Choose languages you think your learners will have heard (e.g. from the learners' part of the world). Try to choose videos that don't conform to stereotypes (e.g. a Caucasian speaking Chinese, etc.).
Technical requirements	One internet-enabled computer in the classroom, with a projector (or IWB).

Procedure

1 Tell the learners that you are going to play a selection of videos of people speaking different languages, with the sound turned off, and that you want them to concentrate on any visual clues they can find (lip shape, jaw tension, etc.), in order to determine what languages the speakers are using. Tell them the languages that the people are speaking (i.e. *two people are speaking English, one person is speaking Spanish, two people are speaking French*, etc.). Ask the learners not to guess the language based on the person's appearance or other types of clues (i.e. body language and gestures, etc.).

2 Show the first video with the sound turned down. Then ask the learners to guess what language the person was speaking. Play the video with the sound turned up, directly afterwards, so the learners know what language it was.

3 Continue with the next video, and repeat the same procedure. Then repeat the procedure with the other videos. As you continue, hopefully the learners will become better at determining the language. If this is the case, ask them to try to tell you what clues gave them the answer.

Variation

Instead of using non-famous people, choose videos of famous people speaking foreign languages. Ask the learners to guess which languages they are speaking based on the same steps above.

9.14 Re-recording speeches and scenes

Main goals	Awareness of the intonation of connected speech
Level	Upper-intermediate (B2) and above
Time	20 minutes
Learning focus	Intonation; chunking
Preparation	Find a website with recordings of famous speeches or scenes from famous films. Try to find recordings that at least some of your learners will be familiar with.
Technical requirements	A computer room, or class set of laptops/tablets/netbooks, with audio software installed (see Appendix B 9.13 for suggestions), or one computer in the classroom, with a projector. Alternatively, ask the learners to come to class with their mobile phones, and use these as voice recorders.

Procedure

1 Ask the learners to go to the website you have chosen and to select a recording of a famous speech or an extract from a film to listen to (if you are using multiple computers), or choose a recording together to listen to.

2 Play part of the text (20–30 seconds), and ask the learners to transcribe this part. Then play the text again, asking the learners to listen carefully to the speaker's intonation and to where he/she pauses, marking both of these on the transcript they have made. Tell them they should concentrate on rising intonation, marking it above the relevant place on the transcript with a diagonal arrow pointing upwards ↗, and falling intonation, marking this with a diagonal arrow pointing downwards ↘.

3 After the learners have listened to the recording, ask them to listen to each sentence, in turn, and to make their own recording. Tell them they should try, as best they can, to match the intonation and pausing of the original speaker.

4 When the learners have finished, they can listen to the recordings. Encourage them to record the sentences again if they think they can do better.

10   Project work

This chapter looks at how technology can be used to support project work, especially (but not only) for young learners and teenagers. Projects can help learners 'develop confidence in using English in the real world, the world outside the classroom' (Fried-Booth, 2002: 5).

Projects are also a means by which learners become active participants in an *experiential learning* model. Experiential learning 'is based on the ideals of active and reflective learning ... requiring the personal involvement of the learner', and it 'encourages learners to develop the target language skills through the experience of working together on a specific task, rather than only examining discrete elements of the target language' (Knutson, 2003: 52). One approach to experiential learning that is common in communicative language teaching is task-based learning (TBL), which focuses on learners doing meaningful tasks using the target language.

One such meaningful task is project collaboration. Through collaboration on projects, learners can work together to use language in communicative and meaningful ways, learning to help themselves and often using language in real settings.

In this chapter, the technology provides the support for some interesting projects, a very motivating way for learners to practise language. There is a focus on collaborative writing to produce an online magazine (10.2), an e-book (10.1), a class recipe book (10.8) or a short film (10.6) that can be shown in a film festival (10.7). Other activities focus on speaking to make a TV programme (10.5) or podcast, an audio file made available for downloading on the Web (10.4), or on working together to produce a time capsule (10.3). Still others ask learners to work through a webquest, a structured, enquiry-based activity using the Web (10.9), or to use the interactive whiteboard (IWB) to create an island (10.10) that can be used as the basis for a long-term class project.

Project work here follows Wilhelm's (1999) suggestion that it best occurs in situations encouraging negotiation of meaning, with the active participation and collaboration of the learners in tasks where they make decisions and plans.

Knutson (2003) divides all projects into phases. The phases used in this chapter are:

- *Exposure*. Learners are introduced to the idea of the project in a way that activates past experiences and previous knowledge of the subject.
- *Participation*. This is when the actual activity or experience takes place.
- *Internalisation*. After the activity, learners can reflect on the experience and can also be questioned about the language learning that took place.

When conducting a project, instructions for learners should be clear, and a teacher should also be sure that there are definite outcomes when it comes to language use, content and participation. These outcomes should also be explained to the learners so they know the purpose of the project. Finally, you should emphasise to learners that you expect all members of the project groups to actively participate in the project.

References

Fried-Booth, D. L. (2002) *Project Work*, Oxford: Oxford University Press.

Knutson, S. (2003) 'Experiential learning in second-language classrooms', *TESL Canada Journal / Revue TESL du Canada*, 20 (2). Available online at: http://journals.sfu.ca/tesl/index.php/tesl/article/viewFile/948/767 [accessed March 2012].

Wilhelm, K. H. (1999) 'Collaborative dos and don'ts', *TESOL Journal*, 8, 14–19.

10.1 Our e-book

Main goals	Motivating learners to write together; sharing learner work
Level	All levels
Time	Variable (several classes)
Learning focus	Collaborative writing
Preparation	If you are doing the activity with young learners, choose a book-creation website suitable for your class (see Appendix B 10.1 for more information and suggested websites). Alternatively, you can create your book in Word and make it available as a PDF file, or in another e-book format.
Technical requirements	A computer room, or class set of laptops/tablets/netbooks. Alternatively, the planning and drafts of the learners' texts can be done in class, and the learners can produce their digital contributions for the book at home.

Procedure

1 Tell the learners that the class is going to work together to produce an e-book, which will be published online. Relate the contents of the book to whatever you are doing in class, or brainstorm with the learners what they would like the e-book to be about. Some examples (depending on the level of the learners) could be:

Ghost stories	*Urban legends*	*Myths and legends*
Short stories	*Book/film reviews*	*Festivals and traditions*
City guidebook	*Student guide*	*Our favourite games*

2 Once the class has decided what the book is about, it's time to decide who does what. You can take on the role of the editor, helping the learners with the writing and deciding the order of the content. Alternatively, the learners can vote for a classmate to take on this role. The editor can also be responsible for writing the introduction to the book and writing the table of contents.

3 Learners next brainstorm possible chapters (or sections) of their book, with the teacher helping with grammar and vocabulary. For example, for a book of ghost stories, the learners could brainstorm different ghost stories they have heard.

4 As the learners produce their writing, give help with grammar and vocabulary; corrections should be made at this point. If you want to encourage peer correction, ask the learners to form editorial committees. Then ask them to read their classmates' writing, correct any mistakes in grammar and vocabulary, and suggest any changes to structure, etc.

5 Once the learners are happy with the content, the book can be compiled and turned into a PDF file, or into another e-book format (see Appendix B 10.1 for more information on how to do this). It's now time to make the book available online. You can make it available on the class website, wiki or blog. Also look at the website accompanying this book (http://languagelearningtechnology. com) for other online publishing options. If you want to, you can also make the book available for sale through an online e-book store.

6 The next step is to promote the book. In class, you can create flyers that the learners can distribute throughout the school. They can hold a press conference and invite other classes. Learners from other classes can be encouraged to interview the writers. Outside the class, the learners can ask their friends and family to download and read the book.

10.2 Class magazine

Main goals	Creating a class magazine
Level	All levels
Time	20 minutes
Learning focus	Writing about hobbies and interests
Preparation	Requires a class *wiki* (a simple website that allows multiple users to write and edit content). Choose wiki software that you are happy with using (see Appendix B 10.2 for suggestions), and set up a class wiki if you don't already have one.
Technical requirements	A computer room, or class set of laptops/tablets/netbooks. Alternatively, the planning can be done in class and the writing at home, if the learners have computers and internet access.

Procedure

1   Tell the learners they are going to be working together on a class online magazine for other language learners, and ask them to brainstorm some of the pages a magazine might have. Suggestions may include:

Editorial	*News*	*Sports articles*	*Horoscopes*	*Gossip column*
Interviews	*Events*	*Fashion section*	*Reviews*	*Advertisements*

For lower-level learners, keep the content of these pages very simple.

2   Ask the learners to work in pairs and decide which sections they want to work on. You can appoint (or learners can vote for) an editor, who will be responsible for the order of the pages, making sure the other writers meet their deadlines and writing an editorial letter or introduction to the magazine.

3   Once the learners have talked about the page(s) they will write, hold an editorial meeting, with each pair presenting their ideas to the class. Encourage the others to ask questions / make suggestions. Tell the learners that the editor has the final say if there are differences of opinion.

4   Once the learners have decided on content, ask them to join the class wiki and to start writing the magazine. They can do this either in class or for homework. If writing from home, each pair should agree on what content each person will write.

5   When the magazine is finished, encourage the class to read the sections written by others by asking each pair of writers to formulate two to three questions about what they have written. Collect these questions, compile them and give them out next class or for homework, asking the learners to read the wiki and to answer all of the questions individually.

10.3 Culture capsule

Main goals	Skills work; cultural awareness
Level	Elementary (A2) and above
Time	Variable (several classes)
Learning focus	Collaborating together; integrated skills
Preparation	Set up a basic webpage for the class (or a wiki). See Appendix B 10.3 for information on how best to do this.
Technical requirements	A computer room, or class set of laptops/tablets/netbooks. Alternatively, you can do the project work on paper and scan, or take digital photos, and upload the learners' work.

Procedure

1 Tell the learners that they are going to create a 'culture capsule', and ask them to guess what that is. The idea is to make a website with descriptions of different aspects of the culture and traditions of where the learners come from.

2 Ask the learners to work in groups or pairs and think about what they would like to contribute to the culture capsule. Tell them that their contribution could be a combination of writing, images, audio or video, and can be about anything related to their own local or national culture. You could write some of these ideas on the board to help them:

A local festival	*Typical food*	*My hometown*	*Traditions*
National dress	*People and places*	*Song and dance*	*Folk tales*

3 Ask the learners to start preparing their contributions, and help them with language as they do so. Learners may choose to take photographs with their mobile phone and then write descriptions to go with them. They may create video or audio files, either using their phones or using computers, in which case you will need to use software to create the files (see Appendix B 10.3 for help with this). This project could be an activity that is spread over several classes.

4 As the learners finish the culture capsule, help them upload their content to the website, wiki or blog.

5 Finish the project by asking each of the groups of learners to present their contribution to the rest of the class.

Variation

If you teach a monolingual class, you could do this activity as an exchange project with a class from another country. This would make the activity more motivating for the learners because their culture capsule would have an audience.

10.4 Class weekly learning podcast

Main goals	Reflecting on what has been done; recording work done
Level	Elementary (A2) and above
Time	Ongoing (15 minutes per class)
Learning focus	Motivating speaking; reflecting on learning
Preparation	Choose a podcast website, and sign up for an account to use with the class (see Appendix B 10.4 for suggestions).
Technical requirements	Voice recorder (a mobile phone will usually do) and access to audio-editing software (see Appendix B 10.4 for suggestions), and a computer with internet access to upload the podcast when finished

Procedure

1   Tell the learners that the class is going to produce a weekly podcast which will become a spoken record of what they have learned in class. The podcast needn't be more than five minutes long, but could be longer if desired. Tell the learners that they will create their podcast at the end of each week, in the last 15 minutes of class.

2   At the end of the class, write the following questions on the board (vary the questions each week, asking ones that are more appropriate to what you have done that week):

What have you learned this week?   *What did we do in class that you liked?*
What did you find easy/difficult?   *Would you like more practice on this week's lesson?*

3   Ask the learners to discuss the questions for five minutes in pairs, and tell them that you are going to ask for volunteers to create the podcast.

4   Ask the questions, and ask for volunteers to answer them, speaking into the voice recorder. Encourage a discussion, rather than just monologues.

5   Now the voice recording can be uploaded to the podcast site as a record of what has been done in class. Be sure to label the recording with some indication of the contents of the class, which will make it more useful in the future.

6   From time to time, return to previous podcasts in class, and use them to show how the learners' speaking has improved.

Variation

Instead of making this a class activity, ask the learners to record and post their individual reflections orally. This option can be done as a podcast, publicly available to all learners or just to you as an audio file (see Appendix B 8.1 for suggestions for audio websites). Once the learners have posted their reflections, you should reply to the voicemail messages they have left.

10.5 TV magazine programme

Main goals	Integrated-skills work
Level	Pre-intermediate (B1) and above (especially pre-teens and teenagers)
Time	Variable (several classes)
Learning focus	Integrated skills (especially speaking; writing)
Preparation	Test the video-camera equipment, and make sure you can connect the camera – to display the video later in the classroom. See Appendix B 10.5 for help with using this equipment.
Technical requirements	Video camera and TV, or a computer in the classroom with projector (or IWB) for displaying the programme when finished

Procedure

1 Write *TV magazine programme* on the board, and ask the learners to tell you what such a programme is. If they don't know, tell them it's a TV programme that presents a variety of topics, and ask them to think of any examples of TV magazine programmes they may know.

2 Tell the learners that the class is going to make a TV magazine programme for people of their age, and ask them what kinds of sections they think the programme should have. Some ideas might be:

News	*Teen advice*	*Dealing with parents*	*Mobile phones*
Sports	*Video games*	*Celebrity interviews*	*Going out*

3 Split the class into small groups and ask each group to prepare a script for their section. Although one or two sections may be in the form of presentations, most of the scripts will be dialogues or interviews, with each of the learners taking turns to say something. Each group should decide who is going to say what on camera. Monitor the groups at this stage, and help them with language.

4 After the groups have finished preparing their scripts (this is probably the next class), ask them to rehearse their sections until they are able to record them without notes. Watch each group rehearse, and help them with pronunciation, etc.

5 Film the programme in front of a live audience (the rest of the class), with the sections in order (to make it easier to edit together later).

10.6 Short film

Main goals	Motivating learners to write and speak by doing a film project
Level	Pre-intermediate (B1)
Time	Several classes (40+ minutes each class)
Learning focus	Integrated skills
Preparation	Find a few good examples of short films to inspire the class before you start (see Appendix B 10.6 for suggestions).
Technical requirements	Video camera; computer and projector to show the film in class later

Procedure

1 Tell the learners that they are going to be working in groups to make a short film, and tell them that you are going to show them a few short films first so they get an idea of what makes a good one.

2 Once the learners have seen the two to three short films, ask them to talk about what makes a good short. Their answers may include: *an original idea, good acting, no repetition, a strong story,* etc.

3 Ask the learners to work in groups of four to six to talk about, and take notes on, the plan for a short film of their own. They should start with the general idea in mind of the beginning, middle and end of the film. At the end of this group session, ask the learners to present their ideas to the rest of the class, and encourage the other learners to give feedback.

4 In the second class, the learners should now write a script together. Ask them to split the plan of their short film up so pairs can work on particular scenes. Monitor and help the learners with vocabulary and grammar, as required. Ask the learners to submit the screenplays to you, and go over them before the next class. Tell the learners that they should also bring any props they need for the film to the next class.

5 Tell the learners that they are now ready to film. How this is done depends on the facilities/space you have available. The learners can film one group at a time, while the others are working on something else, or each group can be filmed live, with the other groups being the audience. In most situations, these will be amateur films, but if you have any learners with experience of acting, they could take the lead in directing the others.

6 Filming the scenes in order should avoid the need for editing. If, however, your learners are confident or keen, then you can suggest they use editing software at home to add the final touches to the film (opening and closing credits, music, etc.). See the website accompanying this book (http:// languagelearningtechnology.com) for suggestions of editing software, and for websites for copyright-free music that can be used. The learners could also add subtitles if they want.

Variation 1

Instead of making a film, the learners can create a photo story. They can pose for photos, and cartoon bubbles can be added with photo-editing software (see Appendix B 10.6 for suggestions). Alternatively, the photo story can be made into a video, and the learners can add a voiceover. See the website accompanying this book for examples of this alternative.

Variation 2

Instead of making a short film, the learners could be encouraged to create a documentary. Alternatively, another type of project (learner interviews, comic sketches, etc.) could be turned into a video.

10.7 Film festival

Main goals	Extending the film project; motivating writing and speaking
Level	Pre-intermediate (B1) and above
Time	Two classes of 45–60 minutes (one for preparation and press conferences, the other for the festival and awards ceremony)
Learning focus	Integrated skills
Preparation	The learners should have created films (see Activity 10.6). Prepare voting slips, and optionally have prizes available for the winners.
Technical requirements	One computer in the classroom, with a projector to show the films

Procedure

1 Tell the learners they are going to take part in a film festival, and ask them if they know what takes place in an event such as this. Tell them that in the class film festival, each film will be presented first at a press conference; then all of the films will be screened and, finally, there will be an awards ceremony.

2 Tell each group to prepare first for a short press conference and to write a short description of the film. Tell the learners that they should also prepare acceptance speeches, in case they win an award. Help the learners with the speeches, giving suggestions of what they should say (e.g. they should thank the other learners who helped them, etc.).

3 When the learners are ready, start the press conference. While one group is presenting their film, the other learners will be taking the role of the press and asking questions. You may want to suggest that, before starting the press conference, the learners brainstorm questions to ask. Depending on time, you may also want to leave the screening of the films and the awards ceremony for the next class.

4 After the press conference, at the end of the first class, decide on the award categories, and suggest a voting system (e.g. learners cannot vote for themselves, one vote per person per category, etc.). Award categories could include the following:

Best fi lm   Best director   Best actor   Best actress

5 Next class, hold the film festival. After the screening of the films, hold the awards ceremony, and organise the voting of each category – to be followed by the prize-giving ceremony and speeches.

10.8 Our cookbook

Main goals	Collaborating together to produce a book of recipes
Level	Pre-intermediate (B1)
Time	60+ minutes (two classes)
Learning focus	Integrated skills
Preparation	Set up a website, wiki or create an e-book (PDF, or other format) for this project (see Appendix B 10.8 for suggestions).
Technical requirements	A computer room, or class set of laptops/netbooks/tablets. Alternatively, the learners can plan the project in class, write the recipes for homework and share them with you via email.

Procedure

1   Ask the learners to think of a local, or national, dish that they like and can make, or one that someone they know can tell them how to make. If possible, ask each learner to choose a different dish. If you have a large class, then learners can do this step in pairs or small groups.

2   Once the learners have chosen their dishes, tell them that, as part of this activity, they will prepare the dish at home, write the recipe and take a picture of the dish to illustrate it in a class cookbook. If some learners are uncomfortable about cooking, encourage them to ask someone else to prepare the dish for them, and they can concentrate on taking photographs and documenting the steps.

3   In class, ask the learners to write out the ingredients and the steps that need to be followed to create the dish. Tell them not to worry if they don't remember all of the steps at the moment, as they can check them when they go home. Ask the learners to consult their dictionaries for new words, and help them with language, as required. If they don't finish writing the steps in class, they can do so at home.

4   Before next class, ask the learners to cook the dish (or persuade someone they know to cook it, if possible), and to take a picture of the final result (and of them cooking it, if they wish). They should make any needed corrections to the ingredients and steps in preparation for submitting their recipes.

5   The learners can now write their recipes to the wiki or website; or ask them to submit the finished recipes to you in Word with their photographs, and you can compile them into an e-book.

Variation 1
This project could be the basis of a class exchange with another class in a different country.

Variation 2
Instead of producing a book, the learners could video themselves making the recipes and explaining in English how to prepare the dishes. The videos could be compiled to create a TV cooking programme instead.

10.9 Make your own webquest

Main goals	Learner autonomy; cooperative learning
Level	Intermediate (B1+)
Time	60 minutes
Learning focus	Integrated skills
Preparation	A webquest is an enquiry-oriented activity in which some, or all, of the information that learners interact with comes from resources on the Web. The activity here is best done after you have done at least one prior webquest with learners (see Appendix B 10.9 for example webquests). The webquests that you do with learners, including this activity, will be added to the class wiki.
Technical requirements	A class set of netbooks/laptops/tablets, or a computer room, with internet access. Alternatively, you can ask the learners to plan this activity in class and write it up for homework.

Procedure

1 After doing at least one webquest together, tell the learners that they are going to work in groups to create their own webquest, which they will add to the class wiki for their classmates to do.

2 Tell the learners that, when researching their webquest, they should keep a record of where they get the information and images they use. Give them the handout below, and ask some comprehension questions, e.g. *What is a webquest? How many parts does it have?* etc.

What is a webquest?

A webquest is a structured activity that asks learners to solve a problem, using the Internet. It consists of the following parts:

- *Introduction.* Includes the reason for doing the webquest and the big question (what problem the website will solve, or what question the webquest will answer)
- *Task.* A description of the end result of the learners' activities, plus mention of the tools required to be able to do the webquest (i.e. links to specific websites, search engines, etc.)
- *Process.* A step-by-step procedure of how the learners will conduct their research, plus guidance on how to record the information collected
- *Evaluation.* A brief description of how the learners will be evaluated; for example, the end product may be answers to a series of questions, a report or a presentation
- *Conclusion.* A brief summary of what has been learned about the topic, with an indication of where to go to learn more
- *Credits and references.* Information about who designed the webquest, and credits for sources, images, etc. used

---

3   The learners work in groups to design a webquest on a topic they decide. Each group should choose a different topic; other groups will then use the webquest at a later date to learn about the subject. Give the learners some examples:

Finding out about a particular city or country   *Researching a period of history*
An unfamiliar sport or hobby   *An endangered species*
An animal or science project   *Wonders of the world*
A particular film, book or game genre   *Unusual jobs*

4   Ask the learners to start planning the webquest and to create a new page for it on the class wiki. This new page should be divided into sections, as per the handout (above), and each section should be completed with instructions, along with links to resources to help the other learners find their information. Monitor the learners while they are writing, and help them with language.

5   When the webquests are ready, ask the other learners to choose one of their classmates' webquests to complete for homework.

Note
The webquest format was developed by Bernie Dodge, http://webquest.org/

10.10 IWB island

Main goals	Setting up the basis of a long-term class project
Level	Intermediate (B1+) and above
Time	60+ minutes (with the island being used for future activities as needed)
Learning focus	Integrated skills
Preparation	The IWB island involves the learners drawing an island on an interactive whiteboard, and then using this island as the basis for activities in future classes.
Technical requirements	An IWB

Procedure

1 Tell the learners they are going to help you draw an imaginary island which will be the basis of a classroom project: the learners will be helping the virtual island promote its tourism. Open a flipchart on the IWB, and ask a volunteer to take the pen and to draw the outline of a large island, filling up most of the space on the flipchart. Ask the other learners if they are happy with the shape, etc., or if they would like some changes made.

2 Once the learners are happy with the island, ask volunteers to add some features to the island. Make sure the features are negotiated, and that the class is happy about whatever is added to the island. Go through the following, in turn, and add any others the class suggest:

Natural features: *rivers, lakes, mountains, hills, forests, swamps*, etc.
Man-made features: *cities, towns, villages, ports, roads, factories*, etc.

3 Once the island has been created, tell the learners that the island is divided into four countries. Decide together what the boundaries of these countries are, drawing them onto the map. Ask the learners to decide names for the island and for the four countries.

4 Tell the learners that they will play the role of the government of one of the four countries, and split the learners into groups accordingly (either select learners for each group, or ask the learners to choose which country they want to represent).

5 Roll a dice for each group to decide the population (1 = small, 3 = medium, 6 = large); and then roll the dice again to decide what the economic situation is (1 = poor, 3 = average, 6 = rich).

6 Ask the groups to work together and to decide briefly the following for each of the four fictional countries, which should be consistent with the results of the geography/population/economy:

Type of government   *Major industry*   *Education level*   *Unemployment*

7 As the group discussions continue, tell the learners they can add features to their part of the map, in the above categories, that represent the information about the island that they have imagined. At this point, it may be appropriate to create separate country maps on four new flipcharts so that each of the groups can add more detail, if needed.

8 Tell the learners in each group to decide which of them is the leader (king or queen / president / prime minister, etc. depending on type of government), and what the other members of the group do. Suggestions to give them include:

Treasurer   *Foreign-office representative*   *Employment minister*
Minister for education   *Cultural minister*   *PR representative*

Make sure each person in the group has a responsibility.

9 Now tell the learners that there is an island congress, and each of the leaders, education ministers, etc. are going to be discussing island policy together. Tell them that the island has attracted a lot of international press recently, and there will certainly be an increase in tourism next year. The policies they need to discuss could include: *building new hotels, increasing the number of roads, expanding the airport or seaport, building a theme park, etc.*

10 Ask the learners to regroup to talk to the representatives of the other countries (e.g. all of the treasurers form one group; all of the foreign-office representatives form another group, etc.). Each group should talk about what they are planning to do to increase tourism, and they should discuss how the different countries can work together to promote tourism and develop facilities for visitors (hotels, theme parks, resorts, etc.).

11 If successful, you can use the IWB island as the basis for future classes.

Note

This activity is compatible with the Island project outlined in Fried-Booth, D. L. (2002) *Project Work*, Oxford: Oxford University Press: 101.

11 Assessment and evaluation

Assessment, evaluation and *testing* are commonly confused terms. For the purposes of this book, *assessment* refers to the *testing* of learner performance, and *evaluation* is used to mean any means of getting information about the course. The latter can refer to whether the material is appropriate to the level, how the learners are coping with the workload or whether the methodology used is appropriate. As such, assessment of learners is often undertaken before evaluation can take place.

Assessment, for many teachers, means testing, followed by grade giving. Grades and marks, however, offer limited information to both learners and teacher, whereas complimentary written comments, indicating where learners can improve and where they are doing well, can be more enlightening.

Lucantoni (2002: 57) states there are three reasons for assessment:

- *Formative assessment.* The purpose of this type of assessment is to evaluate the current progress of learners, in order to determine what needs to be done in the future. Formative assessment is undertaken regularly and is an ongoing process. The main focus is on helping learners with the learning process.
- *Summative assessment.* The reason for this type of assessment is to measure how much learners have achieved up to a certain point in time. Summative assessment is done occasionally, at the end of a term or year. The challenge with these *low-stakes tests* (i.e. tests that are internal, not leading to qualifications) is to create meaningful tests that show corrections of mistakes and provide comments to help learners know how to improve.
- *Formal qualification.* Undertaken through external examination, formal qualification depends on the learners' language level and needs. Preparing learners for these tests is often an important part of a teacher's role. More and more examinations for formal qualifications (*high-stakes tests,* i.e. those which could have a major impact on learners' lives) are being conducted now through computer-based and internet-based testing.

Exploiting technology for formative assessment can be learner-centred and used to give learners extra practice. An example in this chapter is the use of screen-capture software to give individual feedback on writing (11.6). Not only is this software an example of technology being used to save the teacher time when marking writing (spoken feedback is provided, which is quicker than written feedback), but the learners receive both extra listening practice and individualised attention.

Formative assessment of this type can help learners become more autonomous learners, which is increasingly important as we move towards the idea of lifelong learning (i.e. learning that continues beyond school and university). Another way in which technology can support the idea of lifelong learning is through the use of electronic portfolios (or *e-portfolios*), such as the European Language Portfolio (Council of Europe, 2000). Portfolios have long been a standard way for a number of professionals (artists, architects, etc.) to collect and showcase their work. Increasingly, portfolios are being used by teachers and learners of all subjects.

One way of using online e-portfolios is presented in this chapter (11.1). The advantages of using online e-portfolios, rather than paper copies, include portability (i.e. they can be easily accessed and shared), and the potential for multimedia (including digital images of learner work, and audio and video files of learners speaking, etc.). E-portfolios can also be used for summative assessment of learners, as the e-portfolio becomes an ongoing record of learner progress.

Another activity in this chapter that deals with summative assessment is 11.2, which proposes using the idea of *gamification* (i.e. the use of game-design techniques and game thinking to enhance non-game contexts) to add fun to assessment. As Lee Sheldon states in *The Multiplayer Classroom* (2012: xv), assessment 'tends to focus attention more on grades than content', and this is why assessment is often disliked by learners. Few learners look forward to tests with relish because traditional assessment usually highlights the mistakes learners make, punishing them for their failure, rather than rewarding them for their success. One way of remedying this problem, through the awarding of badges, is presented in this activity.

Gamification can also help with formal assessment, especially when dealing with young learners and teenagers. The adoption of experience points, and a level system more usually found in a computer adventure game than in a classroom, is suggested in 11.9 – to make practising for formal examinations more fun.

Formal assessment is also dealt with in Activities 11.3, 11.4 and 11.5, which look at ways in which technology can be used with testing to encourage learners to reflect on assessment, and to make assessment more learner-centred.

Evaluation of a language course is often left until the last moment, and, more often than not, evaluation seems to be an afterthought. This doesn't have to be the case, however, and information about the choice of teaching materials, etc. can be collected throughout the course. One way of collecting this information is through the use of surveys, and there is an example activity in this chapter (11.8) focusing on information collection.

References

Council of Europe (2000) *European Language Portfolio*. Available online at: http://www.coe.int/portfolio [accessed May 2012].

Lucantoni, P. (2002) *Teaching and Assessing Skills in English as a Second Language,* Cambridge: Cambridge University Press.

Sheldon, L. (2012) *The Multiplayer Classroom: Designing Coursework as a Game,* Boston: Cengage Learning.

11.1 E-portfolio archive and showcase

Main goals	Recording and showcasing learners' work online
Level	All levels
Time	20 minutes
Learning focus	Formative assessment; creating a record of learners' work
Preparation	Choose a blogging platform, one where learners can email attachments (documents, photos, audio, video) that will be published online (see Appendix B 11.1 for suggested blogs). Also choose a simple website-creation tool, which will act as the showcase for the best of the learners' work (see Appendix B 11.1 for suggestions).
Technical requirements	A computer room, or class set of laptops/netbooks/tablets. Alternatively, the learners can do the activity from home.

Procedure

1   Tell the learners they are going to be creating an e-portfolio, and explain what this means (a collection of learners' work that tells the story of a learner's efforts and progress in language learning). Tell them there will be two parts to the e-portfolio: an *archive* (all of the work they choose to save), and a *showcase* (what they choose to share with the world, i.e. their best work).

2   Tell the learners that they will start with the archive, and ask them to go to the blog you have chosen to create an account. Then ask them to send something via email that they have written, to show them how easy it is to keep a digital record of the work they do.

3   Ask the learners to continue with the concept of sending their work electronically, and ask them to send copies to the e-portfolio blog / archive of what they produce. In a future lesson (or this one), show them how they can also upload/link to audio files and videos that they produce.

4   Once the learners have a body of work saved to the e-portfolio, introduce them to the idea of choosing the best examples of what they have done and using a showcase for this work. Tell the learners these examples may be pieces of work they receive the best marks for and/or ones they are particularly pleased with. Introduce the learners to the website-creation tool that they will use to showcase their work, and ask them each to set up an account and create a simple website.

5   Once the learners have set up the website, ask them to choose their best work from their archives and publish it on their website. Encourage the learners to choose a broad selection, and to include examples of both writing and speaking. Tell them that they now have the basics of an e-portfolio that they can share with anyone who wants to see what they are capable of in English.

11.2 Awarding badges

Main goals	Reward learners with badges for their work
Level	All levels (young learners and pre-teens)
Time	Ongoing
Learning focus	Motivation for work done; summative assessment
Preparation	This activity works if you are using blogs or wikis with learners. You will also need an account with an image-sharing website (see Appendix B 11.2 for suggestions).
Technical requirements	A computer room, or class set of laptops/netbooks/tablets. Alternatively, you can use just one internet-enabled computer in the classroom, with a projector. Access to a drawing program, or a scanner / digital camera, is also needed.

Procedure

1 Tell the learners that you are going to award badges for the work that they do on their blogs, and talk about what these possible awards could be. Some examples may be:

100% correct	*Good effort*	*Well written*	*Great vocabulary*
Grammar star	*Amazing work!*	*Great listener*	*Well read*

2 With each badge, you need to negotiate with the learners when it will be awarded (i.e. to everyone who does something well, or just to one person per lesson, etc.).

3 Once you have a list of badges that you have agreed on, the learners can design them. This can be done with a computer drawing program or on paper. If done on paper, you will need to scan or photograph the badges. When the learners have finished designing the badges, you can upload them to the image-sharing site.

4 When a learner earns a badge, they can display the badge on their blog/wiki page. If using a class wiki, it would be a good idea for each learner to have a special page where they can display their badges.

11.3 Comparing placement tests

Main goals	Encouraging learners to reflect on their 'level' of English
Level	Pre-intermediate (B1) and above
Time	20 minutes
Learning focus	Reflecting on formal assessment
Preparation	Choose two online placement tests (see Appendix B 11.3 for suggestions).
Technical requirements	A computer room, or class set of laptops/netbooks/tablets. Alternatively, the learners can do the tests at home.

Procedure

1 Ask the learners if they have had to take a placement test, and what they had to do in the test. Ask them if they thought the test was a good way of making sure learners were placed in the correct class.

2 Tell the learners they are going to take two free placement tests and compare the results to see if they correspond. Tell them that they are doing this activity just for fun, and that the tests will concentrate on the vocabulary and grammar that the learners know.

3 Give the learners the addresses of the two tests. Ask them to record the scores that are generated electronically and also to make a note of what the questions were about (testing grammar, vocabulary, etc.).

4 When the learners have taken the tests, hold a class discussion on what they thought of the tests, including which test they thought was the most accurate, the easiest to do, etc.

11.4 Testing you

Main goals	Raising awareness of tests; creating tests
Level	Pre-intermediate (B1) or above
Time	30 minutes
Learning focus	Revision
Preparation	Choose a website which has a number of computer-based English tests and which allows users to create their own tests (see Appendix B 11.4 for suggestions).
Technical requirements	A class set of netbooks/laptops/tablets, or a computer room, with internet access. Alternatively, the learners can do this activity from home.

Procedure

1   Ask the learners what they think of tests and exams. Do they like them? Are they a necessary evil? Are they fair? Are there better ways of evaluating learners? If so, what are they? Share some of the comments that are often made about tests and exams, and ask the learners if they agree or disagree with them:

Exams and tests are stressful.
Some good learners don't do well in exams.
Tests show the results of one day.
Continuous assessment is a better way of grading learners.
Exams don't reward collaboration (this is copying!).

2   Write the following question on the board. Ask the learners to discuss it in pairs, asking them to complete the second sentence.

What makes a good test? A good test ...

3   Ask the learners to share their answers. Some of the things they may mention could include:

... is short.
... is fair.
... only tests work that learners have done.
... is where a learner does well if they understand the material.

4   Tell the learners that they are going to browse a number of language tests on a website. The tests have been created by learners and teachers. Ask them to choose one they think is a good test and suitable for the rest of the class.

5   Talk about the tests together. Which ones did the learners find most useful?

11.5 Testing me

Main goals	Raising awareness of tests
Level	Pre-intermediate (B1) and above
Time	30 minutes
Learning focus	Revision of language
Preparation	Choose a website which has a number of computer-based English tests and which allows users to create their own tests (see Appendix B 11.4 for suggestions). Create a class account with the website.
Technical requirements	A class set of laptops/netbooks/tablets, or a computer room, with internet access.

Procedure

1 Tell the learners they are going to create a multiple-choice test for the rest of the class. Give them the login details of the test-creation website, and ask them to sign in.

2 Divide the learners into pairs or small groups, and ask each pair/group to choose an area of language (i.e. a grammar point or some vocabulary) that the class has been doing recently.

3 Tell the learners that to create a multiple-choice test, they need to have some example sentences (e.g. ten), featuring the vocabulary or grammar point they chose, and that, for each sentence, they need to think of two other possible answers that might be correct. Show the learners an example or two, such as the one below:

I have not been to the theatre _____ a) still b) yet c) already.

4 Help the learners as they prepare their tests. When each pair or group has finished, ask them to check the test by doing it themselves.

5 Finally, ask the learners to share the links to their tests with the rest of the class and to try some of the tests for homework.

6 Talk about the tests next class. Were they difficult? Did they help the learners?

11.6 Screen-capture video feedback

Main goals	Personalised feedback, and listening practice, for homework
Level	Pre-intermediate (B1) and above
Time	5+ minutes per learner, to create the screen-capture video
Learning focus	Evaluation of writing
Preparation	Choose screen-capture software that you find easy to use (see Appendix B 11.6 for suggestions). The best option is software that allows you to save the screen-capture video online, so you can send a link to the learners for downloading.
Technical requirements	A computer and headset, or microphone and headphones. The learners should all have internet access at home, and you will need to have their email addresses to send them the link to the resulting video.

Procedure

1   Ask the learners to send you a piece of their writing via email. You are going to produce a video, which will consist of a screen capture of learners' writing with sections highlighted, along with accompanying audio.

2   Open up the learner's document, and start the screen-capture software. This software allows you to make a video of the learner's work while you highlight different parts of it, talking the learner through what needs to be changed to make the writing better. The advantages of using this software include being able to say more than you would be able to write in the same amount of time, and giving the learner personalised listening practice.

3   Read the learner's writing, and speak about it while highlighting various parts. Limit yourself to about three minutes of commentary. Start by talking in general terms about the writing: *Is the content appropriate? Did the learner complete the task well?* Then talk about the choice of vocabulary and grammar: *Is the language formal/informal enough?*

4   Rather than correct the learner when it comes to details, indicate the areas of the writing that need changing/correcting, and ask the learner to think about something specific (the tense, word order, register, etc.). Finish the commentary by telling the learner what you would like him/her to do (revise the piece of writing).

5   Save the resulting video, and send it (or the link to it) to the learner. The learner receives personalised feedback on his/her writing, and also listening practice. The correction of learner writing will also take you less time than it would otherwise.

Note
Adapted from an original idea by Russell Stannard: http://www.teachertrainingvideos.com/feedback. html

11.7 Self-assessing presentations

Main goals	Self-assessment of speaking through video
Level	Intermediate (B1+) and above
Time	20 minutes
Learning focus	Self-assessing speaking; improving oral presentations
Preparation	Introduce the learners to ways of filming themselves when giving a presentation, and ask them to practise at home (see Appendix B 11.7 for help with this).
Technical requirements	One internet-enabled computer in the classroom, with a projector and a webcam. Alternatively, you can video the learners with a digital camera, or mobile phone, when they are giving their presentations.

Procedure

1 Ask the learners to prepare a short presentation and film it, using either a webcam or digital camera. Alternatively, ask the learners to video each other delivering their presentations, using their mobile phones so they can watch themselves later.

2 Before the learners make their videos, talk to them about what makes a good oral presentation, and turn the ideas into a checklist the learners can use for evaluation. Some ideas that may be mentioned include:

The presenter is well prepared.
The talk is not too long or too short.
The presenter is expressive.
The presentation should seem natural (i.e. not read).
The talk has a clear beginning, middle and end.
The presenter's message is clear and understandable.

When you have a list that you and the learners are happy with, ask the learners to keep the points in mind when they film their presentations.

3 Make sure the learners have the video of their own presentations to watch at home. Ask them to assess their own speaking and make notes on what they think they did well and what they could improve on. After they have gone through the items on the checklist, ask them to write up their notes as a short report.

4 You should also make notes on the presentations, and write a similar short report for each learner. Give the reports to the learners to compare with what they have written.

5 Ask the learners to prepare to give the presentation again and to revise what they do based on the feedback you and the other learners have given. Tell them to experiment with filming themselves at home, before the presentation in class.

6 After the presentations are held again, ask the learners how they felt about watching themselves present, and if they learned much from this. Recording presentations should help with pronunciation, naturalness and delivery, and help learners improve presentation skills in general.

Note
Thanks to Ian James (http://teflteacher.wordpress.com) for inspiring this activity.

11.8 Evaluating classroom activities

Main goals	Reviewing work done; reflecting on learning; learner training
Level	Intermediate (B1+)
Time	20 minutes
Learning focus	Revision of work done
Preparation	This activity is best done towards the end of a term, before an important assessment. Choose a survey tool to use with the learners (see Appendix B 11.8 for suggestions). Set up an account, and write the initial questions (below). Then finish the survey with the help of the learners.
Technical requirements	One internet-enabled computer in the classroom, with a projector

Procedure

1   Tell the learners that they are going to help you design a survey about what the class has learned so far. Write some of the following examples of questions on the board, and ask the learners if they can think of some other questions to ask:

Which of the following activities helped you learn vocabulary best?
Which of the following activities helped you learn verb tenses best?
What format did you prefer for grammar/vocabulary exercises?
Which of the activities best helped you with writing?
How did you become better at listening?
Which speaking activities did you find most useful?
Which reading comprehension activities did you think worked best?
What kind of homework did you think helped you?

2   Ask the learners to work in groups and to choose one of the questions. Expand the question by listing the different kinds of activities done in class. Show the learners an example of what they should aim for:

Which of the following activities helped you learn vocabulary best?

writing out the words	studying the words at home
saying the words aloud	testing vocabulary with a partner
reading the words in context	playing games with the words
writing examples with the words	using flashcards on the computer
hearing the words	another way_____

---

3   As the learners are working, open the learning survey tool, and start to add the questions from Step 1 to it. Then ask volunteers from each group to add to the list of activity types for each question, or wait until each group has finished generating their own lists first.

4   Once all of the questions are entered in the survey, ask the learners to complete it for homework. The learners will answer the questions, selecting preferences so that you know which activities they rate highest. Use the information they provide to change what you do in class with the learners next term.

11.9 Levelling up

Main goals	Using game terminology and a *level system* to motivate learners to do more practice tests for homework; formal assessment
Level	Intermediate (B1+) or above (best with pre-teen or teenage learners), preparing for an external exam
Time	20 minutes
Learning focus	Helping learners understand the link between practice and results
Preparation	This activity is best undertaken at the beginning of a course, or at a moment during the academic year when you want learners to do more homework. You can set up a wiki, using the instructions below, or adapt a ready-made *level system* (see Appendix B 11.9 for help with this).
Technical requirements	One internet-enabled computer in the classroom, with a projector

Procedure

1 Talk to the learners about the differences between the word *level* when talking about learning a language and when talking about an adventure game on a computer:

Language level refers to how proficient you are when it comes to a language. You make progress by practising and studying, and you usually change from one level to another when a teacher, or examiner, evaluates your progress and considers you have a higher level. Usually your level doesn't change until you have finished a course.

In many computer adventure games, level can refer to the progress your character makes in skills and abilities. You make progress by experiencing the game, and you increase in level when you have collected enough experience points (XP). You accumulate experience points by playing the game, discovering new things and practising your skills and abilities.

2 Now tell the learners that you are going to make English exam-preparation class more like an adventure game by using a different level system and awarding experience points. Tell the learners you are doing this to give them a better sense of progress and (hopefully) to motivate them to practise and study more.

3 Present the scale of levels to the learners (see example), recorded on the wiki you've set up. Tell them you are going to use the wiki to record their progress and that they will start at Level 1 and level up, depending on the amount of exam practice they do.

Level	Experience points (XP)	Grade (%)
Level 12	12,000	A+ (100%)
Level 11	11,000	A (90%)
Level 10	10,000	A- (80%)
Level 9	9,000	B+ (79%)
Level 8	8,000	B (77%)
Level 7	7,000	B- (75%)
Level 6	6,000	C+ (74%)
Level 5	5,000	C (70%)
Level 4	4,000	C- (60%)
Level 3	3,000	D (59%)
Level 2	2,000	E (45%)
Level 1	1,000	F (44%)

4 Tell the learners that the levels refer to a particular language area of the exam they are taking (e.g. University of Cambridge ESOL Examinations, *First Certificate in English*: Reading / Writing / Speaking / Listening / Use of English) and that you want them to predict their level, based on the results of previous practice tests they have done. If they have not yet done any exam practice, then tell them to just take a guess.

5 After the learners have predicted their level, tell them you are going to give them a practice test to check if their prediction was correct. Give them the practice test for the language area you have chosen.

6 Once you have the results of the practice tests, record them in the wiki, in the form of a table (see below for an example). For these results, produce one page on the wiki per language area.

Reading	Test 1	Test 2	Test 3	Test 4	XP	Level
Xavi	55%				2,000	2
Abdul	45%				2,000	2
Montse	52%				2,000	2
Pierre	67%				4,000	4
Francis	49%				2,000	2
Neveen	59%				3,000	3
Julian	59%				3,000	3

7 Tell the learners that their level in the future will depend on the results of the last three practice tests they do, and that they will earn 200 experience points for each practice test they do. Tell them that experience points will always be adjusted up to their level, so, for example, if a learner averages 59% for the last three tests, then that learner's XP will be raised to 3,000 to match the percentage.

8 Create a separate page for each learner on the wiki, and list the average test score for each skill (see example below). Teachers should keep an ongoing record of the learners' scores and use this page to write comments once a month or so about each learner's progress, giving the learners help by telling them what they should focus on.

Neveen

	Reading	Writing	Use of English	Listening	Speaking	Average %	Overall Level
Level	3 (59%)	2 (49%)	2 (54%)	4 (60%)	4 (68%)	58%	2

9 Continue recording the learners' results for each language area, and encourage each learner to work on areas of weakness.

Variation

The above activity assumes the teacher will be doing all of the record keeping as well as writing the comments about each learner. You may want to encourage the learners to self-assess and write their own comments about what they need to work on.

Note

Idea and level scale adapted from Sheldon, L. (2012) *The Multiplayer Classroom: Designing Coursework as a Game*, Boston: Cengage Learning.

Appendix A: Learning technologies guide

Here is a list of all the learning technologies referred to in the book, along with some general notes about each technology. For websites and software for the activities in this book, see Appendix B: *Technical notes and suggested websites/software by chapter*.

Audio recording and editing

The best free software is *Audacity* (http://audacity.sourceforge.net). It is available for Windows, Mac and Linux and is easy to use. More information and links to tutorials can be found at the website accompanying this book (http://www.languagelearningtechnology.com). Some activities that involve audio recording and/or editing include 4.1, 5.1, 5.6–5.10, 5.12, 5.13, 8.1–8.4, 8.6, 8.8, 9.1, 9.6 and 10.4.

Blogging

Recommended blogging platforms include *Blogger* (http://blogger.com), which is ideal for beginners, and *WordPress* (http://wordpress.com), which is more flexible, but a little more complex.

Before starting to blog with learners, carefully consider who is going to be blogging and how many blogs you want to manage. If you are new to blogging, then I recommend starting with a *class blog*. If you want to give the learners more freedom, then consider a combination of a *tutor blog* and a *learner blog* (either one per group of learners, or one per learner – but remember, the more blogs you have, the more time it will take you to manage them and respond to posts, etc.).

- *Class blog.* This is the easiest way to blog, and is recommended if it is the first time you are going to blog with learners. You administer the blog and ask each of the learners to sign up as writers (you can do this by entering their emails and inviting them to be writers on the blog). Having a class blog means there is only one blog for you to visit to read learner work, but it is less motivating for learners because they don't *own* the writing space.
- *Learner blogs.* Giving each learner a blog is more motivating (because they own the writing space and can personalise it), but learner blogs are harder for you to manage because you have to visit each learner's blog individually. If you decide to use learner blogs, be sure to add links from each of these blogs to your own blog (the tutor blog). A compromise, so that you don't have as many blogs to visit, would be for groups of learners (three to four) to set up their own blog.
- *Tutor blog.* This is the teacher's blog, which will act as a hub between the learner blogs. You can use it to post tasks (homework, etc.) and links for the learners. It is not necessary to start a tutor blog if you are not setting up learner blogs. Because learners will be accessing the tutor blog (to see tasks that you post), it is generally a good idea to post a list of links to the learner blogs on one side of the tutor blog, to make it easier for learners to find each other's blogs.

Some activities for blogging can be found here: 2.4–2.6, 7.3, 7.4, 11.1 and 11.2.

CMS (Course Management System)

Course Management Systems are also known as Virtual Learning Environments (VLEs). See Appendix B 1.6 for more information on this.

Digital poster

Digital-poster software lets learners mix text, images, audio and video in order to represent ideas or tell a story. An example of this is *Glogster* (http://www.glogster.com). See Activity 3.6 for an example of the use of digital posters.

Google Forms

Google Forms, which is a document type you can create with *Google Drive* (https://drive.google.com), allows you to set up a simple survey. To begin, press the *create* button, and select *form*. Give the form a name, and follow the instructions to create your survey. When you have finished, you can email the link for the published form to the people you want to respond, or publish this link on your class blog or wiki. See Activity 1.2 for an activity using Google Forms.

LMS (Learning Management System)

Learning Management Systems are also known as Virtual Learning Environments (VLEs). See Appendix B 1.6 for more information on this.

Recording audio

Recording audio can be done with either a computer with a built-in, or separate, microphone (or headset), or a voice recorder (see *Voice recorders*). If using a computer, you will need specialist software (see *Audio recording and editing*).

Screen capture

Taking *screenshots* (i.e. an image of whatever is on your screen) can be done by simply pressing the 'print-screen' button if you want a still image, or by using specialist software if you want video. Recommended free software includes *CamStudio* (http://camstudio.org) and *Jing* (http://www. techsmith.com/jing.html). Activities that use screen capturing can be found in Chapter 11.

Search engines

Google and other search engines have a number of advanced features that can be useful for you and your learners, especially when searching for specific grammar strings. Here are a few examples:

- *Using quotes (").* Using quotes when searching will find an exact word, or set of words in order. Search on "can't ever end", for example, and you will find more example sentences containing this phrase than if you search without quotes. This technique is very useful for searching for song lyrics or poetry.

- *Using the plus symbol (+).* If you are looking for word combinations, using this symbol will give you examples where the two words occur together. However, this does not always work. Phrasal verbs, for example, are often separated, so will not necessarily appear in a verb + particle search. Also, unless you are using a database which is tagged for part of speech, you can't key in something as general as verb + preposition – in actual fact, a search with the + symbol is purely lexical.

Two activities that use search engines are Activities 4.5 and 4.8.

VLE (Virtual Learning Environment)

See Appendix B 1.6 for more information on this.

Voice recorders

In the book, *voice recorder* refers to the software on most mobile phones and portable devices specifically designed for recording speech, as well as the simple *sound-recorder* software on a PC. The microphone quality is usually better on portable devices than on mp3 players or mobile phones, although the latter can be used, instead. If you are buying a voice recorder, look for one which saves the audio as *WAV* or *mp3* audio format, so that you can play the audio on any computer without the need to convert file formats. A built-in speaker is also desirable, as you can immediately play back what you have recorded for your learners to listen to. Audio can also be recorded using a computer with a microphone (see *Recording audio*). The following activities use voice recorders: 4.1, 5.1, 5.7, 5.9, 5.10, 5.12, 8.1–8.4, 8.6, 9.1, 9.6, 9.12 and 9.14.

Appendix B: Technical notes and suggested software/websites by chapter

Here is a list of suggested software/websites for the activities in this book and technical notes, organised by chapter. Please note that inclusion in this book does not necessarily mean that the author or the publisher endorse all the websites or their content.

Where activities are not listed, there are no additional notes or suggested websites.

Cambridge University Press has no responsibility for the persistence or accuracy of URLs for external or third-party internet websites referred to in this publication, and does not guarantee that any content on such websites is, or will remain, accurate or appropriate.

You can find updates on the website accompanying this book, (http://www.languagelearning technology.com).

Chapter 1

1.1 Getting to know you
The best way of recording learners is to use the voice recorders in their mobile phones. See Appendix A, *Voice recorders* for more information.

1.2 Technological survey
There are a number of free online survey tools that you can use. Recommendations include *Survey Monkey* (http://www.surveymonkey.com) and *eSurveysPro* (http://www.esurveyspro.com). You can use *Google Drive* (https://drive.google.com) – see Appendix A, *Google Forms* – to share and store documents. For some ready-made example surveys you can use with your class, go to the website accompanying this book (http://www.languagelearningtechnology.com/surveys).

1.5 Plan B
It is not possible to cover all contexts here, but here are some tips for some specific contexts.

- *Interactive whiteboard (IWB) and PowerPoint.* Most IWB software allows you to create PDF copies of your files. If you know in advance that the projector and/or computer doesn't work and, therefore, that you will not be able to use PowerPoint, then you can make photocopies of the files you have stored on the IWB.
- *Online video.* Download a copy of the video you want to watch in class (providing the website's Terms of Service allow for this), using tools such as *Keep Vid* (http://keepvid.com) or *SaveMedia* (http://savemedia.com).
- *General.* Always have a plan B that doesn't rely on using any technology. This will probably be a prepared lesson plan on a general topic that you can do anytime with a class.

1.6 Our VLE

- *Educadium* offers a free VLE (up to 25 users) at http://www.educadium.com
- *Free Web Class* (http://freewebclass.com) offers a similar hosted VLE for up to 35 users.
- *Moodle* is currently the most popular VLE for education. Please note that *Moodle* (http://moodle. org) requires you to have your own server space from a Web-hosting service company (see *Dummies.com* for additional information: http://www.dummies.com/how-to/content/getting-web-server-space.html), so there is a cost, although when you buy server space, setting up a VLE is usually automated and easy to do.

  An alternative is to use a server space that is already hosted on *Moodle*. Organisations that create server space on *Moodle*, specifically for education, include *Freemoodle.org* (http://www. freemoodle.org – completely free) and *Key To School* (http://www.keytoschool.com – free trial). You can find more help here: http://moodle.com/partners

- *Blackboard* (http://www.blackboard.com) is another popular VLE with organisations, but it is not free. If you are looking for an institution-wide solution that you don't want to host yourself, then *Blackboard* is worth considering.

Alternatives to the above (if you are looking for a simpler solution) include the social network *Edmodo* (http://www.edmodo.com), which is free and easy to use, although lacking the powerful course-management tools of a VLE.

1.7 Dictionary race

There are many online electronic dictionaries available, with similar features, such as *Cambridge Dictionaries Online* (http://dictionary.cambridge.org) and *Oxford Dictionaries* (http:// oxforddictionaries.com). Try a few, and then choose one you and your learners like.

1.8 Class audio recording

You can use a voice recorder for recording. Either buy a special voice recorder (better quality), or use the one built into your mobile phone. See Appendix A for more help with voice recorders.

1.9 Unlocked achievements

If you want to reward your learners with badges, as well as notify them of the points they have earned, then you can use *Mozilla's Open Badges* (http://openbadges.org) to reward learners. If you teach young learners, then *Class Dojo* (http://www.classdojo.com) is a good alternative for awarding points to learners.

1.10 Flip your classroom

Apart from *YouTube* (http://www.youtube.com), recommended video-sharing websites include *Vimeo* (http://vimeo.com) and *Viddler* (http://www.viddler.com).

Chapter 2

2.1 Learning together online

Edmodo (http://www.edmodo.com) is the best private social network to use for this activity. It has similar features to *Facebook*, and so most learners will find it easy to use, but is completely free. Once you have set up an account and created a network, you will need to invite your learners via email. An alternative is *9th Period* (http://www.9thperiod.com). Another good private social network is *Ning* (http://www.ning.com), but there is a charge to use it.

2.2 Who are my classmates?

For suggestions on private social networks to use, see 2.1 above.

2.3 Personal learning online

Starting a Personal Learning Environment (PLE) means creating accounts with a number of social tools which are linked together. I suggest learners join a *class wiki* and set up personal accounts with three tools: a *microblog* (e.g. *Twitter*), a *blog* (e.g. *Blogger*) and a *social network* (e.g. *Facebook*).

- *Wiki.* Set up a wiki for the class with tools such as *Wikispaces* (http://www.wikispaces.com) or *PBworks* (http://www.pbworks.com). This will be the class shared space, where learners can share project work, writing, etc.
- *Microblog. Twitter* (http://www.twitter.com) is now the dominant microblog, and is the one I recommend. Ask the learners to create an account and to follow each other. You should do the same. Ask the learners to use *Twitter* to communicate in English between classes, and to share interesting links with each other. An interesting alternative to *Twitter* is *Plurk* (http://www.plurk.com).
- *Social network.* If your learners already have accounts with *Facebook* (http://www.facebook.com) and are happy to make use of them for English, then this is fine. You can set up a private group for the class, which means the learners aren't forced to add each other as friends. Alternatively, you could use another public social network, such as *Google Plus* (https://plus.google.com), or a private one, such as *Edmodo* (see 2.1).
- *Blog.* This will be used for reflection on learning by the learners, and for writing work in draft (if you use the wiki for finished writing work). The easiest blogging software to begin with is *Blogger* (http://blogger.com). An alternative is *WordPress* (http://www.wordpress.com).

Rather than creating accounts with all of the social tools above, you may want to start with one tool first (the microblog or social network, for example), and then add others as the term goes on. You may find that some learners end up preferring one tool over another – this is fine: it is after all a *personal* learning environment.

2.4 Class blog

Using *WordPress* (http://www.wordpress.com) for the class blog will help you manage contributions from learners. When you add your learners as users to a *WordPress* blog, you can assign them to one of a number of roles:

- *Administrator.* The person who creates the blog is the administrator. You can preview all of the comments that are posted on the blog (a good idea, especially if you teach young learners, and to avoid spam).

- *Editor*. This role will let learners edit the contributions of other learners. The role of editor is probably not useful unless you want to encourage group writing and peer correction on the blog.
- *Author*. This is the role recommended for learners. They can write their own posts, publish them and comment on the posts of others.
- *Contributor*. This role is similar to the role of author, but the learners cannot publish their own posts.
- *Subscriber*. This role just lets people read the posts on the blog. If you decide on making the blog private (i.e. not available to be read by anyone on the Web), then readers will need to subscribe. The role of subscriber could be used for parents, other teachers, etc.

2.7 Language wiki

Setting up a class wiki is easy. I recommend using *Wikispaces* (http://www.wikispaces.com) or *PBworks* (http://www.pbworks.com). First, create the account, and then invite your learners to join via email. Although not necessary, it is better for each learner to have an account because that way you can see the work each learner does (for this, you need to look at the 'Recent changes' (in *Wikispaces*) or 'Page history' (in *PBworks*). Once you have set up the wiki, create new pages as required.

2.8 What we need English for

Recommended online noticeboard sites include *Wallwisher* (http://wallwisher.com), *Corkboard Me* (http://corkboard.me) and *Lino* (http://en.linoit.com). For digital posters, *Glogster* (http://www. glogster.com) and *Webdoc* (http://www.webdoc.com) are both free and easy to use.

2.9 Safety online

There are now many online safety resources that can be adapted for use in class. I recommend the following: *KidSmart* (http://www.kidsmart.org.uk), *SafeKids.com* (http://www.safekids.com) and *SafeTeens.com* (http://www.safeteens.com).

Chapter 3

3.1 In context

Online learner dictionaries that work well with this activity include the *Cambridge Learner's Dictionary* (http://dictionary.cambridge.org/dictionary/learner-english) and *Merriam Webster's Learners Dictionary* (http://www.learnersdictionary.com). Alternatively, you can use a concordancer such as *JusttheWord* (http://www.just-the-word.com).

3.3 Online word-game tournament

Suggested online word games for this activity include those on *Facebook*, such as *Scrabble* (http://www.facebook.com/ScrabbleEA) or, for young learners, *LearnEnglish Kids* (http://learnenglishkids.britishcouncil.org/en/play-words), which has a number of different word games. There are more suggestions in 3.4 below.

3.4 Word puzzles

Recommended word-puzzle sites include *Wordia* (http://www.wordia.com) and *Puzzlemaker* (http://www.discoveryeducation.com/free-puzzlemaker).

3.5 Learner-generated quizzes

Test-/quiz-generator websites you can use include *Quia* (http://www.quia.com/shared/english), *Quizlet* (http://www.quizlet.com) and *Vocab Test* (http://www.vocabtest.com).

3.6 Memory posters

Digital-poster sites, such as *Glogster* (http://www.glogster.com) and the online scrapbook tool *Scrapblog* (http://www.scrapblog.com), let learners mix text, images, audio and video in order to represent ideas or tell a story.

3.8 Word associations

A visual-dictionary website, such as *Visuwords* (http://www.visuwords.com) or *Snappy Words* (http://www.snappywords.com), works well with this activity.

3.9 Making word games

Recommended word-game sites include *Wordia* (http://www.wordia.com) and *Puzzlemaker* (http://www.discoveryeducation.com/free-puzzlemaker).

3.10 Words and phrases

To conduct a concordance search, you need to use a concordancer, such as *Compleat Lexical Tutor* (http://www.lextutor.ca/concordancers). When you search for a word or phrase, the website will return a number of examples of the language in use, which you can then display to learners to show how the word or phrase is used. You can then look at the examples and examine multiple meanings or different parts of speech. Go to the website accompanying this book (http://www.languagelearningtechnology.com) for a more detailed explanation of concordancers, and a video showing you how best to conduct this search.

3.11 Synonym swap

For this activity, you can use *Synonym.com* (http://www.synonym.com). Alternatives include *Visual Thesaurus* (http://www.visualthesaurus.com) and *Thesaurus.com* (http://thesaurus.com). Other websites that can be used for this activity include *Thesaurus.net* (http://www.thesaurus.net) and the thesaurus search on *Merriam-Webster* (http://www.merriam-webster.com).

3.12 Experimenting with antonyms

Use *Synonym.com*, as with 3.11, but for antonyms, use http://www.synonym.com/antonym

3.13 Slang, register and style

One of the best sources of slang is the *Urban Dictionary* (http://www.urbandictionary.com). Other dictionaries of slang include *A Dictionary of Slang* (http://www.peevish.co.uk/slang) and the *Online Slang Dictionary* (http://onlineslangdictionary.com).

3.14 Multiple-meaning presentations

For this activity, use a concordancer that produces example sentences, and which is easy for learners to use. A good example of this is *JustTheWord* (http://www.just-the-word.com). Other concordancers you can use include *Corpus.byu.edu* (http://corpus.byu.edu), *Compleat Lexical Tutor* (http://www.lextutor.ca/concordancers) and *WebCorpLive* (http://www.webcorp.org.uk/live).

3.15 Noticing collocations

The *Compleat Lexical Tutor* (http://www.lextutor.ca) is probably the best tool for this activity. Alternatives include *WebCorpLive* (http://www.webcorp.org.uk/live) and *British National Corpus* (http://sara.natcorp.ox.ac.uk).

Chapter 4

4.2 Grammar check

Most word-processing programs, such as *Microsoft Word* or *Open Office*, have built-in grammar-checkers you can use. You can also use external ones for this activity, such as *Ghotit* (http://www.ghotit.com) or *LanguageTool* (http://www.languagetool.org).

4.3 Automatic cloze tests

Cloze-test generator websites that work well with this activity include *L. Georges Cloze Test Generator* (http://l.georges.online.fr/tools/cloze.html) and *Quizlet* (http://quizlet.com).

4.4 Questioning infographics

Infographic repositories include *Infographic List* (http://infographiclist.com) and *Cool Infographics* (http://www.coolinfographics.com). Other sources include *Daily Infographic* (http://dailyinfographic.com) and *Info Graphic World* (http://infographicworld.com).

4.5 Grammar fight

The best website for this activity is *Googlefight* (http://www.googlefight.com). If you want an alternative, then *Wolfram Alpha* (http://www.wolframalpha.com) is interesting, as it will show the frequency of both written and spoken forms of structures.

4.6 Grammar-reference sites

Here are some grammar-reference websites you can use for this activity:

- *LearnEnglish*: http://learnenglish.britishcouncil.org/en/grammar-and-vocabulary
- *BBC Learning English*: http://www.bbc.co.uk/worldservice/learningenglish/language
- *Internet Grammar of English*: http://www.ucl.ac.uk/internet-grammar
- *About.com Grammar and Composition*: http://grammar.about.com/

Three additional sites you can use are:

- *onestopenglish*(http://www.onestopenglish.com/grammar/grammar-reference)
- *About.com* (http://esl.about.com/blgrammar.htm)
- *UsingEnglish.com* (http://www.usingenglish.com/glossary.html)

4.7 Common grammatical errors
Grammar-checking websites you can use for this activity include:

- *Ghotit*: http://www.ghotit.com
- *LanguageTool*: http://www.languagetool.org

4.8 Real-world grammar
Just about any shopping site for DVDs and books will work with this activity. Try *Amazon* (http://www.amazon.co.uk) or *Barnes & Noble* (http://www.barnesandnoble.com).

4.10 Authentic word clouds
There are now lots of word-cloud creator sites. *Wordle* (http://www.wordle.net) is the most popular, but *Tagxedo* (http://www.tagxedo.com) and *Word It Out* (http://worditout.com) are just as good.

4.11 If only …
Mind-mapping software which works well with this activity includes *Popplet* (http://popplet.com), *MindMeister* (http://www.mindmeister.com) and *SpicyNodes* (http://www.spicynodes.org).

4.12 Grammar in context
Twitter (http://www.twitter.com) is the best microblogging website to use for this activity. Searching on the grammar in question will lead to a number of examples you can choose from.

Chapter 5

5.1 Guess what I'm talking about
Make sure you choose a quiet place without background noise when making the recordings with the voice recorder. Always check the sound quality before recording the full interview. A mobile phone or mp3 player with built-in microphone can be used if you do not have a specific device made for voice recording (see Appendix A, *Voice recorders* for more information). You can also use a computer with audio software to record the audio (see Appendix A, *Audio recording and editing* for more information).

5.2 Other people's interests
The best website to use is *Voxopop* (http://voxopop.com). Here are some example recordings:

- Hobbies:
  http://bit.ly/cuIhzh
  http://bit.ly/OOWVQc

- Sports:
  http://bit.ly/NRzuC6
  http://bit.ly/PxOmY9

5.3 Search the tube

The following internet *memes* are a good place to start, but you may want to look for a current one to use as an example, too (search for 'best Internet memes' and the year).

- General memes:
  Lolcats.com: http://www.lolcats.com;
  Karate Kyle: http://knowyourmeme.com/memes/karate-kyle

- Viral YouTube videos:
  Star Wars Kid: http://bit.ly/bojNQ
  Charlie Bit Me: http://bit.ly/KukYV
  Numa Numa: http://bit.ly/15sokw
  David After Dentist: http://bit.ly/9VjSKP
  Nyan Cat: http://bit.ly/hhnjc9
  Can't Hug Every Cat: http://bit.ly/055VYH

5.4 Reordered video story

To make screenshots of the video, you can simply press the 'print-screen' button on your computer, but if you do this, you will have to crop the image to get rid of the images of the browser and video player, which appear on the screen. To crop the images, paste the screenshots into a Word document and using the 'crop' tool, remove the unwanted parts of the image.

Another way of capturing the screen is by using free software such as *Jing* (http://www.techsmith.com/jing.html) or *CamStudio* (http://camstudio.org), which will also let you record video. See the website accompanying this book (http://www.languagelearningtechnology.com) for more help.

5.6 Guided tours

The best way of doing this activity is by using the website *World Voices* or *Woices* (http://woices.com), which allows you to upload audio directly and match it to a particular place. Alternatives include combining map-making software, such as https://maps.google.com, with an audio or podcasting website, such as http://soundcloud.com. For more information, with an example, on how to combine map-making software with an audio or podcasting site, see the website accompanying this book (http://www.languagelearningtechnology.com).

5.7 Recorded poetry

There are many videos of poems that work well with this activity, such as Michael Rosen's 'We're going on a bear hunt' (http://bit.ly/OUS9K) and Spike Milligan's 'Ning Nang Nong' (http://bit.ly/OVQYp).

5.8 Online classroom guest

The most popular free internet telephony software is *Skype* (http://www.skype.com). Alternatives include *iCall* (http://www.icall.com) and *Viber* (http://www.viber.com).

5.9 Recorded stories

See Appendix A for help with *Voice recorders*.

5.10 Voice-recorder dictation

See Appendix A for help with *Voice recorders*.

5.12 Someone I know

See Appendix A for help with *Voice recorders*.

5.13 Altered interviews

Audacity (http://audacity.sourceforge.net) is the best free software to use for this activity. Cutting and pasting can be done in a similar way to cutting and pasting text. See the website accompanying this book (http://www.languagelearningtechnology.com) for an example video of how this can be done.

Chapter 6

6.1 Word-cloud warmer

Word-cloud sites that can be used for this activity include *Tagxedo* (http://www.tagxedo.com), *Wordle* (http://www.wordle.net) and *Word It Out* (http://worditout.com).

6.2 Video pre-reading warmer

You can easily create a short film to use as a warmer, using *Go Animate* (http://goanimate.com) to make an animated film, or *Search Stories* (http://searchstories-intl.appspot.com) to make a video based on a Google search.

6.3 Quick-response reading race

You can create QR codes at *ClassTools.net* (http://www.classtools.net/QR), *Kaywa QR code* (http://qrcode.kaywa.com) and *QR Code Generator* (http://qrdroid.com/generate).

Rather than use a wiki to host the content the QR code links to, it is better to set up a separate webpage for each text, with a site such as *Pen.io* (http://pen.io) or *Tidypub* (http://tidypub.org). This way, learners can't cheat by looking at the other texts before they come across the QR codes for them.

6.4 IWB skimming and scanning

Finding suitable online texts for advanced learners is easy, as any of the news websites will have suitable articles you can use. For lower levels, *Breaking News English* (http://www.breakingnewsenglish.com) or *English Online* (http://www.english-online.at) are two good sites, with lots of articles at different levels. You can also find relevant texts at *Simple English Wikipedia* (http://simple.wikipedia.com).

6.5 Pre-reading presentation

The easiest way to do this activity is to make use of the presentation software already on your computer. There are now also some interesting alternatives available online, including *Prezi* (http://prezi.com), *SlideRocket* (http://www.sliderocket.com) and *BrinkPad* (http://www.brinkpad.com).

6.6 Readathon

Recommended virtual-classroom software includes *Wiz-IQ* (http://www.wiz-iq.com) and *Vyew* (http://vyew.com). Others include the 'Platforms/Collaborate' section of *Blackboard* (http://www.blackboard.com) and *Adobe Connect* (http://www.adobe.com/products/adobeconnect.html).

6.9 Coded message trail

You can use the cipher tools at *Rumkin* (http://rumkin.com/tools/cipher) or *Secret Code Breaker* (http://www.secretcodebreaker.com/codes.html). For the QR codes, *QR Treasure Hunt Generator* (http://www.classtools.net/QR) or *Kaywa QR Code* (http://qrcode.kaywa.com) can be used.

6.12 Big events

For higher levels, any online newspaper websites in English will be appropriate, such as *The BBC* (http://bbc.co.uk), *The Guardian* (http://www.guardian.co.uk) and *The New York Times* (http://www.nytimes.com). For lower levels, try *Breaking News English* (http://www.breakingnewsenglish.com), *News for Beginners* (http://newsforbeginners.com) and *English Online* (http://www.english-online.at).

6.13 Kids' storytelling

Storytelling websites for kids include the British Council's *Learn English Kids* (http://learnenglishkids.britishcouncil.org), *Children's Storybooks Online* (http://www.magickeys.com/books) and *KidsStoriesOnline.com* (http://www.kidsstoriesonline.com).

6.14 Interactive fiction

Interactive fiction (IF) suitable for your class can be found at *If Only* (http://www.theswanstation.com/wordpress/author/joe-pereira). The IF Guide is located at *The People's Republic of Interactive Fiction* (http://pr-if.org/doc/play-if-card).

6.15 Fan fiction

Legally, fan fiction has been argued to fall under 'fair use' when it comes to copyright, and the Organization for Transformative Works, believing that fan fiction 'is a creative, transformative process' (http://transformativeworks.org), exists to uphold the legality of non-profit fan fiction under the fair-use doctrine. Some authors such as JK Rowling (*Harry Potter*) and Stephanie Meyer (*Twilight*) have declared to be in favour of fan fiction; it is only this legal fan fiction, generally that published on *FanFiction.Net* (http://www.fanfiction.net), that I suggest teachers use.

Chapter 7

7.1 Social-networking writing group
Recommended social networks include private ones, such as *Edmodo* (http://www.edmodo.com), and public ones, such as *Facebook* (http://www.facebook.com), where private groups can be set up. With Business English learners, setting up a private group on LinkedIn (http://www.linkedin.com) would be a good idea.

7.2 Writing on a class wiki
Suggestions for wikis include *Wikispaces* (http://www.wikispaces.com), *PBworks* (http://www.pbworks.com) and *Wetpaint* (http://www.wetpaint.com).

7.3 Using learner blogs
Blogger (http://www.blogger.com) or *WordPress* (http://www.wordpress.com) are two blogging platforms that work well. For more information on the difference between a *tutor blog*, a *class blog* and *learner blogs*, see Appendix A, *Blogging*.

7.6 Five-sentence photo story
Instead of just using *Google Images* search (http://www.google.com), try searching *Flickr* (http://www.flickr.com) or *Photobucket* (http://photobucket.com) in order to find more interesting images. In *Flickr*, you can sort the results by 'relevant', 'recent' or 'interesting'. If you use the 'advanced' search, then you can choose to search using a *Creative Commons licence* (i.e. where copyright is not an issue), and also select which types of images (photographs, screenshots, art, etc.) to include or exclude. Other collections of photographs worth looking at include 'eltpics' on *Flickr* (http://www.flickr.com/photos/eltpics) and *Getty Images* (http://www.gettyimages.com).

7.8 Interactive story
Storytelling websites such as *StoryMaker* (http://www.clpgh.org/kids/storymaker), or the animated storytelling website *Zimmer Twins* (http://www.zimmertwins.com), can be used for this activity.

7.9 Developing a story
Story Starters by Scholastic (http://teacher.scholastic.com/activities/storystarters) and the animated story site *Zimmer Twins* (http://www.zimmertwins.com) can be used for this activity.

7.10 Crazy stories or poems
There are lots of text-generator websites, such as *Mad Takes* (http://www.madtakes.com), *Education Place* (http://www.eduplace.com/tales) and *Crazy Tales* (http://www.rinkworks.com/crazytales).

7.11 Art stories
A search on *Google* will find specific paintings, but the *Famous Artists Gallery* (http://www.famousartistsgallery.com) and *Artcyclopedia* (http://www.artcyclopedia.com) have large collections of famous paintings.

7.12 Do you dream?

Learners can use an image library such as *Flickr* (http://www.flickr.com) to find images. The dreams can be interpreted using a dream dictionary, such as *Dreamdoze* (http://dreamdoze.com) or *Smartgirl* (http:// www.smartgirl.org/dreamdictionary.html).

7.13 Message from the past

There are a number of 'future email' websites, such as *EmailFuture.com* (http://emailfuture.com) and *FutureMe* (http://www.futureme.org).

7.14 Report writing

Recommended survey-question websites include *Kwik Surveys* (http://kwiksurveys.com), *SurveyMonkey* (http://www.surveymonkey.com) and *LimeSurvey* (http://www.limesurvey.org).

7.15 Sensationalist reporting

Any online tabloid newspaper in English, such as *The Sun* (http://www.thesun.co.uk) or *The Daily Mail* (http://www.dailymail.co.uk), would be suitable for this activity.

7.16 Biographies

Dipity (http://www.dipity.com) or *X Timeline* (http://www.xtimeline.com) can be used for this activity.

7.17 Translate to SMS

Websites that show and translate standard English to SMS messages include *Transl8it!* (http:// transl8it.com) and *Lingo2 Word* (http://www.lingo2word.com).

7.18 Pros and cons

Pro / Con Lists (http://www.proconlists.com) is probably the best website to use for this activity.

7.19 Social network CVs

The professionally focused social network *LinkedIn* (http://www.linkedin.com), or the social networks *Muxi* (http://www.muxi.com) or *BranchOut*, which is part of *Facebook* (http://apps.facebook.com/branchout), can be used for this activity.

Chapter 8

8.1 Spoken journals

Simple audio-recording tools, such as *Vocaroo* (http://vocaroo.com), are best for this activity. Alternatives include *Audio Boo* (http://audioboo.fm), especially if your learners have a smartphone and can download the Audio Boo app. If you want to use video, too, then *MailVu* (http://mailvu.com) is a good tool.

8.2 Speaking pictures

Blabberize (http://blabberize.com) works well with young learners and teenagers. *Fotobabble* (http://www.fotobabble.com) is a similar website. For older learners, *VoiceThread* (http://www.voicethread.com) may be a more appropriate tool.

8.4 Unscripted and scripted dialogues

Audio tools that are appropriate for this activity include *Vocaroo* (http://vocaroo.com) and *Audio Boo* (http://audioboo.fm). For advice on voice recorders, see Appendix A, *Voice recorders*.

8.6 Guided tour

The *Woices* (World Voices) website (http://www.woices.com) is ideal for this. You can also use a personalised travel-guide website, such as *Community Walk* (http://www.communitywalk.com), and add audio to places on the map, using tools such as *Vocaroo* (http://vocaroo.com) and *Audio Boo* (http://audioboo.fm).

8.7 Virtual-world tourists

The virtual world *Second Life* (http://www.secondlife.com) can be used for this activity. The software will need to be downloaded and installed, and an account set up. Once this has been done, you can search for real-world places from within *Second Life* – there are plenty to choose from, but I recommend you check them before class and choose the best ones to visit. An alternative to *Second Life* is *Twinity* (http://www.twinity.com), but the real-life places are limited to a few European cities, such as London and Berlin.

8.8 Talk-radio speaking

Recommended audio-editing software includes *Audacity*, which can be downloaded here: http://audacity.sourceforge.net. If you need an online tool, then *Myna* (http://advanced.aviary.com/tools/audio-editor) can be used instead. See Appendix A, *Audio recording and editing* for more help with using audio-editing software.

8.9 Current affairs

Video-interview websites that work well with this activity include *Intervue* (http://intervue.me), which lets learners post replies at any time. If you want to hold the interviews in real time, a tool such as *ooVoo* (http://www.oovoo.com) will let you do this.

8.10 Train or coach?

The National Express coach and train journey planners that were used in this activity are here: http://www.nationalexpress.com

8.11 Discussions of interest

The audio-voice forum website *Voxopop* (http://www.voxopop.com) is the best website for this activity.

8.12 Animated film

Go! Animate (http://goanimate.com) is ideal for this activity, because it is online, easy to use and audio can be recorded and uploaded. *Artoonix* (http://www.artoonix.com) allows you to create cartoons and add your own audio, but the software needs to be downloaded first. Other animated video sites, such as *Zimmer Twins* (http://www.zimmertwins.com) and *Dvolver* (http://www.dvolver.com/moviemaker), do not allow you to upload your own audio.

Chapter 9

9.1 Class-vocabulary audio notebook

Podcasting websites, such as *SoundCloud* (http://www.soundcloud.com), *Audio Boo* (http://www.audioboo.com) and *Podomatic* (http://www.podomatic.com), can be used for this activity.

9.2 Phonemic dialogues

Two websites that can be used for this activity include *Phonetizer* (http://www.phonetizer.com) and *Text2Phonetics* (http://www.photransedit.com/Online/Text2Phonetics.aspx).

9.3 Howdjasayit?

Talking pronunciation-dictionary websites include *Howjsay.com* (http://howjsay.com) and *Forvo* (http://www.forvo.com). For minimal pairs, *Shiporsheep.com* (http://www.shiporsheep.com) is useful.

9.4 Schwa what?

There are several online phonemic charts available. The British Council has one on *TeachingEnglish* (http://www.teachingenglish.org.uk/activities/phonemic-chart) and there's one on *onestopenglish* (http://www.onestopenglish.com/skills/pronunciation/phonemic-chart-and-app/interactive-phonemic-chart) and on *English Club* (http://www.englishclub.com/pronunciation/phonemic-chart-ia.htm).

9.5 Phonetic games

One website with lots of phonetic games on it is *Phonetics Focus* (http://cambridgeenglishonline.com/Phonetics_Focus).

9.6 Minimal-pair poems

Websites with pronunciation help for minimal pairs include *Shiporsheep.com* (http://www.shiporsheep.com) and *Ted Power*, where an index of common mistakes is given (http://www.btinternet.com/~ted.power/l1all.html).

9.7 Newsreader

There are teleprompters that can be used at *CuePrompter.com* (http://cueprompter.com), *EasyPrompter* (http://www.easyprompter.com) and *Teleprompter Software* (http://www.freetelepromptersoftware.com).

9.9 Voice recognition

Voice-recognition software to use can be either on the computer (Windows 7 and above has speech recognition built in); on learner smartphones (*Siri* is built into the iPhone, and *Vlingo*: http://www. vlingo.com can be downloaded for Android phones); or on a website (both *e-Speaking*: http://www. e-speaking.com and *iSpeech*: http://www.ispeech.org can be used for this activity).

9.10 Smartphone app

Asking the learners to search the *Android App Store* or *iTunes* is the best way of finding an English-pronunciation app that will work on your learners' smartphone. *Phonetics Focus* from *Cambridge English Online* (http://cambridgeenglishonline.com/Phonetics_Focus), *Sounds* from Macmillan Education (http://www.soundspronapp.com) and *Sounds Right* from the British Council (http:// learnenglish.britishcouncil.org/en/mobile-learning/sounds-right) are all recommended.

9.11 What's the intonation?

The following websites can be used for this activity: *Fonetiks.org* (http://www.fonetiks.org), *Sounds* (http://sounds.bl.uk/Accents-and-dialects) and the *Speech Accent Archive* (http://accent.gmu.edu).

9.12 Different accents

Searching for English accents or specific accents (Scottish, Welsh, etc.) on *YouTube* (http://www. youtube.com) will return results. You can also go to the website accomanying this book (http://www. languagelearningtechnology.com) for example videos of people speaking English with different accents.

9.14 Re-recording speeches and scenes

Audacity (http://audacity.sourceforge.net) is the best choice for audio-recording editing. See Appendix A, *Audio recording and editing* for help with this. Alternatively, voice recorders can be used (see Appendix A, *Voice recorders*).

Chapter 10

10.1 Our e-book

Kerpoof (http://www.kerpoof.com/#/activity/storybook) and *Storybird* (http://storybird.com) can be used with young learners for this activity. With adults, you can create the book in a word-processing program and save it in PDF format. Then it can be uploaded to a site, such as *Issuu* (http://issuu.com) or *Scribd* (http://www.scribd.com).

10.2 Class magazine

A class wiki can be set up at *Wikispaces* (http://www.wikispaces.com) or *PBworks* (http://www. pbworks.com).

10.3 Culture capsule

A wiki (see 10.2) or a basic webpage can be used for this activity. Simple webpages can be set up, using *Pen.io* (http://pen.io) and *Tidy Pub* (http://tidypub.org), and more complex sites can be created for free, using *Weebly* (http://www.weebly.com) or *Wix* (http://www.wix.com). Any audio files that are created can be stored on a site such as *SoundCloud* (http://www.soundcloud.com), and video can be uploaded to *Vimeo* (http://www.vimeo.com), *Viddler* (http://www.viddler.com) or *YouTube* (http://www.youtube.com). Alternatively, if the audio and video files are small, they can all be stored, along with the text, on a *Posterous Spaces* site (http://www.posterous.com).

10.4 Class weekly learning podcast

Audacity (http://audacity.sourceforge.net) is the best choice for audio-recording editing. See Appendix A, *Audio recording and editing* for help with this.

10.5 TV magazine programme

The easiest equipment for shooting videos in class these days may be a camera phone, which is now available on most phones. If you use a camera phone, then make sure you can get the videos off the camera (via a cable, etc.). For better-quality video, use a special video camera or the video function of a digital still camera. In all of these cases, a tripod is recommended (to keep the camera steady).

10.6 Short film

Good examples of short films to inspire the class can be found at the *Future Shorts YouTube* channel (http://www.youtube.com/user/futureshorts). Others will be shared on the website accompanying this book (http://www.languagelearningtechnology.com).

For the photo-story variation, *ProjectRome* (http://rome.adobe.com), or other desktop publishing software, can be used to create interesting documents.

10.8 Our cookbook

A wiki (see 10.2) or a basic website can be used for this activity. The website can be created for free, using *Weebly* (http://www.weebly.com) or *Wix* (http://www.wix.com). To create an e-book, create the book in a word-processing program, and save it in PDF format. Then it can be uploaded to a site such as *Issuu* (http://issuu.com) or *Scribd* (http://www.scribd.com).

10.9 Make your own webquest

Example webquests can be found at *WebQuest.org* (http://webquest.org). You will also find more on the website accompanying this book (http://www.languagelearningtechnology.com).

Chapter 11

11.1 E-portfolio archive and showcase

Recommended blogs for the e-portfolio archive include *Posterous Spaces* (http://www.posterous.com) or *Tumblr* (http://www.tumblr.com).

For the e-portfolio showcase, create a website, using a template for free, using *Weebly* (http://www.weebly.com) or *Wix* (http://www.wix.com).

11.2 Awarding badges

Recommended image-sharing websites include *Flickr* (http://www.flickr.com) and *Photobucket* (http://www.photobucket.com).

11.3 Comparing placement tests

There are lots of online placement tests for learners. *StudyCom* (http://www.study.com/tests.html) and *English English* (http://englishenglish.com/englishtest.htm) are recommended for this activity.

11.4 Testing you

The following websites have example computer-based English tests. They also allow users to create their own tests: *Quia* (http://www.quia.com/shared/english), *Quizlet* (http://www.quizlet.com) and *Vocab Test* (http://www.vocabtest.com).

11.6 Screen-capture video feedback

Screen-capture software that can be used for this activity includes *Jing* (http://www.techsmith.com/jing.html) and *CamStudio* (http://camstudio.org).

11.7 Self-assessing presentations

The website *Present.me* (http://present.me) can be used by learners. Alternatively, they can film themselves with digital cameras or their mobile phones.

11.8 Evaluating classroom activities

Survey tools that can be used for this activity include *SurveyMonkey* (http://www.surveymonkey.com), *Urtak* (https://urtak.com), *Tricider* (https://tricider.com), *Kwik Surveys* (http://kwiksurveys.com) or *LimeSurvey* (http://www.limesurvey.org). They are all slightly different, so which one you choose will depend on your requirements.

11.9 Levelling up

You can either adapt a ready-made level system for gamification, such as *Chore Wars* (http://www.chorewars.com), or use the suggested tables in this book and incorporate them into a wiki, such as *Wikispaces* (http://www.wikispaces.com) or *PBworks* (http://www.pbworks.com).

Index

Academic writing 146
accents, Different accents 185
accuracy
Animated film 167
Reading aloud 153
Talk-radio speaking 160
Unscripted and scripted dialogues 154
Virtual world tourists 158–9
activating interest in reading, Pre-reading presentation 105
activating schema, Pre-reading presentation 105
active listening 81
Against all odds computer game 169
Alien vocabulary 48–9
Altered interviews 96–7
Animated film 167
antonyms, Experimenting with antonyms 55
argumentative essay, Pros and cons 144
Art stories 136
Ask the Internet 112
assessment and evaluation
evaluation of a language course 204
feedback for learners 203
for formal qualification 203, 204
formative assessment 203–4
gamification of assessments 204
learner-centred assessment 203
low-stakes tests 203
reasons for assessment 203
summative assessment 203–4
technology support for 203–4
assessment and evaluation activities
Awarding badges 206
Comparing placement tests 207
E-portfolio archive and showcase 205
Evaluating classroom activities 212
Levelling up 213–15
Screen-capture video feedback 210
Self-assessing presentations 211
Testing me 209
Testing you 208

asynchronous web communication 3
Audacity tool 82
audio-editing software 148, 160
Altered interviews 96–7
Audio gap-fills 63
audio-guide websites 156–7
audio recording
Class audio recording 19–20
guide to recording and editing 217, 218
Re-recording speeches and scenes 187
tools 150
web sources 2
websites 148
audio-voice forum websites 165–6
authentic listening, Other people's interests 84–5
Authentic word clouds 75–6
autocue 179–80
Automatic cloze tests 65
automatic text generators 134–5
automatic-translation websites 61
Awarding badges 206
awareness, Guess the language 186
awareness of tests
Testing me 209
Testing you 208

Back-up if technology fails, Plan B 10, 16
Big events 114–15
Biographies 141
Blackboard (VLE) 10, 11
blended-learning approach 10
blogs 2, 3, 25, 121
Awarding badges 206
Blog exchange 34
blogging guide 217
Blogging summary 127
Class blog 32, 33, 34
E-portfolio archive and showcase 205
types of 25
Using learner blogs 126

book creation, Our e-book 191
book-creation website 191
book titles 72
browser tools 74
Business English, Social network CVs 145

cameras *see* digital cameras
catchphrases, Common grammatical errors 71
chunking, Re-recording speeches and scenes 187
Class audio recording 19–20
class blog 25, 121
   Class blog 32, 33, 34
Class magazine 192
class record of language/vocabulary, Language wiki 35
Class-vocabulary audio notebook 173
class web pages 3
Class weekly learning podcast 194
class wiki 122
   Awarding badges 206
   Biographies 141
   Class magazine 192
   Class-vocabulary audio notebook 173
   Language wiki 35
   Make your own webquest 199–200
   Writing on a class wiki 125
classroom management
   Plan B (back-up if technology fails) 10, 16
   Visual class list 14
cloze-test generation, Automatic cloze tests 65
Coded message trail 110–11
cohesive texts, Myths and legends 128
collaborative learning 147
collaborative projects 189
   Culture capsule 193
   Our cookbook 198
   Report writing 139
collaborative writing 122
   Our e-book 191
   Writing on a class wiki 125
collocations
   Noticing collocations 58–60
   Words and phrases 53
Common grammatical errors 71
communication, Web 2.0 sites 2–3

community *see* learning community
community of practice 25
comparative language, Train or coach? 163–4
Comparative texts 107–8
comparing images to descriptions, Quick-response reading race 103
Comparing placement tests 207
comprehension, definition 81
computer-aided pronunciation (CAP) 171
computer-assisted language learning (CALL) 4
computer games 148
   World issues 168–9
   see also gamification of assessments
Computer Mediated Communication (CMC) 147
concordance software, Grammar in context 79
concordancer
   In context 40
   Multiple-meaning presentations 57
   Words and phrases 53
conditionals, If only … 77–8
connected speech and pausing, Newsreader 179–80
connected speech intonation, Re-recording speeches and scenes 187
connecting with other L2 speakers, Blog exchange 34
consonant sounds, Schwa what? 176
Content Management System (CMS) 17
context
   Audio gap-fills 63
   In context 40
contrary-to-fact conditionals, If only … 77–8
cookbook, Our cookbook 198
cooperative learning, Make your own webquest 199–200
corpus search, Grammar in context 79
Course Management System (CMS) 218
coursebook, Flip the coursebook 23
Crazy stories or poems 134–5
creating tests
   Testing me 209
   Testing you 208
critical listening, Guided tours 89

critical literacy 99
Culture capsule 193
Current affairs 161–2
CV (curriculum vitae) writing, Social network
    CVs 144

debating, World issues 168–9
description, Guided tour 156–7
descriptive grammar 61
descriptive writing
    Art stories 136
    Do you dream? 137
detail, listening for
    Altered interviews 96–7
    Guided tours 89
    Reordered video story 87
    Someone I know 95
Developing a story 133
dialogue
    Animated film 167
    Discussions of interest 165–6
    Unscripted and scripted dialogues 154
dictation, Voice-recorder dictation 93
dictionaries (online/electronic) 10
    Dictionary race 18
    In context 40
    Slang, register and style 56
    Word associations 50–1
Different accents 185
digital audio, development of 81
digital cameras 3
    Alien vocabulary 48–9
    Digital camera scavenger hunt 41–2
    Visual class list 14
digital generation gap 4
digital literacy skills 99, 122
digital poster-creation website, Memory
    posters 46–7
digital poster guide 218
digital poster site 36
digital sticky notes 36
discussion
    Current affairs 161–2
    Discussions of interest 165–6
Do you dream? 137
documentary, Short film 196

drafting/re-drafting
    Developing a story 133
    Interactive story 131–2
    Writing on a class wiki 125
dream dictionary 137

e-book creation, Our e-book 191
editing, Crazy stories or poems 134–5
electronic dictionaries *see* dictionaries
    (online/electronic)
electronic portfolios *see* e-portfolios
electronic texts 99
email 25
    Message from the past 138
encouraging participation, Mystery guest 33
English accents, Different accents 185
English for Academic Purposes (EAP),
    Academic writing 146
English for Special Purposes (ESP) 150
e-portfolios (electronic portfolios) 122, 203–4
    E-portfolio archive and showcase 205
error correction
    Automatic cloze tests 65
    Common grammatical errors 71
    Grammar check 64
    Minimal-pair poems 178
    Noticing collocations 58–60
European Language Portfolio 203
evaluation
    Evaluating classroom activities 212
    see also assessment and evaluation
examination
    exam practice 61
    see also assessment and evaluation
experiential learning 189
Experimenting with antonyms 55
expressing likes, Other people's interests 84–5

Facebook 26, 122
Fan fiction 119
Favourite websites 15
films
    Animated film 167
    Film festival 197
    film titles 72
    Short film 196

Five-sentence photo story 129
Flip the coursebook 23
Flip your classroom 23
flipped classroom 10
fluency
   Discussions of interest 165–6
   Guided tour 156–7
   Mobile circle game 155
   Reading aloud 153
   Talk-radio speaking 160
   Train or coach? 163–4
   Unscripted and scripted dialogues 154
   Virtual world tourists 158–9
   World issues 168–9
formal assessment 203, 204
   Comparing placement tests 207
   Levelling up 213–15
formal language, Report writing 139
formative assessment 203–4
   E-portfolio archive and showcase 205
forum discussions 25
fun *see* motivation/fun

gamification of assessments 204
   Levelling up 213–15
generating ideas, Five-sentence photo story 129
genres
   Academic writing 146
   Pros and cons 144
   Recorded stories 92
   Sensationalist reporting 140
getting to know each other
   Class blog 32
   Getting to know you 12
   What we need English for 36
gist
   Guess what I'm talking about 83
   Quick-response reading race 103
   Reordered video story 87
giving advice, World issues 168–9
Google 68
Google Forms guide 218
Google Images 2
Googlefight website 68–9
grammar
   definition 61

descriptive grammar 61
   online tools 61
   prescriptive grammar 61
   technology-supported approach 61
grammar activities
   Audio gap-fills 63
   Authentic word clouds 75–6
   Automatic cloze tests 65
   Common grammatical errors 71
   Grammar check 64
   Grammar fight 68–9
   Grammar in context 79
   Grammar-reference sites 70
   Grammar safari 74
   If only … 77–8
   Questioning infographics 66–7
   Real-world grammar 72–3
grammar-checking sites, Common
     grammatical errors 71
grammar-checking tools 61, 64
grammatical accuracy
   Crazy stories or poems 134–5
   Speed writing 130
Guess the language 186
Guess what I'm talking about 83
Guided tour 156–7
Guided tours 89

hardware technologies 6
hobbies and interests, Class magazine 192
homework 150
   Flip your classroom 23
   Learning together online 27–8
   Levelling up 213–15
Howdjasayit? 175

ice-breaking, Getting to know you 12
Identifying text-types 113
If only … 77–8
image bank 137
image search engine 129
In context 40
inferencing
   Guess what I'm talking about 83
   Fan fiction 119
infographics, Questioning infographics 66–7

information, using the Internet 2
information (listening for)
  Guided tours 89
  Interview bingo 94
  Online classroom guest 91
  Recorded stories 92
  Talk-radio listening 88
information (reading for)
  Big events 114–15
  Coded message trail 110–11
  Interactive fiction 117–18
  Reviewer role play 109
information gathering
  Favourite websites 15
  Technological survey 13
information sharing
  Blog exchange 34
  Mobile circle game 155
integrated skills
  Culture capsule 193
  Film festival 197
  IWB island 201–2
  Make your own webquest 199–200
  Our cookbook 198
  Short film 196
  TV magazine programme 195
integrating reading and writing
  Ask the Internet 112
  Interactive fiction 117–18
integrating technology
  back-up plan if technology fails 10, 16
  blended-learning approach 10
  flipped classroom 10
  learners' views on 9
  Learning Management System (LMS)
    10, 11
  Personal Learning Environment
    (PLE) 10
  resources available 9
  Virtual Learning Environment (VLE)
    10, 11
integrating technology activities
  Class audio recording 19–20
  Dictionary race 18
  Favourite websites 15
  Flip your classroom 23

  Getting to know you 12
  Our VLE 17
  Plan B 16
  Technological survey 13
  Unlocked achievements 21–2
  Visual class list 14
Interactive fiction 117–18
interactive speaking
  Current affairs 161–2
  Talk-radio speaking 160
  World issues 168–9
Interactive story 131–2
interactive whiteboard *see* IWB
International Phonetic Alphabet 174
International Reading Association 99
Internet
  as an information source 2
  Ask the Internet 112
  opportunities for writing 121
  range of uses in language learning 2–3
  Internet technologies 6
internet telephony 148
Interview bingo 94
interviewing
  Altered interviews 96–7
  Someone I know 95
intonation
  Re-recording speeches and scenes 187
  What's the intonation? 184
iPad 152
iPhone 152
iTunes, Search the tube 86
IWB (interactive whiteboard) 4
  criticism of 5
  effective use of 5
  IWB island 201–2
  skimming and scanning 104
  Unlocked achievements 21–2
  use of clickers 5

journals, Spoken journals 149–50
journey-planning language, Train or coach?
    163–4
journey-planning websites 163–4

Kids' storytelling 116

language feedback, Class audio recording
   19–20
language laboratories 81
Language wiki 35
learner autonomy
  and lifelong learning 203
  Dictionary race 18
  Flip your classroom 23
  Grammar-reference sites 70
  Make your own webquest 199–200
  Noticing collocations 58–60
  Our VLE 17
  Personal learning online 30–1
  Smartphone app 183
  Spoken journals 149–50
  using technology 2
  Words and phrases 53
learner blogs 25, 121
  Blogging summary 127
  Using learner blogs 126
learner feedback, Screen-capture video
   feedback 210
learner-to-learner interaction 150
  Discussions of interest 165–6
  Unscripted and scripted dialogues 154
learner training 147
  Dictionary race 18
  Evaluating classroom activities 212
  Our VLE 17
learners, views on using technology 9
learning community
  building 25–6
  online communities 25
learning community activities
  Blog exchange 34
  Class blog 32, 33, 34
  Language wiki 35
  Learning together online 27–8
  Mystery guest 33
  Personal learning online 30–1
  Safety online 37
  What we need English for 36
  Who are my classmates? 29
Learning Management System (LMS)
   10, 11
Learning together online 27–8

level of learning, Levelling up 213–15
lifelong learning concept 203
limericks 181
Linguaphone 81
listening
  and comprehension 81
  teaching approach 81–2
  technology support for 81–2
listening activities
  Altered interviews 96–7
  Guess what I'm talking about 83
  Guided tours 89
  Interview bingo 94
  Online classroom guest 91
  Other people's interests 84–5
  Recorded poetry 90
  Recorded stories 92
  Reordered video story 87
  Screen-capture video feedback 210
  Search the tube 86
  Someone I know 95
  Talk-radio listening 88
  Voice-recorder dictation 93
listening material, on the Web 2
listening skills
  and pronunciation 171
  Schwa what? 176
  Voice-recorder dictation 93
long-term class project, IWB island 201–2

Make your own webquest 199–200
Making word games 52
meanings of words, Multiple-meaning
   presentations 57
memes, Search the tube 86
Memory posters 46–7
Message from the past 138
microblogging websites 26
  Grammar in context 79
mind-mapping software 66–7
  If only … 77–8
Minimal-pair poems 178
Mobile circle game 155
mobile devices 3
mobile-phone vocabulary, Mobile circle
   game 155

mobile phones 3, 148
  Getting to know you 12
  voice recorders 172
  see also smartphones
monologue
  Guided tour 156–7
  Speaking pictures 151–2
Moodle (VLE) 10, 11
motivation/fun
  Altered interviews 96–7
  Awarding badges 206
  Class weekly learning podcast 194
  Coded message trail 110–11
  Fan fiction 119
  Film festival 197
  Interactive fiction 117–18
  Kids, storytelling 116
  Levelling up 213–15
  Making word games 52
  Mystery guest 33
  Online classroom guest 91
  Readathon 106
  Short film 196
  Talk-radio listening 88
  Tongue twisters 181
  Unlocked achievements 21–2
  Virtual world tourists 158–9
  Voice recognition 182
  Word puzzles 44
mp3 players 3
Multiple-meaning presentations 57
multimodality, Do you dream? 137
music software online 73
Mystery guest 33
Myths and legends 128

narrative tenses
  Animated film 167
  Recorded stories 92
narrative writing
  Art stories 136
  Crazy stories or poems 134–5
  Developing a story 133
  Five-sentence photo story 129
  Interactive story 131–2
  Speed writing 130

natural speech, Interview bingo 94
needs analysis, Favourite websites 15
negotiation, World issues 168–9
networking tools 25–6
news articles, Sensationalist reporting 140
newspaper language, Big events 114–15
Newsreader 179–80
non-standard expressions, Common
    grammatical errors 71
normalisation of technology 4
note taking, Myths and legends 128
Noticing collocations 58–60
noticing grammar usage, Grammar safari 74

online audio 81–2
Online classroom guest 91
online communities 25
online dictionaries *see* dictionaries (online/
    electronic)
online notice board 36
online thesaurus *see* thesaurus (online)
Online word-game tournament 43
Other people's interests 84–5
Our cookbook 198
Our VLE 17

pedagogy, and technology 3–4
personal information, Mobile circle game 155
Personal Learning Environment (PLE) 10
  Personal learning online 30–1
Personal Learning Network (PLN) 26
  Personal learning online 30–1
personal writing
  Message from the past 138
  Speed writing 130
personalised feedback, Screen-capture video
    feedback 210
phonemic charts 176, 177
Phonemic dialogues 174
phonemic script websites 174, 176
phonemic spelling, Phonetic games 177
phonetic alphabets 174
Phonetic games 177
photo story 196
placement tests, Comparing placement tests 207
Plan B (back-up if technology fails) 10, 16

planning, Five-sentence photo story 129
podcast websites 194
podcasts 81, 82, 171–2
    Class-vocabulary audio notebook 173
    Class weekly learning podcast 194
    definition 82
    Search the tube 86
poetry
    Crazy stories or poems 134–5
    Minimal-pair poems 178
    Recorded poetry 90
portfolios 203–4
post-reading task 102
predicting before listening, Interview bingo 94
pre-reading tasks
    Pre-reading presentation 105
    Video pre-reading warmer 102
    Word-cloud warmer 101
prescriptive grammar 61
presentations, Self-assessing presentations 211
process writing
    Blogging summary 127
    Myths and legends 128
    Social-networking writing group 123–4
    Using learner blogs 126
professional writing
    Biographies 141
    Report writing 139
    Social network CVs 144
project work
    collaboration on projects 189
    experiential learning 189
    phases of projects 189
    teaching approach 189
    technology support for 189
project work activities
    Class magazine 192
    Class weekly learning podcast 194
    Culture capsule 193
    Film festival 197
    IWB island 201–2
    Make your own webquest 199–200
    Our cookbook 198
    Our e-book 191
    Short film 196
    TV magazine programme 195

pronunciation
    importance of 171
    teaching approach 171–2
    technology support for 171–2
pronunciation activities
    Class-vocabulary audio notebook 173
    Different accents 185
    Guess the language 186
    Howdjasayit? 175
    Kids' storytelling 116
    Minimal-pair poems 178
    Newsreader 179–80
    Phonemic dialogues 174
    Phonetic games 177
    Reading aloud 153
    Re-recording speeches and scenes 187
    Schwa what? 176
    Smartphone app 183
    Speaking pictures 151–2
    Talk-radio speaking 160
    Tongue twisters 181
    Unscripted and scripted dialogues 154
    Virtual world tourists 158–9
    Voice recognition 182
    What's the intonation? 184
pronunciation-dictionary websites 175
Pros and cons 143
publishing learners' work online 3

Questioning infographics 66–7
quick-response (QR) code generator 110–11
quick-response (QR) codes 103
    Coded message trail 110–11
    Quick-response reading race 103
quiz-generator website, Learner-generated
    quizzes 45

range of speakers
    Guess what I'm talking about 83
    Other people's interests 84–5
Readathon 106
reading
    critical literacy 99
    digital literacy 99
    new genres of text 99
    skills for new media 99

teaching approach 99
technology support for 99
reading activities
Ask the Internet 112
Big events 114–15
Coded message trail 110–11
Comparative texts 107–8
Fan fiction 119
Identifying text-types 113
Interactive fiction 117–18
IWB skimming and scanning 104
Kids' storytelling 116
Pre-reading presentation 105
Quick response reading race 103
Readathon 106
Reviewer role play 109
Video pre-reading warmer 102
Word-cloud warmer 101
reading aloud
Kids' storytelling 116
Readathon 106
Reading aloud 153
reading and writing
Ask the Internet 112
Interactive fiction 117–18
reading extensively
Fan fiction 119
Readathon 106
reading for pleasure 99
Fan fiction 119
Interactive fiction 117–18
Kids' storytelling 116
Readathon 106
real-world communication, Grammar in
context 79
Real-world grammar 72–3
recipes, Our cookbook 198
record of learners' work, E-portfolio archive
and showcase 205
Recorded poetry 90
Recorded stories 92
recording audio *see* audio recording; voice
recording
reflection on formal assessment, Comparing
placement tests 207
reflection on learning

Class weekly learning podcast 194
Evaluating classroom activities 212
register
Academic writing 146
Slang, register and style 56
Reordered video story 87
Report writing 139
reporting, Blogging summary 127
review of work done, Evaluating classroom
activities 212
Reviewer role play 109
revision
Evaluating classroom activities 212
Grammar in context 79
Language wiki 35
Learner-generated quizzes 45
Making word games 52
Memory posters 46–7
Real-world grammar 72–3
Testing me 209
Testing you 208
rhyming words, Recorded poetry 90

safety online 26
Safety online 37
scanning
Coded message trail 110–11
IWB skimming and scanning 104
scavenger hunt, Digital camera scavenger
hunt 41–2
Schwa what? 176
screen capture, guide 218
screen-capture software 203, 210
Screen-capture video feedback 210
search engines 74
guide 218–19
Search the tube 86
Self-assessing presentations 211
self-correction
Recorded stories 92
Voice-recorder dictation 93
semantics, Word associations 50–1
Sensationalist reporting 140
Sheldon, Lee 204
Short film 196
Simple English Wikipedia 122

skimming, IWB skimming and scanning 104
Skype 147
  Online classroom guest 91
Slang, register and style 56
sleep and dreaming, Do you dream? 137
smartphones 3, 9
  apps 150
  audio-guide app 156
  Smartphone app 183
SMS messages, Translate to SMS 142
social learning 25
social media 25–6
  safety online 26
social networking 25–6
  Learning together online 27–8
  platforms 121
  private and public networks 26
  sites 2
  Social network CVs 144
  Social-networking writing group 123–4
  Who are my classmates? 29
  writing on social networks 122
software technologies 6
Someone I know 95
song titles 73
speaking
  benefits of voice recording 147
  teaching approach 147–8
  technology support for 147–8
speaking activities
  Animated film 167
  Current affairs 161–2
  Discussions of interest 165–6
  Guided tour 156–7
  Mobile circle game 155
  Reading aloud 153
  Self-assessing presentations 211
  Speaking pictures 151–2
  Spoken journals 149–50
  Talk-radio speaking 160
  Train or coach 163–4
  Unscripted and scripted dialogues 154
  Virtual world tourists 158–9
  Voice-recorder dictation 93
  World issues 168–9
spellcheck tools 61, 64

spelling, Translate to SMS 143
Spent computer game 169
Spoken journals 149–50
spoken narrative, Animated film 167
Stop disasters computer game 168–9
stories, If only … 77–8
story-starter websites 133
storytelling website 131–2
stress and rhythm of speech, Newsreader 179–80
stress patterns
  Howdjasayit? 175
  What's the intonation? 184
structuring texts, Crazy stories or poems 134–5
style
  Academic writing 146
  Slang, register and style 56
summarising
  Big events 114–15
  Biographies 141
  Blogging summary 127
  Myths and legends 128
  Report writing 139
summative assessment 203–4
  Awarding badges 206
supporting learning online, Personal learning online 30–1
survey tools 212
surveys
  Evaluating classroom activities 212
  Technological survey 13
synchronous web communication 3
Synonym swap 54

tablets 3
Talk-radio listening 88
Talk-radio speaking 160
task-based learning (TBL) 189
teachers
  guidelines for using technology 4–5
  principled approach to technology 4–5
  training in use of technologies 5
Technological survey 13
technology
  and pedagogy 3–4
  avoiding Everest syndrome 3, 4

back-up plan if it fails 10, 16
benefits of learning technology 2
constant development 4
guidelines for teachers 4–5
guides to 3–4 *see also* Appendices
normalisation in language education 4
principled approach for teachers 4–5
promoting learner autonomy 2
range of hand-held devices 3
range of learning technologies 6
range of uses for the Internet 2
range of uses in language learning 1
telephony software, Online classroom guest 91
teleprompter 179–80
teleprompter websites 179–80
test-generator website, Learner-generated
    quizzes 45
testing
  Testing me 209
  Testing you 208
  see also assessment and evaluation
texting language, Translate to SMS 142
text-types
  Comparative texts 107–8
  Identifying text-types 113
  Message from the past 138
  Pros and cons 144
  Sensationalist reporting 140
  Social network CVs 145
thesaurus (online) 10
  Experimenting with antonyms 55
  Synonym swap 54
timeline websites, Biographies 141
tone groups, Newsreader 179–80
Tongue twisters 181
Train or coach 163–4
Translate to SMS 142
travel, Train or coach 163–4
tutor blog 25, 121
TV magazine programme 195
Twitter 26, 122

unfamiliar vocabulary, Alien vocabulary 48–9
Unlocked achievements 21–2
Unscripted and scripted dialogues 154
user-centred tools 25

video
  Reordered video story 87
  Screen-capture video feedback 210
  Search the tube 86
  Self-assessing presentations 211
  Video pre-reading warmer 102
  Web sources of video clips 2
video-interview websites 148
video presentation, Flip your classroom 23
video-sharing sites 2, 185, 186
video tools 150
virtual classroom 23
virtual communities 2–3
virtual island, IWB island 201–2
Virtual Learning Environment (VLE) 10, 11
  Our VLE 17
  VLE guide 222
virtual worlds 148
  Virtual world tourists 158–9
Visual class list 14
visual clues, Guess the language 186
visual dictionary, Word associations 50–1
vocabulary
  teaching approach 39
  use of technology to help learners 39
vocabulary activities
  Alien vocabulary 48–9
  Art stories 136
  Digital camera scavenger hunt 41–2
  Experimenting with antonyms 55
  In context 40
  Learner-generated quizzes 45
  Making word games 52
  Memory posters 46–7
  Multiple-meaning presentations 57
  Noticing collocations 58–60
  Online word-game tournament 43
  Slang, register and style 56
  Synonym swap 54
  Word associations 50–1
  Word puzzles 44
  Words and phrases 53
Voice recognition 182
voice-recognition software (VRS) 182
voice recorders 3, 147–8
  guide to 219

voice recording
  benefits to learners 147
  Class audio recording 19–20
  Getting to know you 12
  to help with pronunciation 171–2
  Voice-recorder dictation 93
  see also listening activities
VoiceThread tool 152
vowel sounds
  Recorded poetry 90
  Schwa what? 176

Web
  source of information 2
  source of listening material 2
Web 2.0
  opportunities for real communication 2–3
  publishing learners' work online 3
  tools 25
  user-generated content 2–3
webcams 148
webquest, Make your own webquest 199–200
websites, Favourite websites 15
What we need English for 36
What's the intonation? 184
Who are my classmates? 29
wiki software 192
Wikipedia 122
wikis 2, 3, 25, 121, 122
Word associations 50–1
word-cloud creator 75–6
word clouds
  Authentic word clouds 75–6
  Word-cloud warmer 101
word definitions, Word puzzles 44
word frequency, Words and phrases 53
word-game site 52
word games
  Making word games 52
  Online word-game tournament 43
word identification, Digital camera scavenger hunt 41–2
word-processor tools 61, 64
Word puzzles 44
word stress, Howdjasayit? 175

Words and phrases 53
World issues 168–9
writing
  collaborative 122
  opportunities on the Internet 121
  publishing learners' work online 3
  teaching approach 121–2
  technology support for 121–2
writing activities
  Academic writing 146
  Art stories 136
  Authentic word clouds 75–6
  Automatic cloze tests 65
  Biographies 141
  Blogging summary 127
  Class blog 32
  Crazy stories or poems 134–5
  Developing a story 133
  Do you dream? 137
  Five-sentence photo story 129
  Interactive story 131–2
  Message from the past 138
  Myths and legends 128
  Pros and cons 143
  Report writing 139
  Sensationalist reporting 140
  Social network CVs 145
  Social-networking writing group 123–4
  Speed writing 130
  Translate to SMS 142
  Using learner blogs 126
  Writing on a class wiki 125
writing and reading
  Ask the Internet 112
  Interactive fiction 117–18
writing fluency
  Social-networking writing group 123–4
  Speed writing 130
  Using learner blogs 126
writing paragraphs, Social-networking writing group 123–4
writing tools, Grammar check 64

YouTube 2, 94, 185
  Search the tube 86

Made in the USA
Middletown, DE
01 July 2020